Edith & I
On the trail of an Edwardian traveller in Kosovo

For travellers, and all those who make them welcome.

And for my favourite fellow-traveller, Rob,
who has taken me to such wonderful places
and helped me feel welcome there.

First published in 2013 by Elbow Publishing

Second edition: February 2014

Copyright © Elizabeth Gowing, 2013

A catalogue record for this book is available from the British Library

ISBN 978-0-957409-01-9

Cover design and images: Su Jones and Paddy McEntaggart

Inline photographs © Elizabeth Gowing, except where others are acknowledged alongside the photograph

Design & typesetting: Sally Ellis

Edith & I
On the trail of an Edwardian traveller in Kosovo

Elizabeth Gowing

For Diane
Thank you for
having me!
Elizabeth Gowing
Kennington 9 June '14

Elbow Publishing
Cornwall

CONTENTS

Thanks & acknowledgements

I have been lucky to have support from some wonderful travelling companions, both literal and metaphorical, over the four years that it took to write this book. Many of them are mentioned by name in the text, but some deserve a particular thank you here, and I also want to take the chance here to thank those who offered help behind the scenes and between the lines.

Deep gratitude and a huge *faleminderit* to Antonia Young and Bejtullah Destani for inspiration and generous sharing of their knowledge and contacts relating to Edith's life and work. Thanks too, to Edith's family, including all those mentioned in the book, but particularly Dr James Hickson for his help as Edith's literary executor, and kind permission to reproduce the extracts from her books.

For continuing to be interested in the various quests I've been engaged on, and support along the various trails I've followed over the years a special thank you to my wonderful family – Gowing, Greenslade, Wilton, Ward and Lucas.

For comments that made *Edith & I; on the trail of an Edwardian traveller in Kosovo* a better text, I'd like to thank Keith and Christine Gowing, Robert Wilton, Barbara Wilton, Paula Bowles, Su Jones and the members of the writers groups I belong to who've met with me on Monday nights at *Dit e Nat* in Pristina, and with Magnetic North in Greenwich.

Others who helped behind the scenes and during the research and publication process include Anne Goldgar, Sheila Gunn, Chris Hall, Peter Warburton, and John McTernan, who, when I met him at a drinks party in 2008, told me this was a story worth telling – and gave me the wise advice to keep a notebook as I followed the trail, and to send a thank you letter every day. So thank you!

Su Jones and Paddy McEntaggart deserve thanks not only for excellent company over games of Jenga in at least three countries, but for the stunning cover design of the book. Thanks, too, to Sally Ellis for the elegant insides.

I have also been lucky to have support in my quest from numerous libraries, archives and museums, as will be evident from the story that unfolds here. Anyone who has tried researching their family or similar stories from history will understand the huge power held by institutional gatekeepers to the past, and will know what a delight it is when the gatekeepers exercise their power with encouragement, kindness and sympathy. Thanks to all those who helped at the Archaeological and Anthropological Museum in Cambridge, the Bankfield Museum, the Bodleian Library, the British Library, the British Museum, the Ethnological Museum in Pristina, the Pitt Rivers Museum, the Somerset Heritage Centre, and in particular to Sarah Walpole at the Royal Anthropological Institute.

cont.

I am grateful for permission from the Royal Anthropological Institute to quote from those of Edith Durham's notebooks and diaries which they hold, to Wiley to reproduce the extract from the speech of HJ Braunholtz published in the journal, *Man*, on pages 50-51 and 237, for permission to quote from Henry Nevinson's diaries★ from the Ayrton Estate and the Bodleian Libraries, University of Oxford as the owners of the diaries, and from the British Library to quote from the correspondence of Marie Stopes which they own.

Edith Durham has been an inspiration to me, as to many others, and I thank everyone who has made it possible for me to share what I've learned from, with and about her.

★Bodleian shelfmark e616/4 5 September 1911 ff, 30 November, and 27 and 31 December and e617/1 for 11 January and 28 March 1911.

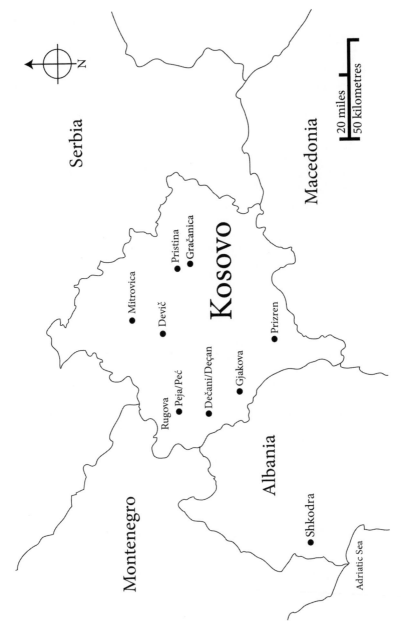

1 AyDIT DourHAM

'So why do some Albanian men wear little domed white felt hats and some wear black berets?' It seemed a reasonable question – the white 'plis' hat is a striking feature of national dress among Kosovo's older Albanians, but not all grandfathers wear it. I'd been in Kosovo a few weeks and was curious. Were the men in white felt from different clans from the men in black? Was there only one person per family entitled to wear the *plis*? I had started to construct some theories.

The Albanian girl I was talking to frowned.

'There's no reason really. What are you, AyDIT DourHAM?'

I smiled politely and incomprehendingly back at her.

A few weeks later I had my first experience of an Albanian wedding. Rob and I were invited by a new friend of mine, and I was offered a place in the car with the bride's sister. We travelled in convoy with horns blaring and ornamental handkerchiefs dangled out of windows. Under our windscreen wiper, and under the windscreen wiper of every other car in our procession, was a teatowel.

That seems odd to you? Worthy of comment?

'So, umm, what's the reason for the teatowels that I keep seeing on the cars in Kosovan wedding processions?'

My friend smiled vaguely. 'There's no reason really. What are you, AyDIT DourHAM?'

I'd tasted *flija*, the national dish of Kosovo's Albanians, a few days after arriving in Pristina, but only later that summer did I learn the almost identical word, meaning 'sacrifice'. I asked a guy I knew who had studied Albanian at university in Pristina – 'do you think there's any connection, given the traditional sun-ray design of the food and the ancient sun-worship I've read about here?'

'I really don't know. You're quite an AyDIT DourHAM aren't you.'

So now I wanted to find out not just about the teatowels and the old men's headwear and the etymology of carbohydrates, but about this person that kept being mentioned.

The first name sounded Turkish, but the surname was clearly Anglo-Saxon, and after some repetitions I was able to transcribe what was being repeated here. Edith Durham is clearly a celebrity in Kosovo, and there is an assumption that as a British woman – especially one asking questions about traditional hats – I must have heard of her.

Shortly afterwards, I had to work a little harder at my acquaintance with Miss Durham because I was paid to. One of the jobs I fell into in the first few months in Pristina was private English tutoring. My favourite student was Fatmir, a good-looking refugee from the Albanian-majority area of Preshevo, within Serbia. Fatmir's interest in learning English was limited, but his love of England itself was boundless. He was a particular fan of Winston Churchill, so my early lessons focused on texts around the great man. But after a few lessons like this, and once Fatmir had learned how to pronounce 'Marlborough' correctly, we clearly needed some new material. Fatmir and I had talked about the national histories contained in ordinary objects; he had described for me the ethnographic collection he had gathered, with eagle motifs woven into blood-coloured rugs, the wooden carved bowls, incorporating a little plinth, designed for washing your guests' feet, the elaborate fetish around the three traditional layers of footwear – and he'd told me of how his collection was burned in the 1999 war; the objects blackening, crumbling, disappearing as the latest phase of national history was played out in objects. He was another Albanian who had talked to me about AyDIT DourHAM so for our next lesson I found some internet text on the woman. Painstakingly, we completed together a cloze procedure

Edith Durham was _____ in 1863. For most of her life she _____ in North London. Until the age of 37 she _____ her time with watercolour painting (exhibiting at the Royal Academy) and _____ for her sick mother but by 1901 she was becoming ill herself and her doctor _____ her to travel. The journey she _____ that year changed her life. She _____ the Balkans and _____ in love with the life she _____ there. When she _____ back to London she told her mother she would continue to nurse her for ten months of every year on condition that she could _____ to the Balkans for two months each year. On her visits to the Balkans she _____ artefacts for museums in Britain and _____ anthropological notes. Back in London she _____ a Fellow of the Royal Anthropological Institute. She _____ seven books about the Balkans. She _____ in the Balkans during the Balkan wars of 1912 and 1913 and _____ tirelessly to give humanitarian aid. As a result of all her work, the Albanian people _____ her the title 'Queen of the Mountain People'. She _____ to lobby for the Albanian cause until her death in 1944.

When we compared it with a biography of someone still alive it was a good example text for the differences between the simple past and the present perfect ('For most of her life she lived in North London ...' but is now dead; 'For most of his life he has lived in North London ...' and still does). Grammar has a ruthless way of reminding you of mortality.

Despite my grammatical certainties, preparing the English exercise really only underlined the gaps in my knowledge of Edith's life. They might have stayed incomplete but for an article that appeared in a Sunday paper about my work as a volunteer with the Ethnological Museum in Pristina. Amongst the exaggerated compliments was a generous comparison of my work with Edith Durham's.

There's nothing like being told you have just the same nose as someone to make you overly interested in the exact flare of their nostrils. It was time that I read something written by ED. My entry point was her book, *High Albania*, in which she describes one of her journeys through Kosovo. Despite the nearly 30 years which divided her death from my birth, now I could feel the faltering beginning of a relationship.

She recounts a conversation familiar to me in ongoing debates with Kosovan taxi drivers about why I don't want to have children:

We had arrived at questions which – even in Servian – were most embarrassingly personal and physiological, when luckily one of the pigs got its head jammed in the petroleum can, rushed thus bonneted shrieking through the yard, and diverted the conversation.

and experiences I'd never had – the harem she visits just outside Pristina:

Was shown into an apartment full of stout, pallid, collopy females ... Shrieks of laughter at idea of my going round alone with a man ... Their conversation is much what one would expect of a cow if it could talk.

I warmed to her sense of humour, her intrepidity, her frankness and comment on what she found on her travels, and back home – describing an elaborate hairdo found in Kosovo:

Ends of both curls fastened to leather band under chin sewn with large turquoise beads. Whole making a solid block of hair – grotesque and extraordinary, at least

I thought so till I came back to England and found everyone's head swollen to double its size with stuffings, frizettes and 'transformations'.

I pitied Edith's return to London, and going through her writing gave me a new way to appreciate my luck in being in Kosovo. Reading something based in the country you are in gives your walk a filmstar swagger; you are allowed occasionally to believe you are a character from a book.

And then one day, my swagger came to an abrupt halt. Rob came home from work with news. With the end of his contract in Kosovo he was being offered an excellent new job – back in London, the capital of the land of stuffings and frizettes.

We discussed the decision over dinner. We discussed it again in the middle of the night after we had both lain silently for hours in bed trying to imagine Whitehall, trying to remember what the London Underground was like.

We made our decision, and yet we continued to discuss it for days. Was Rob right to leave his Balkan adventure and the sharp sunlight and shadows of July in Kosovo and go back to a better salary and a duller working day? Could I be happy following him to Pimlico? What would I do there?

Meanwhile, we got packing, with the sensible decision sitting like a solid, immoveable and wearying weight in our suitcases. It felt like the end of a long hot summer – the end of a way of life we'd grown into over three years in a country where people were more important – and frequently more efficient – than systems, where activities were based on spontaneity, and where we'd been apprenticed in long hours of sitting talking over coffee, and savouring tastes we'd not known before – of smoked pepper relish, chestnut honey, wedges of *flija* with homegrown tomatoes. In Kosovo I'd become a beekeeper, articles had been written about me in the Sunday papers, I'd learned to speak Albanian, learned the feel of it on my mouth. I'd made daring new friendships with people I wouldn't have known how to talk to just a few years before; leaving the country was saying goodbye to someone I was really fond of: the Kosovan me.

It felt like no-one in London, welcoming me back to the cold comfort of cheddar cheese, would understand. But as I sorted out our bookshelves into the pile to give away and the pile To Keep with the well-thumbed copy of *High Albania* on the top, I realised that of course there was one Englishwoman who could sympathise; we'd be moving to within a few miles of Edith's birthplace.

2 Life might, after all, be worth living

Our new flat in London was not a good place to spend long days alone. Small and in a strange mobile telephone black spot, it was in full view of Big Ben and – even without Radio 4 on; even when I averted my eyes from the clockface – my days were punctuated by the heavy resonant reminders of time passing me by. Every fifteen minutes I thought of Mrs Dalloway, as the 'leaden circles dissolved into air'.

I tried to fill the minutes with purposeful activity, not just waiting for Rob's weary return from his new high-pressure job. Control-C; Control-V – I copied and pasted CVs into emails to an increasingly speculative range of addresses. I applied for work as a translator, desperate to use my most-treasured souvenir of our time in Kosovo. I applied to the London offices of some of the international charities with whom I'd worked as a consultant in Pristina, I offered myself as a volunteer in local schools, libraries, refugee centres, support groups ... But the radio was full of the financial crisis and no-one was hiring; few people were even replying, except my Kosovan friends. They sent me envious messages about the flat in view of Big Ben, about the 'dinamik' life they'd heard of in London. I sent back careful messages; yes, my family was well and I was happy to see them again. No, I hadn't found work yet. Roberti was well and his job was good. I would be coming back to visit Kosovo – when I had some money.

I sent messages to the guides at the Ethnological Museum who were dreaming of twinning the museum with a collection in Britain. The museum had opened shortly after I'd arrived to live in the city, three years previously so I had a sense that my growth in familiarity with its beautifully restored buildings was in tune with the rest of the population's slow move to appreciation of the treasures, and now maybe we could take it further. I wrote up loving descriptions of the museum's group of eighteenth and nineteenth century buildings set in a pretty little garden under the shade of a walnut tree, and its exhibits of jewellery, embroidered costume and elaborate socks, and contacted museums in England who might share my enthusiasms. I longed to share the intricate handcrafts I'd learned and the lives they reflected. I ached to be back among those lives.

Meanwhile, I tried to make myself feel better by gorging on the cheddar cheese, salt and vinegar crisps, the Cadbury's, Heinz mushroom soup, Ambrosia custard ... all the things I had missed in Kosovo. I put on weight.

My London friends welcomed me 'home' and got on with their lives and their families that had expanded and moved on and out during the years I'd been away. Children had been born and needed mothering; house prices had increased and families were relocating – away from Big Ben, and in on themselves. I read a lot, mainly about Kosovo, but it didn't help. I didn't need to be reminded of the landscapes I couldn't see out of the smart London window. What I needed were some guidebooks to the new situation I found myself in. A melodramatic phrase came back to me – 'the future stretched before me as endless years of grey monotony, and escape seemed hopeless'.

It was Edith. Not the Edith striding the mountains, riding for four days to send the telegram that would hold Korça against Greek invasion, scouring the markets for Albanian weavings like those I had self-consciously draped over the sofa in our small Pimlico sitting room. This wasn't Edith the heroine, but Edith the frustrated 37 year-old in her stifling London home. This was someone who understood.

I remembered an evening in Kosovo when I'd been invited to dinner to meet a visiting British Balkan expert. Antonia Young has been coming to Albanian lands every year for the last fifty. She started when she was twenty, and is now an inspiring white-haired grande dame. She is soft-spoken, maybe even shy, until she starts talking about the subjects she is passionate about; and one of these is Edith Durham. She has written articles about Edith, and led a tour through Albania in the 'nineties in the footsteps of Edith Durham. As we had sat with our hosts in the warmth of a Balkan summer evening in the restaurant courtyard, Antonia told me animatedly that there is a small museum in Halifax where she had curated a room dedicated to Edith Durham's travels and collections.

So when another empty day dawned over London's crowded skyline I decided I would travel north to see what I could learn there, not about Edith the Queen of the Mountain People, but about Edith the petulant Englishwoman; Edith after she returned from Kosovo – a rather stout lady stuck in Hampstead with some strange stories to tell.

As I got out of the train at Halifax I thought of Edith being prescribed 'travel' for her nervous breakdown. Not that my trip felt exactly like a Cure; I saw more chip shops in my journey from the station to the Bankfield museum than I had seen in all the weeks since my return to London. So this couldn't compare with her cruise down the Dalmatian coast but I could still feel my spirits lifting, as Edith had written of that first untethering from London; that 'life might, after all, be worth living'.

Halifax is a town to be navigated in three dimensions, thanks to its position over gorges and in valleys. Bold Victorian bridges stride the chasms, and walled pathways in chunky liver-coloured stone lead not just left and right but also up and down. I got lost as in a miniature Gotham, walking up the stone walkway when I should have been directly underneath it, and apparently unable ever to get where I wanted to be, like an Escher drawing. But as I asked for help from people with unfamiliar accents I was reminded that I was somewhere new, and on a quest, and the wrong turns acquired some of the whiff of adventure.

I found the Bankfield museum eventually – a large house set in parkland. It had had an established textile collection by 1935, and when ED was considering where to give the clothes she had collected on her Balkan travels it promised a good home. One room gave an idea of what it would have been like in her day – a finely-proportioned drawing room with glass cases inset into the fitted bookcases round the edges. They were labelled in neat gold-painted lettering with names of countries, and each country was represented by a few pinned pieces of fabric. I dawdled round Burma, the West Indies, basketwork hats, frayed fabrics, velvets with the nap worn – the world's Oxfam shop. And then I saw a flash of familiar designs – the geometric patterns I had last seen in the glass cases of Pristina's Ethnological Museum. I knew the words for them – the labels in self-conscious italics here were part of my vocabulary. *Jelek, marama, opinga* ... I mouthed the names for the items of traditional costume, old friends.

Squinting into the case I could just make out the neat script on the small tags attached to each exhibit. They were her initials – MED. So I knew the exact journey these decorative towels and cloths had taken. I could imagine, from her writing, the bustle of Albanian commerce in which she'd haggled for them in Prizren or Pristina. Then there would have been the packing up – I thought about my own miserable loading of boxes a few months previously – and eventually their arrival in London where they could be unfolded like a narrative for friends and guests to read. I stared at the glass, and caught my own reflection squinting back.

But this was just one display case and I left The Balkans, and the pieces pinned like butterflies among the other textile collectors' world treasures, to search out the room dedicated to the travels of Edith Durham. The exhibition was called 'Bread, Salt and our Hearts' after the traditional Albanian offer of hospitality even in the most straitened circumstances. It told and illustrated the story of Edith's adventures across the Balkans and I gained a new respect for her, crossing rivers by raft

The stream was swift and strong. Stark naked men, with inflated sheepskins bound before them pranced about the shore, playing like kittens. The crazy contraption was half full of water. We piled ourselves and the saddles on the centre plank. Three men … guided the affair to the end of the promontory; there the current caught us up, whirled us around like a straw, and spun us along the water slopping over the gunwales.

and dealing with suspicious officials

In Nish they all imagined, as I learnt later, that I was bound for Bulgaria with evil intentions; messages from Montenegro for the undoing of Serbia. But I had come to see carpet making – and I saw it.

Pictures of wrinkled faced, twinkling-eyed Albanian men carrying their prized guns were illustrated with quotes from her books about days

chewing sheep-cheese and firing rifles and revolvers indoors; a noisy joy that peppers oneself and the refreshments with burnt powder and wads.

A postcard from the Balkan States exhibition of 1907 at Earl's Court illustrated the work that Edith did as King Nikola of Montenegro's 'Commissioner' for the exhibition but there was also information about her role in aid work – the months she spent as part of the Macedonian Relief Committee in 1903 where she visited more than a thousand houses offering aid, and then worked in the hospital in Ohrid

suppurating gunshot wounds were quite a new experience to me and I found them most fascinating.

A two-dimensional Edith was there, in photographs familiar from what I had read about her: a pre-Raphaelite picture of a late teenager with an intelligent half-smile and long hair (before she cut it short in her more rebellious or practical years), along with an image I hadn't seen before – on horseback, off to distribute aid in Macedonia. There were scrapbooks, too, with her photographs stuck in with neatly-lettered captions, and picture postcards from her travels.

But more than that, a three-dimensional Edith emerged.

In Kosovo I had taken my shoes off before entering any house; from the footwear scuffed off at the door of a home you could tell who was inside the building. Opening the front door of the house where I had lodged with a Kosovan family, I could tell whether my landlord (long brown shoes) was in, and whether my fellow lodger (fancy strappy sandals) was back yet. I left my own dusty boots to show that I was home, and thought about the elaborate sliding panels in gold-lettered oak in my grandparents' mansion block on the south coast where residents elegantly recorded their movements *in* or *out* of the apartments. Here at the Bankfield was the suggestion that Edith was *in*. Her shoes here could have been just scuffed off by her while she popped in for coffee. They were the twine-and-hide knotted traditional *opinga* I had first seen on display in Pristina's museum. Unlike the fine embroidery of the traditional wedding dress, or the elegant silks and linens elsewhere in the collection, these were valuable because they were practical; important because of all the rocks and mud and mountain sides they had rubbed up against, significant because of the heels that had been chafed inside them, and had eventually worn them down so you could see how the body's weight had been distributed over them, the exact gait of the woman who had walked seven moons (and more) in these moccasins.

Her note on the slippers accompanied them in their display case,

when newly made the shoes are soaked in oil till pliable. They then mould themselves to the feet and give the toes and sole a good grip on rocks. The soles of this pair are worn through as I traipsed many miles in them.

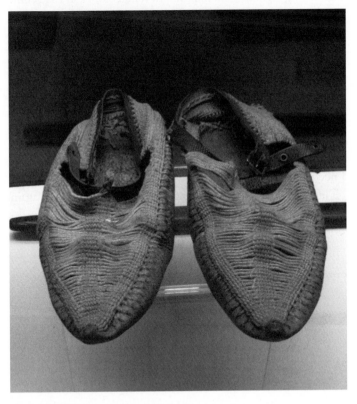

With thanks to Calderdale MBC Museums

I stared at them for a long time, thinking about their former owner, the landscapes she had 'traipsed', in Kosovo, Albania and beyond, but also the villages she had helped, the lives she had saved through her distribution of corn and quinine, roof felting and public awareness in the forgotten regions on the other side of Europe. And I remembered that each time, after her adventures, with her saddlebags packed with hand-woven souvenirs and her sharp mind stuffed with impressions and prejudice, her diaries with telling vignettes and impromptu watercolours, she had come back to London. In England, she had worked at a patient, lively, intelligent explanation of the Balkans to the Britons. Through seven books, her many articles, her lectures and endless letters to politicians and to the Foreign Office, she had found a way to bring Kosovo alive in England; I needed to learn from her.

I stared at the *opinga* and vowed that I would learn to follow them – but not just into former war zones and smoky hans, through the incense swirls of Orthodox monasteries, across the Accursed Mountains and for resting stops in Ottoman harems. I needed to learn from her how to walk your goat hide slippers off into adventure and wear them meaningfully back home again.

𝟥 Seeing things through Edith's eyes in Bloomsbury

I emailed friends in Kosovo to tell them about the museum in Halifax, and the ethnologists from the Pristina museum replied asking for more details. I uploaded more of the blurry photographs I'd taken so that I could send the *opinga* back to the land they had come from, and realised how crazy this was. The Bankfield museum, nestling amid the chip shops of Halifax, had a greater richness of Kosovan costume than the well-loved little Ethnological Museum in Pristina's old town. As a British woman I could, for the price of a day return to Yorkshire, see more of Kosovo's history in textiles than could the professionals in the country itself. It felt unfair and I wondered what could be done.

The more I thought about the Bread, Salt and our Hearts exhibition, focused on the Albanian idea of hospitality, the more the idea grew of helping the collection which Edith had cared for so conscientiously – these long-term British guests – return home. I imagined display boards, information panels, and the rich embroideries and fabrics, as well as the everyday towels and shoes, which help us to put ourselves – and our finery, our frippery, our domestic tasks – in perspective. These things tell us where we come from, tell us we are not alone, inspire us with what we might become. And maybe an exhibition would attract attention to Edith's battle for independence and give hope to other women. Not just those like me, but also women trapped in the care of invalid relatives and the inflexible gender roles of most Kosovan families. I wondered how you put together an international touring exhibition, how much it cost, what the insurance arrangements were, whether it would be possible.

Of course, the exhibition of objects would have to be modest in size – but for the information panels, there was wider scope. I remembered something else that Antonia Young had told me: that there were albums full of Edith's photographs which had never been published. Maybe reproductions of these would be possible?

At that dinner, Antonia had described the photographs, and our eyes had lit up. It was the sort of conversation that travellers have on hot evenings in foreign courtyards – stories of the rich pickings to be had in little-known corners of the world, tips on how to hunt down treasure. Such conversations don't usually lead to Bloomsbury, but Antonia had said the photos were held by the British Museum.

As a young teenager I read an influential novel about a couple of kids who fell in love when one bumped into the other on the way out of the British Museum. It was a carefully-written story for a particular market – the kind of kid who was reading books rather than spending time with boys – and it added a romantic frisson to the stone-cold beauty of the building and its contents. When I was older, suffering real heart-ache, it had been the Assyrian section here where I took refuge, and on many other less dramatic occasions I had gone – perhaps as Edith had on a free afternoon – to the museum to remove myself from a world of neat squares and over-priced tea shops and wander the halls of a building offering signs like 'right: Asia; left: Africa'. It is like spending an hour or two at Cape Horn in the middle of a day's shopping.

I gathered that the Museum had no Balkans displays so I went to the information desk to ask how I might be able to find Edith's photographs in the archives. They told me I needed the anthropology department and gave me a map of the museum on which the helpful information officer drew the route – down the stairs to a room that wasn't labelled on the map. 'But it's below this room' the assistant assured me, planting an x in biro on another square of the map, like a pirate might.

'How will I know when I'm there? Will it have a sign?'

'Look for the bell set in the wall,' she advised, and so, feeling like Alice in Wonderland off to catch the Hogwarts Express, I made my way to the bell-in-the-wall by the unmarked room which houses Anthropology Section.

They answered my ring, and strangely muttering, immensely kind men and women dealt with my enquiries. Yes, they had some of the photographs Antonia had told me about. But did I know about the other items that had been bequeathed to the Museum by Miss Durham? They pulled details off the catalogues of the items. In a mixture of 1914 and 2008 I was given both a colour printout of the digitised catalogue showing photographs of the items associated with Edith's name in the elaborate electronic search results, but also a copy of the pages from the exquisite Edwardian catalogue where the acquisitions were first recorded. There, in those final pre-war days of June 1914, the slippers, gloves, socks and belt, along with a spoon, flute, guitar and bow – an impromptu party on one page – had been listed in elegant script, each item accompanied by a fine, pedantic drawing a few centimetres wide. These sketches would literally fit on a thumbnail, and I imagined the archivist – probably muttering and kindly like his 21st century descendants – bending over his tiny two-dimensional museum with pride. For my own adventures in two dimensions they sat me down at a long table and presented me with bulging photograph albums. These weren't the originals, and they left me alone with them.

I wondered quite what I would find as I lifted the cover of the first one.

It was like listening to the ramblings of an old woman. The images were powerful, jumbled together, unmarked, unconnected with one another. I grasped at a few definitely recognisable sites from Balkan cities. This must be Serbia. This Macedonia. So if they were in order, would this one be Kosovo? There was no way of telling, and as I turned the pages I became increasingly lost. Lakes, mountains, weddings, guns, markets, homes … in the end I surrendered myself without a map to the strange, familiar wandering through long ago and faraway.

I thought about my exhibition, looking out for likely images. Some photographs were beautiful – wonderful faces, caught in natural glimpses, as you might see people in passing train carriages, or on the down escalator as you go up. And as with people on the Tube, the photographs were ultimately frustrating – they told me so little about themselves, and even less about the woman behind the camera. At least I was learning one thing about Edith – she wasn't the kind of girl to offer her camera to strangers and ask them to snap her standing next to a famous monastery. She wrote in a letter when she was in her sixties of her 'long life as a looker on, who sometimes sees most of the case'. That is what she had done on her travels, and all you could see of her was the look in the eyes of the people she was staring out.

But perhaps, I realised, that is all that we ever know about ourselves. I don't see myself for even a fraction of the time that my friends and colleagues see me. One brief check in the mirror in the morning, a sneaked look at a reflection in a shop window as I pass by, but otherwise my view of myself is the view I have of other people looking at me and talking to me as I move through my day.

The staff allowed me to photocopy some of the pictures, and so I kept with me some of the most striking portraits, images that could accompany the exhibition which was growing each time I thought about it. My favourite was the musician with his *çifteli* just in frame, staring boldly straight at me, exactly as he had stared at Edith.

4 The purple slippers

In the library at the British Museum I had been told that I could apply to have a look at the items Edith had brought back, so I filled in the necessary form and asked for an audience with a pair of slippers. I was sure that there was nothing like them that had survived in Kosovo, and the description of them suggested they could be a beautiful centerpiece for an exhibition of Albanian artefacts.

While I had been in Kosovo I had learned how significant a part was played by footwear in Kosovan homes, in understanding of cleanliness, of 'the other'. The whole country had a foot fetish. Businessmen and politicians would carry in their pocket a small wipe for polishing their shoes, to be applied just before a meeting started – the Pristina equivalent of a breath freshener spray perhaps. Visiting a home (or even some offices) you will take your shoes off as an absolutely inviolable rule. Even in circumstances where I have been moving in and out of a house, carrying tables to set up a birthday party, for example, it was considered quite reasonable that I should stop each time at the threshold and change into or out of my outdoor shoes.

Just as it is an unbreakable social requirement to remove your shoes at the entrance to a home, it is considered good hosting to provide indoor footwear for your guests. So arriving at classy houses for dinner parties in my carefully co-ordinated smart shoes, I would be slightly crestfallen to be handed in exchange the standard pair of carpet slippers which are kept by the door in a variety of shades and sizes for the visitor. On my visit to the Prime Minister's home where I had been nervous about looking my very best, I had been surprised to discover that these footwear rules applied even in exalted company, and both he and I sat dangling large slippers from our feet at Kosovo's equivalent of Chequers.

Though you must also be careful how you dangle. Showing the soles of your feet to someone else is considered a great offence to them. As a result, Kosovan footwear is elaborate. Today this more often means fragile and glittery sandals, but in the past (and still in evidence in the country's handcrafts) the foot fetish showed itself in hand-knitted socks or slippers. Three layers of footwear made for practicality, and perhaps the kind of indulgence shown in Victorian petticoats. The outer layer was made of strips of leather – the *opinga* that ED had had made for her which had been on display at the Bankfield Museum. The inner layer was a sock. The middle layer was an often gorgeous knitted slipper, protected from the elements on one side and from sweat on the other.

The pair in that catalogue photograph I'd seen at the British Museum were a deep Liberty purple, with gold thread and intricate stitching. They would be an inspiring part of the exhibition and while I waited for a response on when I could go and see them in the museum stores I started researching how one might put on an exhibition.

What I found out was not immediately encouraging. Museums had different requirements but the most stringent included provision for handmade wooden boxes stuffed with protective material for each item to be shipped. One pair of earrings; one custom-made box. An additional brooch: an additional custom-made box. Artefacts had to be displayed in a locked case and this case could not be unlocked unless a member of the loaning museum staff was present. If the item was sharing a case with an item from another museum, this meant both members of staff would have to be present at the same time, and the hotel bills for one would have to be footed while awaiting the arrival of the other. Travel of museum staff had to be business class, and if they were taking the items hand luggage, the museum warned that they might require an additional seat booked for the hand carry case. These couriers' accommodation in the town of the exhibition venue of course had to be covered and this would be for a minimum of three days 'to take into account the need for artefact acclimatisation'… and curators' jollies, I supposed.

But I wasn't panicking yet – this was all a matter of money, and perhaps money could be found. First, I had to pull together a convincing catalogue for the exhibition, and that meant seeing these slippers, for example, with my own eyes.

Judy from the museum replied to the request I'd submitted and we set up a date when I could come out to the Museum store in West London. The stores in Olympia are housed in a former mail sorting office – an eminent Victorian building of many floors and, now, fire escapes. Security is high and I was buzzed through a turnstile gate and escorted through a series of electronically locked doors before I arrived at the stores themselves. Together with what I'd read about the exhibition loan arrangements, I began to question whether ED's exhibits were in prison awaiting bail rather than respected guests. I wondered whether the slippers had ever made a bid for escape, trying to tiptoe unobtrusively along the passages, setting their pointed toes on a course for Albanian lands. Maybe my exhibition could offer something like what Edith was seeking when she set off for the Balkans – if not exactly an escape bid, then at least a form of parole.

I thought about the parcels and envelopes ('letters of thanks, letters from banks,/ letters of joy for the girl and boy') that had moved through these complicated corridors in the past, and had a sudden vision of the accumulated treasures of the world held by the British Museum being a slow, infinitely slow form of mail too. They are brought here with careful details of their address, classified, directed to their destination, and held safely in the meantime.

How long that time might be is, of course, a topic of healthy debate. But having come from a country where nearly half of all homes were burned in the interethnic conflict of 1998/9 and beyond, I had seen how fragile was the survival of anthropological artefacts. As Edith had seen first-hand in the Balkan wars of 1912 and 1913, if you are fleeing for your life, or running from your burning home, Grandma's wedding dress or Grandad's best handmade slippers are not the things you are going to save.

Poverty has played its part too, in the stripping of Kosovo's traditional costumes and the record of what they were like. I have been amazed by how few photographs my Kosovan friends have of themselves and their families in childhood. Cameras were rare in Kosovo at a time when my parents and grandparents were taking holiday snaps for granted. So glimpses are rare of Kosovo's past. Increasingly I could understand the British Museum as a place of sanctuary, asylum, for objects too vulnerable in their homeland.

Of course that didn't help in deciding how, when, or if they should then be returned. Or whether it was reasonable to request a business class ticket for a member of museum staff and their hand luggage to take items like these in their custom-constructed boxes to be shown elsewhere, and then to fly back out to collect them, with acclimatisation time in hotels included.

But for today I was just thrilled that ED had rescued these, and that the British Museum had then taken them in – one of the pretty little pairs shuffled in two-by-two to this extraordinary ark.

Judy was ready to show me the slippers when I arrived. She was glamorous in a gorgeous coat (Uzbekistan) and gestured round the warehouse of rolls and wooden boxes where her stock was held like a very up-market department store.

When we had finished introducing ourselves she went up a little metal ladder to the top shelf and brought down a package wrapped in tissue paper. Truly, this was a more up-market store than I had ever shopped in.

She laid a sheet on the table and then, sweeping the tissue paper back like a stage whisper, revealed the slippers. They were exquisite – the colour undimmed by the hundred years since ED had packed them up. Judy lent me a magnifying glass to see the stitching more carefully and I was awestruck by the careful handiwork, but also by the odds of their survival. Edith had done the slippers, their owners, and their people, a wonderful service in rescuing them and then passing them on for safekeeping. The British Museum store is a verb as well as a noun.

5 The wax cylinders

Being able to touch those slippers felt like a significant concrete connection with Edith and her world. I told everyone I met at the time about this burgeoning relationship, my new friend. However, most people in London knew as little about Edith as they did about Kosovo and it was a dispiriting quest to be sharing. But there was one person I wanted to tell whom I knew would understand. His name appropriately means 'the dawn' and Agim had marked the beginning of our engagement with Kosovo. In the rushed days before our move to Kosovo, Rob had had a couple of weeks of language lessons with Agim, coming home to me and making noises I couldn't understand – until he taught me how to mimic the shapes his mouth was making, to echo the verbs in a strange, exciting courtship. Everything that I learned then from Rob, he was learning from Agim and eventually I got to meet the third member of the *ménage à trois* whose foreign accents so excited us.

Now I was back in the London which had been Agim's home for ten years, and more recently than it had been mine. He seemed as intrigued to hear about my Kosovo as I was to learn about his London. We arranged to get together for a drink; in Pristina style, not an alcoholic drink, but a coffee. We set a time and he asked me to suggest a place. I thought of an oriental cafe I know, all cushions and hanging lamps and we agreed to meet there.

Sitting down, I was dislocated. At the tables around me, young Londoners tried their first hookahs, and I self-consciously ordered a mint tea. It was made with fresh leaves, and the waiter poured it theatrically in a fragrant stream from a copper pot held high above my glass. It was exotic and oriental – and nothing like anywhere I had ever had a drink in Kosovo, where the mint tea was served practically and without fuss from neat teabags like those you can buy in Sainsbury's. This was the source of my dislocation; a fear that the Balkans of the imagination was already starting to corrode the Balkans of my memory and experience. I worried about why I had chosen this particular café.

Agim arrived and ordered a hot chocolate, as if to prove a point.

We set our drinks thankfully aside when the small talk was over, and Agim asked for details of my ED research. He has a fast, breathless way of talking, his favourite response the enthusiastic vowels of 'aashtuuuu' – 'that's just it'.

He loved the photograph of the slippers, and then I told him about the British Museum photographs too. Agim's ponytail bobbed as he asked for details and I hesitantly sketched my dream of an exhibition and how important it would be for Kosovars to see some of their heritage, even if just in a travelling show.

'Aaashtuu, aaashtuu,' said Agim. 'And what about a soundscape? Do you know that some of her recordings survive too? A few songs she captured on wax cylinders in Albania'. This eavesdropping on what she would have been listening to might be the next best thing to talking to her directly, and Agim's final words to me when we said our goodbyes were 'don't forget to contact the British Library.'

I needed no further encouragement. For me, the British Library is a model of an ideal community. I was already familiar with some of the quartiers of this wonderful metropolis – the Business district, the government district (in the social sciences reading room), its exhibition areas – the Kensington of the building, as well as all the resources it offered in its public spaces, like any enlightened community should: water fountains and cash point, restaurant and cafe. My favourite facility is its standing chairs

– slightly reclined planes of wood with padding at the points where head and back make contact, placed in a circle outside one of the reading rooms so you can stretch out after hunching over books, whilst remaining on your feet.

And if only it could be properly catalogued, perhaps even more interesting than all the books is the other knowledge that sits at the library's desks and terminals – the connections and ideas stored in the readers' heads. British Library users are a Radio 4 demographic, a good-looking, quirky, eclectic and obviously intelligent bunch of the self-taught.

There is a sense of people making their lives meaningful as you walk past the Library's readers and researchers. Everyone is here because they want to be; they want to come and sit, quiet and civilised; they want to remove lip balms and hand creams from their bags (signs explain carefully that these can damage the books; but the effect of preparing yourself is like getting ready for a sauna or swimming pool), to regress to using pencil only (biro, too, can damage the books) like in primary school; there is even a communal pencil sharpener at the front of the room like I remember Mrs Burnley having on her desk in Year 1.

But the music reading room was new to me and it's not like the other reading rooms. For a start, you get the sense that there is less 'reading' going on here, and more 'listening'. Not just in the designated carrels with headphones, but in people's heads. A girl sat over a score with a ruler in her mouth, fingers involuntarily moving over it as if it were a clarinet. The man opposite me hummed tunefully as he took notes. And I was sure that in everyone's minds there were soundless strains of exotic song. I was reminded of how older generations of Albanians in Kosovo use the verb 'me këndue', now reserved for singing, when they talk about reading.

At the information desk I asked how I could listen to Junio Fatis, a song recorded by Edith in Albania. I was told to 'go past Beethoven, down to Mozart and use the terminal there to log in.' Maybe this is how directions will be given in heaven.

When I reached (the bust of) Mozart, I discovered the computer with those professional headphones which really block out the world outside. Wearing them I could see my fingers moving over the computer keyboard, but could hear no sound – like diving, or dreaming.

And then one click took me far, far away. There was the spatter and spurt of the wax cylinder (I thought of each of them as a bump and a bash of Edith's saddlebags as she travelled back from Albania) and a sudden wail. Albanian singing has a wailing quality even when you hear it live. Hearing it now in my strange otherworldly underwater condition, it was like a ghost from the past, crying to be heard.

The catalogue records Edith's annotation that this was 'Shan's favourite song'. Marko 'Shan' Shantoya was her Albanian guide, an intriguing character who drifts into her narrative, letters and diaries as a close fellow-adventurer. And, yes, the romantic in me had wondered whether he had ever been more to her. I listened again and realised that the song's subject matter is how the eponymous Junio avenged his brother's death. Shan was obviously not the dreamy type.

But nevertheless, listening was evocative. In Kosovo I had grown familiar with this singing style, the narrative songs of Albanian tradition. One day, in a muddy village in the shadow of the Accursed Mountains I had been visiting a girl I had become friendly with. Her father sat in the front room with us, listening in the rather bemused way that fathers listen to their daughters' friends the world over. She had tried to bring him into the conversation – 'tell her about your medal, Dad.' Proudly he had gone to the plasterboard wall where a rough nail had been banged in to hang last year's promotional calendar from the political party popular locally. I realised that draped over February was a ribboned medal. It was explained that some decades earlier, Ymer had won a Yugoslavian music competition. He offered to sing for us, and his voice had lifted in the same fierce wail that I heard from those British Library headphones, although he had sung a strange song of gratitude to NATO, Bill Clinton and Robin Cook for the liberation of Kosovo in 1999. It was his own composition, he explained shyly when he'd finished and had returned to being a rather slight quiet man in a shack who was wary of his daughter's odd friends. It hadn't just been the medal that had seemed to make him a different, more impressive figure a few minutes before.

He was a long way away now, but it was the same lump in my throat that was summoned as I sat in the British Library where the music was generating an unsettling mixture of feelings something like homecoming and homesickness.

When I had surfeited on this haunting singer with his tale of blood from another century I clicked on the second piece, 'Ninety days at sea'. I expected the same querulous male voice. But it wasn't him.

It was her!

I got goosebumps as Edith Durham spoke to me. 'An Albanian song about the sea,' she announced, in a pleasant but straining primary school teacher's voice which seemed as if it was struggling to be heard. Maybe the interference wasn't the wax cylinder, and the songs had actually been recorded in a hailstorm?

The song began and I tried to imagine them crouched round the recording equipment in 1905. And then there was a rasping screech – the kind of noise a goat might make if it swallowed a wax cylinder – and the recording stopped abruptly. But to be honest, I was no longer so interested in the music. I pressed 'play' again and listened to Edith's simple spoken announcement over and over.

So now we had been introduced.

6 The pears under the pear tree

Now Edith had spoken to me, I decided it was time to pay her a house call. After all, we both knew that in the rituals of Albanian hospitality, it was I who would be honouring her through my visit. Through the census returns for 1871 I found out where she had lived. The census listed her father, a surgeon, her mother, Mary just a year older than me, and six children: Mary Edith the eldest, and Arthur, Herbert, Ellen, Caroline, Florence and an as yet unnamed baby. They lived together with their butler, cook, housemaid, nursemaid, nurse, and 'surgical nurse' – a rather uncomfortable sounding female to have about the house – in Lower Brook Street and I set off to the building, past the smart houses of Mayfair. Almost all the houses I passed looked as if they would have been there when seven-year-old Mary Edith lived in the neighbourhood. Letterboxes gleamed, doorbells were as brassy as uniform buttons; the street was intimidating and holier-than-thou in its careful painting and polishing.

Number 82 was still standing although no plaque marked the spot where this extraordinary woman had spent her formative years. I stared at it, thinking of what I'd read about tourists who continued to throng the Louvre, even after the Mona Lisa was stolen, gathering to stare at the space on the wall where she had once hung. I wondered what I should do next.

In one of Durham's articles in 1903 for the *Pall Mall Gazette* she parodies an Albanian she has met and who speaks English with what she calls 'fluent inaccuracy' (rather like my own Albanian) talking about the UK.

'That London! I know him! Five million peoples! And what a lot of criminals! Oh, your people bad people. In my country all kind good mans. Perhaps you all lone, got no money, tired, hungry. You knock at door. "Ullo, what you want?" "I hungry." "Come in." Then he give you bread, wine, tobacco, all what you want. Now, in London if you knock at door he says, "You run 'way or I call a p'leece!"'

So the thought of the response I would probably get if I knocked at this stranger's door was enough to turn me away. I contented myself with the coward's substitute for experience – a quick photograph. Looking at the picture now, I see myself reflected in the panes of the front door. If you don't push it open, I suppose that's all you will ever get for going to visit the places where long-dead people once lived.

My next call on Edith was a week later, and I was determined to be a little more adventurous. Perhaps I could find an 'Ullo, what you want? Come in' even among the millions of peoples in scary old London. I'd learned of three further addresses where Edith had lived. One was the address I had noted from the acquisitions book at the British Museum. This was where she had been living when she donated the objects to the Museum in 1914. The second address I'd found when I was researching other possible exhibits for my possible exhibition in the online catalogue showing the objects she had donated to the Pitt Rivers Museum. She had been living there in the latter years of her life. The third address I knew from her calling card which had formed part of the Bankfield Museum display. All were easily walkable from each other in the area of Hampstead and Belsize Park so on a bright autumnal day, scented with the sweet smell of yellow leaves just turning, I set out for the villas of north west London.

I found the first road easily. As I walked down it, I scanned the house numbers and realised that it was a long road; that this was going to be a long walk.

Walking on and as I looked at the patterning of the numbers and the houses still surviving from the period when Edith was alive, I also realised that this was probably going to be a long walk for little reward – not even a door slammed in my face. What door there had been, and the house – and the life – it might have led to, must have disappeared years ago. All the houses on the right hand side of the road were no more than about 40 years old. I wondered what bomb or modernising frenzy had taken the even numbers and spared the odd.

It was a dispiriting start to my little pilgrimage, feeling the threads of Edith's life so hard to pluck up.

And then suddenly I heard a sound that was as familiar to me as it would have been to Edith. It was the first time I had heard these vowels, the musical swearwords, in a street since Pristina. In fact, the first phrase that was distinct enough for me to be sure was 's'guxojmë' – 'we don't dare'. We bloody well did.

'Are you Albanian?' I asked (in Albanian) of the small family group stood on the pavement.

Yes, they were. They were from Peja, a town that Edith had visited. And where was I from? Well, I explained in Albanian, I had lived in Pristina for two years. We agreed what a small world it was. And how did I learn to speak their language?

I gave the name of my language teacher. Oh yes, his father was the friend of the older gentleman on the pavement. He had got to know my teacher through his work as a judge. And then their daughter had worked on a film with him a while ago. Truly, the Albanian's is a comforting-sized world.

I asked more polite questions of the family and the father presented his family in proper Albanian style. His son had just finished school and was preparing to go to university. What would he be studying? Law, of course, and the young man and the older both smiled at each other.

There was an Albanian expression for this which I had learned with our mutual friend the language teacher. With some effort, I got it out – 'the pear falls under the pear tree, eh.' They smiled and enjoyed their inter-generational similarities.

Then their daughter arrived from the house to join us. Her father took great delight in performing the introductions once again. 'This is Elizabeth. She speaks Albanian – she even knows how to say "the pear falls under the pear tree"'. We all basked in my linguistic achievement.

They asked what I had done in Kosovo and I told them about my work with the ethnological museum – how I had helped to organise weekly events preparing traditional food the traditional way in the museum gardens for visitors. Yes, they had seen it on television. I realised that of all the population of north-west London, I had probably found the only people who would recognise the name of the person I had been coming to see. Did they know, I asked, that Edith Durham had once lived on this street? No! They were as thrilled as I was.

It was a disappointment not to have found the Queen of the Mountain People, but I was almost more excited by finding some mountain people themselves, and the enthusiasm of the family from Peja encouraged me to press on and find the next address. Of course there was always the chance that the pear would have fallen under the pear tree, and some kindred spirit lived in the building which must have housed the strange collections, the battered trunk of Edith Durham.

Glenloch Road had all its houses standing. I could imagine exactly what Edith's walk home might have been like, to right side and left, as I made my way towards her front door. The house was divided into flats, so I had to play Belsize Roulette with the bells, wondering which chamber was full.

I got an answer to the first button on the entryphone so I stood on the path explaining something incoherent about why I was there – my interest in a woman who had lived in this house 70 years previously. Did the current occupant know anything about her?

No, she didn't, but thankfully nor did it seem she was going to call *a p'leece* on me. She said she'd come out to talk to me.

While I waited I tried to pull together a more intelligible explanation of Edith for someone who had never heard of her. It was an odd introduction to be performing, and reminded me of the work I'd done at the Ethnological Museum in Pristina, when Kosovan visitors came to the events we'd organised and I would enthuse to them about the traditional woodwork, the rituals of hospitality, ways of preparing food. I had had three years of such conversations trying to promote to Kosovars the Kosovan culture that attracted more interest from foreigners; it was now ironically appropriate to be trying to promote to the British a British woman who was better loved by Kosovars.

But to my surprise, it turned out that the woman now living in Edith's house was familiar with the Balkans.

'Oh yes, I go regularly to Belgrade,' she said, and I looked at Edith's descendant, standing in front of me on her suburban doorstep with no shoes on, with new respect.

'I even visited Pristina in the early 1990s,' she said, and now I was intrigued. That was the Milošević era, when quietly, and mainly ignored by British ladies from North London, systematic oppression of Kosovo's Albanians was initiated by the Serbian regime in education, employment and policing. I asked her more about her impressions, but we ended up swapping stories about the Grand Hotel and the need to improvise bathplugs, how hellish it is to start the day on Turkish coffee and the local *raki* firewater. The fruit at Edith's 1940s home was certainly falling where you would expect it to.

I carried on to the final house on my list, through streets now darkening, but where a breeze was whirling the dry leaves around me like luck.

Ellerdale Road held the most wildly neo-gothic of the houses I'd seen today. Emphasising the Hansel and Gretel look was creeper running amok across the roof and down over the porch like jungle lianas. As if I had stumbled on some ancient civilisation there was a vast Grecian head, a storey high, with a syphilitic nose, stranded in the driveway.

I could hear voices in the back garden and when I went through the gate cautiously, I found two boys in prep school uniforms trampolining in a lazy kind of way and chatting about their day at school. When I could finally get their attention I asked whether any grown-ups were around. A man shuffled out from the basement when he heard me talking. Not unfriendly, he asked what I wanted.

'Do you live here? I wanted to talk to someone about the history of the house.'

'Try the front door,' he advised. 'There's loads of 'em in there.'

I knocked on the door. A svelte woman in black opened it, and gave me a glimpse of the loads of 'em within. Madonnas smiled from the walls, sculptures posed in every corner; bits of old churches hung from the ceiling. This appeared to be the house of a collector even more committed than the collector who had lived there in 1904.

When I explained what I was here for, the silent woman in black showed me through to the Willie Wonka who ran this house of surprises. Sitting at an enormous old table piled with various forms of beauty – books, print-outs of Baroque women, invitations to vernissages – he invited me to sit down and tell him about Edith Durham.

This time I gave a more accomplished potted biography – the breakdown at 37 which led to her prescription to travel ...

'Thirty seven, you say? Like the Marianne Faithfull song?'

I didn't know what he was talking about. 'Jung – the theory that women have a crisis at the age of 37. Hang on ...' With a little help from the beautiful assistant in black, he found his way onto YouTube, and the rest of our conversation took place to the wailing of Marianne. 'Lucy Jordan/ In a white suburban bedroom.../ At the age of thirty-seven she realised she'd never/ Ride through Paris in a sports car with the warm wind in her hair.'

We talked about Edith, her urge for travel and warm wind in her hair, about Albania (he had visited the beautiful ruins of Butrint in a professional capacity), the North West Frontier and other badlands. He invited me to lunch to talk more.

Over lunch the current resident in Edith's home asked me how I'd found his – Edith's – address. I told him about the visit to the Bankfield Museum, and the calling card that had been included behind glass, along with the other exhibits. At the mention of the exhibits, his eyes sparkled and perhaps his hair stood up on end a little bit more. He knew people who had antiques shops, exhibition spaces – we could put the exhibition on together, he said.

It was a seductive idea.

'But you need more than just the objects,' he urged. 'Let her narrate her story; find manuscripts, tell the story in her own words.'

He paid for lunch and invited me back. I would have loved to have seen more of Edith's house, but Edith was warning me away from the 'white suburban bedroom'. And it was true that I should be focusing on letting Edith narrate her story. I left Hampstead for the Royal Anthropological Institute, where Edith could give me a piece of her mind.

7 In her own words

From my census research I knew Edith had younger sisters. One, born five years after her, shares her name with my own five-year younger sister, Caroline. When I was in Kosovo I had written emails to my Caroline telling her about my strange new life, creating for her a coherent narrative of my confused and confusing experiences. Perhaps Edith, too, had rehearsed some of her raw saddle sores in correspondence with her family. Letters offered a way for a first-hand account, before the need for tact in front of a wider public, or the scalpel of book editors (a friend later showed me a letter from ED to Joseph Swire on the subject of editing where she had discussed the adjective-chopping process, finding a short word that would do as well as each long one, and claimed to have rewritten parts of her first book fourteen times).

I learned that the first entry for ED in the British Foreign Office files, from 1908, reads 'Durham, Miss M. E., Inadvisability of Corresponding With'; this was just the kind of correspondence it would be most interesting to read so I tried to find out where her letters were held. Many of them are at the Royal Anthropological Institute, an organisation which became an increasingly important part of Edith's life. As an old lady she wrote with typical brusque modesty of how she'd first got involved with the RAI,

> I shared a studio with an old fellow student Hannah Myers. And she, interested in the Balkan stuff I had got, said, 'You ought to show this to Sligs.' She invited Dr Seligman to tea and he was much interested and told me I had got information no one else had worked

on. To cut a long tale short, he and Joyce shoved me into the Anthrop and I had to read a paper.

Her relationship with the Institute continued from there and she was to become a member, and ultimately its Vice President (the first woman to hold that post) as well as a minor benefactor, donating a set of 'comfortable chairs' for the lecture room in her will.

I discovered that the RAI now had its headquarters in a part of London that had always intrigued me. Fitzrovia is the area under the BT tower. The tower itself is, of course, visible from much of central London, but have you ever seen its base? I had walked that area frequently – had worked nearby, and strolled the streets in lunch hours. The shadow of the BT tower swings across the neighbourhood like a giant gnomon. But I had never seen the point where it joins the ground. I had begun to believe that it was afloat somewhere off the Tottenham Court Road.

It seemed a suitably magical place to visit to deepen my friendship with a dead woman. I booked myself for an appointment with the archives that lie behind the Georgian front door of the Royal Anthropological Institute in Fitzroy Street.

The place could do with being scrutinised by some anthropologists itself. I was shown into a narrow hallway, down some steps and into a book-lined study. There was a general smell of Oxbridge don. Piles of unidentified anthropological documents towered in box-files around me and I had an uncomfortable feeling that shrunken skulls or unsettling photographs could fall at my feet if I attempted to move any of the teetering columns of learning. On the floor by the window was a battered old leather suitcase, as if some anthropologist had just come back from the field and set it down.

I think Edith would have been itching to sort it out. I read a description of her in the journal of the Institute, *Man*, which described the Institute's move to their former premises in Upper

Bedford Place, 'Not only did Miss Durham help to find us our ... premises ... ; but when the move there took place in great haste and the library was dumped down all over the floor in unmanageable heaps, Miss Durham came to the rescue, sorting out the muddle, and placing the books on their proper shelves – a piece of prolonged and hard physical work.'

She must have been missed in the move to this building.

Far from the British Library's automation and conveyor belts, the RAI still seems to work largely on handwritten entries and connections made in the mind of librarians and archivists, not database search terms. So when I formally presented the accession numbers of the letters I had heard about online, I was told that if these were what I was interested in, there were far more items I should also look at. Gratefully, I allowed the archivist to do my research for me. Once I had been settled in at a spare table next to the desk where the librarian worked, and repeatedly offered tea (perhaps the Royal Anthropologists had been reading ED's accounts of Albanian approaches to hospitality), the librarian went off to bring in the first boxes of documents for me to look at. She reappeared with four or five boxes stacked high in her arms, like a department store bellboy on a Christmas card.

It did feel rather like Christmas. It is an enormous privilege when someone shares a book with you (Edith herself seemed to have been quite a tartar on the subject – there is a series of letters from her to someone to whom she lent a book which begin 'I have only one copy and as it is long out of print it is irreplaceable so I must beg that care be taken to return it shortly'. Three months after she had lent it there is another letter suggesting there had been some exchanges in the intervening time, 'I wrote in fact as a reminder, I have alas lost so many books through not reminding the borrower in time and have had the reply "I sent it back ages ago. Or had forgotten all about it and lost or lent it to someone else". So at pretty regular intervals I whistle for them'.

Of course, in the reference library of the RAI no whistling was required, but I still felt myself honoured to be able to read this material.

Edith had indeed given her sister the first glimpses of her adventures in long, carefully written letters. They weren't written to Caroline, as mine had been, but to the sister closest to Edith in age, 'Dear Nellie', four years Edith's junior. There were also photographs, thankfully annotated to spare me the guessing game I'd had to play at the British Museum, scrapbooks, paintings, book manuscripts and lecture notes.

They were fragile, in some cases crumbled at the edges. There were times when a word was lost at the end or beginning of a line. But these butterfly wings carried the marks of some fascinating travel. Edith's life – or at least selected small parts of it – now became believably real. In one letter she describes the sketches she did of frescoes in a church. Later going through her scrapbooks, I found the sketches.

I felt I got to know Edith properly during the days I spent in the RAI. I was astonished at her clarity of writing – so little hesitation, repetition, correction in a pre-computer age. I don't know whether that was common to all well-educated Edwardians, and it is a skill we have now lost, or whether it was evidence of her bright mind.

But I also I learned her weaknesses of punctuation – her complete lack of use of paragraph divisions, which made some accounts of her journeys feel almost as unending as the long rides she was describing. She narrates the route over the 'Accursed' mountains into Kosovo, where – like the road – the account went 'on and on and on and on'. Fascinating though it was, with the glimpses of country I had been in myself a few months before, and the skilful little vignettes she included of the people she met, I longed occasionally for a short break in the prose, to stop at the literary equivalent of the hans she described, or sometimes for just a comma – the 'wretched cottage' where she had 'smoky milk' as a pause on the ride through the slithering mud.

But the fact of these letters being unedited was what made them so exciting. Much of the material was familiar from what I'd read in *Through The Lands of the Serb* or *High Albania*, but the details which had been left out for the general public made me feel privy to confidences. Her diaries and letters include details of errors by Marko Shantoya, her guide – the time he almost toppled their cart over, or when he overslept and delayed the whole party from leaving the monastery – which she censored in the public version, and there were also some more honest opinions – 'I am afraid I am developing a quite Montenegrin hatred for the Turk. My visit to Turkish territory has not improved my idea of him.'

On her way back from Gračanica monastery, the diary gives cosy detail of her and Marko and a Serbian schoolteacher travelling together huddled under a blanket – which perhaps understandably didn't make it to the public account of an English lady abroad. Indeed, her appetite was suppressed in many ways in the published account I'd read – when she recounts the visit to the Metropolitan in Pristina, she describes their makeshift dinner 'Metrop insisted on beginning with a tinned hors d'oeuvre. Great search in cupboard. Discussed which of various tins should be opened. Contents unknown. Turned out to be potted ham. We emptied tin – I had most – and started on a vast dinner of 5 courses all very filling'. In the book, the incident is recorded but the fact that Edith had most is coyly omitted. I thought of this woman, snuggling under rugs with foreign men and gobbling up tinned ham abroad, and then feeling ashamed of herself on return to Britain. It made me sad.

Almost as much as her time in Kosovo, I was fascinated by the little insights into the work of running a household from the other side of Europe revealed in the personal correspondence with her sister. Thanks to the 'Austrian mail' (and indeed the Austrian male – at least for some of her travels it was through the kindness of the Austrian consul in Prizren that ED had the chance to use this method for sending and receiving letters) it was quite possible to manage a meaningful correspondence from one end of Europe to the other. On 2 August, ED writes to Nellie that she had just received her letter dated 26 July. To have only a seven-day wait seems unthinkable luxury – the British Forces Post (we, too, had had a diplomatic kindness to thank for our being allowed to send and receive letters that way) scarcely managed such a swift journey time to us in Kosovo with all the benefit of modern vans and planes helping our envelopes on their way. And when poor Nellie, back in England, wasn't being given pages of description of her sister's adventures with young officers, Turkish officials and Serbian monks, ED did engage with the practical chores that her absence had saddled Nellie with in London. Mrs Childs had apparently been 'making scenes' and 'must certainly go' although ED adds fairly that 'I promised to pay for her teeth … and will fulfill that promise.'

I made notes to follow up these intriguing details. Who was Mrs Childs? Were any of her family still alive, and might they remember this strange wilful employer and her cluttered sitting room? I wrote my notes as Edith wrote hers; she jotted down about the monastery in Peja,

> **The whole style of art is something Eastern, exotic, quite foreign and one sees that it is the parent of St Mark's Venice. St Mark's ought to be an 'Orthodox' church. I wonder greatly how it came about that St Mark's was built and must look it up.**

I imagined her coming back to London, some of the flea bites from her Balkan beds still fresh, and making time – when her mother was having an afternoon rest? – to come in from Hampstead to a library or booksellers, sitting in a room like the one I was in today, and doing research. Just because she wanted to know how it came about that St Mark's was built.

The days I spent in the fug of the RAI raised far more such questions than they gave answers. The immediate prompt for the next stage of my quest came from a letter not to sister Nellie but to brother-in-law Godfrey. It apparently accompanied a birthday present of two cigarette holders ('one for weekdays and one for Sundays').

The latter is silver. I bought it out of a man's mouth
at Prizren. Pull off the mouth piece and then the three
pieces of filigree pull off and you can clean the tube.
Shantoya – my man – hearing that you have a beard
thinks you will look extremely noble when smoking it.
She signed off,

Adieu and best wishes – mind you wash the pipes.

Just as I had been thrilled to find the sketches that were mentioned elsewhere in the RAI's collection of diaries, now I wanted to see those cigarette holders.

8 The filigree ring

The filigree of which Godfrey's pipes were formed is made through an extraordinary alchemy that changes dull silver rods into intricate doodles of earrings, lacy decorated platters, and fine ornamentation for belts and cups, puffed from the precious metal, into swords, rings and brooches fragile as winter leaf skeletons. My first glimpse of the craft in Kosovo had been, as with so many wonderful things, at the Ethnological Museum in Pristina.

The museum is staffed by an enthusiastic group of good-looking young ethnologists with genuine natural charm and a well-rehearsed patter for visitors coming to the museum. They will take you upstairs to the room of jewellery and traditional costumes, and fling open the doors of a beautifully carved cupboard. Inside, spectacularly lit and displayed on black velvet, is a range of filigree.

With secrets like this being revealed to you, it is easy to fall in love. I had asked the guides, and the museum director, whether I could help in the museum, and soon established a rhythm of weekly English lessons for the group of guides, a weekly treat for me in surroundings which never failed to get my heart racing, however many times I walked through the museum compound's dramatic wooden gates.

As the guides and I talked each week we had come up with ideas for ways that we could promote the museum. We put together a proposal and received enough funding from the British Embassy to enable us to set up a Craftspeople in Residence Week of demonstration and sales at the museum. It was here that I had had my chance to see a filigree magician at work.

The man who came to the museum was from Prizren, which considers itself the crafts capital of Kosovo. In front of him on the table was a scribble of silver wire, in skeins of different thickness. The man took the wire and worked it with his fingers and with small fine tools. Under his hands, spirals, zigzags and flowers appeared which he twisted together into delicate arbours of decoration. He sprinkled silver powder between them like a spell, fired it with a fine blowtorch, and produced jewellery before our very eyes. He brought with him a range of filigree creations including extraordinary ships made from silver. They sat beached among the gewgaws, admired but unsold by the end of the week.

Filigree is sold by weight, a strange pricing structure that seems to have built into it a complete disregard for the artistry and time that has gone into its production. If one 200g lump of silver wire costs the same as any other 200g lump, it is hard to demonstrate how the craftsperson has added value. It also means that heavy lumps of silver shipping are very unlikely to be bought. I saw the visitors to the museum (we had 600 that week in contrast to the 6 per day average we'd recorded on other days) handling the weighty silver bracelets and paperknives and could see them hungry to buy something. But the price – and sometimes the ostentation of the style – was so often prohibitive. I wondered how the simple flowers which the filigranist had produced as part of his demonstration could be presented in a form that people would see a use for. Remembering the difficulties I'd had buying birthday cards in Kosovo, I wondered about greetings cards, and thought how one might go about attaching a silver filigree flower onto card.

A few months before the museum's crafts residency, I'd met a nineteen-year-old girl from a painfully poor family who had told me she was looking for a job. She had shown me the trousseau she was stitching so the one skill I knew she had, other than the initiative and energy to have approached me, was neat needlework. Thinking about the filigree greetings cards idea, I asked Syzana if she'd like to be part of a small project with me and a friend. We'd do the marketing for free, and she would produce the cards, sewn with filigree flowers, and take all the profit. We'd all be supporting the traditional craft of filigree.

The cards she produced, each with a real silver decoration startling against a monochrome card, were beautiful, and the project grew within weeks, with orders for thousands of cards. When the original craftsman couldn't supply the individual flowers quickly enough to keep up with the orders which we were receiving we began working with a filigree co-operative in Prizren.

I visited them in the former tobacco factory where they had set up an old formica-topped workbench, a primus stove for making Turkish coffee, and another for heating up the liquids in which pieces of silver were cleaned. They showed me the crude hand-operated machines which were used for converting metal bars, two fingers thick, into wire of different diameters through extrusion – pulling the bars repeatedly through decreasing spaces until it was fine and pliable. I thought about sucking sticks of seaside rock to a fine point.

I'd watched them work, and sometimes they'd even let me have a go at the unfathomable twists and turns. One day they had showed me a manoeuvre called 'mouse tooth' which involved bending wire backwards and forwards around two tiny pins until it produced a softened zigzag. I tried – and failed. They showed me, slower, and I failed again. Eventually I gave up, and left them to working the piece in a blur of hands and eyes which, within seconds, had created the design.

When I went to leave they presented me with a small box. Inside was a ring made up of mouse-tooth shaped into a flower and cradling a small stone. My eye returned repeatedly to the zigzag so impossible to produce.

'We want to thank you', they said as they gave me the ring. 'For helping us to tell people about filigree. When people have seen our phone number on the back of the greetings cards they have contacted us and commissioned more things from us. We are really grateful.' They were speaking in Albanian, but now they switched to English for a sentence they had obviously prepared with care.

'For us you are the *big momma* of Kosovan filigree.'

I had no idea where they had heard the phrase, or what exactly they thought it meant, but it was clearly intended to be flattering. I smiled, and sighed – I would rather have been the Queen of the Mountain People like Edith, but it was better than nothing.

Much of the filigree that Edith had brought back from Kosovo was now held in Oxford's Pitt Rivers Museum. Hunting through the Pitt Rivers online catalogue for references to her cigarette holder filigree from Prizren, I thought of ShPK Filigran ('Filigree Plc'). I saw them sitting, ten at the one table, with their blow-torches and the alarming old rabbit paw they use to brush off the silver dust. One of the craftspeople is the sixth generation of his family to practise the craft of filigree – it could easily have been his great-grandfather who had produced the earrings or pistol or necklace I was promised sight of at the museum.

So I arranged a visit to Oxford.

It was a strange trip back in time – to my own past as well as Edith's. I had studied at Oxford, and lived there after I left university. It was at Oxford that I had met Rob, who had brought me to Kosovo. This was the beginning of it all. There is always a heady rush of nostalgia for me in visiting the city, and it was all the more powerful, returning to the Pitt Rivers Museum, where so many people's histories were encoded. I had just finished reading *The House in Norham Gardens*, a book where the anthropological collection in a North Oxford attic comes to life and haunts the modern-day inhabitants. I couldn't work out what I really wanted to be haunted by on this trip – my own past in Oxford, or my more recent past in Kosovo, or Edith's past, a hundred years before.

As I walked down Broad Street to get to the museum, I heard two students talking. One was explaining she had just signed up to JACARI, the University's student volunteer home tutoring scheme for primary school pupils newly arrived in the UK; it gave me a heightened sense of my life flashing before me. As a student I had wanted to be part of the JACARI scheme, but had decided to stand instead for election in the college. On the night that I was defeated in the vote I had returned to my room and filled in the application form for the tutoring. I had gone on to spend eye-opening afternoons with a refugee family from Uganda, which persuaded me that after my degree I should train to become a primary school teacher. I was here now fifteen years, four schools and a deputy headship later, and aware of just how much I owed to that Ugandan family.

'But the family aren't answering my phone calls,' said the student to her friend, 'so I'm not sure whether to go ahead with it.'

I turned round and spoke to her. 'I'm sorry, but I couldn't help hearing what you were saying. I did JACARI fifteen years ago. It changed my life. Please try calling them again.'

She looked at me like I was Marley's ghost, and I felt a little other-worldly myself, meddling in someone else's future. So I returned myself to the past. I arrived at the Pitt Rivers back entrance and was met by Elin who was to show me ED's collection. I was learning how such encounters behind the scenes at the museum should go, and was prepared for the relationships now – she had to be interpreter and bodyguard; she would watch my every move, for signs of suspicious activity – writing notes in ink when I should be using pencil, touching things I shouldn't. But she would also be keen to show the exhibits to me, to enable me to understand them.

She was friendly, but she wouldn't shake hands. She apologised, gesturing with her palms held out to me like a minstrel. Her hands were clad in striking purple rubber gloves. Skin condition? Fashion statement?

'Funky colour!' I said.

These were of course gloves to be worn to protect the exhibits. And I was told that once I had been given my own pair, I would be allowed to touch things myself – though not before I had signed a form with guidelines on handling poisoned arrows.

Elin had set out on a table the exhibits I had asked to see. They were lain on the same protective packaging you use in punnets of strawberries to stop soft fruit from spoiling.

I was eager to scrutinise them so I pulled at the gloves I'd been given, keen to put them on so I could handle the objects. But pulling them over my Prizren ring I realised I was going to rip them. Gently, I worked the ring off my finger and put it on the table. There it lay, next to the jumble of silver squiggles that Edith had brought back with her from Kosovo, the latest in a grand ancestral line.

I turned my attention to these other items that had been so much longer out of Kosovo. Along with some rather crude earrings and an intricate necklace, the piece de resistance (possibly literally) was a marvelous pistol. As the catalogue description told me, it was decorated 'cock, cap and frizzen' (the reserved style of the catalogue seemed to have suddenly turned piratical) with filigree. The fine silver thread wove and snaked around the weapon like snail trails in the morning, entirely incongruous with the deathly purpose of the flintlock. It was beautiful. I imagined how delighted Arberita, Bekim and Valon from the Ethnological Museum would be. There was nothing like this in Kosovo that I had seen. I imagined how the eyes of the guys at ShPK Filigran would light up. They'd be copying the designs in no time.

I tried to take photographs but the images were dull and inexpert. Perhaps these were things you had to appreciate while they were in front of you. That, after all, is part of the philosophy of museums.

I read the catalogue descriptions of the objects, I tried to photograph them; I poked them gently with my strange purple fingers, I took some notes. And I wondered what else I should do. I didn't want Elin to feel that I was less than serious. I didn't want her to feel her time had been wasted in preparing the objects for me. I stood reverently in front of them a little longer, thinking about time and place and skill, and people's passing.

Before I moved on to the photographs taken by Edith, which the Museum had also prepared for me to look at, Elin asked me to sign the visitors' book. It was a wonderful document in itself, dating back to 1984. A standard format asked for name, time in, time out, reason for visit; any office reception would require the same. But presumably few offices would have such glorious and multifarious entries. 'Reason for visit: Inspection of Denis Johnson hobby-horse', 'proctor's clothing', 'sealskin map', 'visit grandmother's moccasins', 'The LACE CONVENTION' (in other circumstances I would have assumed this was an acronym but where I was I guessed that, no, this was a group of people getting together to discuss doyleys).

I rapidly began to feel inadequate reading through the reasons why other people had come: *biography for the 'other within' project, Dorling Kindersley photo shoot, tarot card research, the Welsh wiseman's charm, grass raincapes, pudding pans, PhD thesis on mermaid/siren amulets, research on history of dentistry in Nigeria, silk undergarments for armour, crocodile claw, drop off a Chinese robe, design for Oxfam, collection of 160 body paintings, study of Indian rabbit sticks, to photograph ethnographic material concerned with mollusks.*

OK, well at least I was more interesting than the mollusk guy.

The visitors' book was like a brief conversation between all these interesting people. No doubt the grass raincape woman had the same trouble I did in explaining to friends and family what drove her with her particular obsession. But here, she and the pudding pans man and all the others, including Edith and me, were among friends. Some people even felt moved to write comments on their quest – 'researching for a film on face shaving. The Pitt Rivers collection makes sense at last in terms of the history and the ethnography of shaving.'

However, out of all this motley crew, over a period of 24 years, not one single person had come to see anything to do with ED. Once again, I felt that Edith and I had something to prove.

After I'd finished with my new-found researcher friends, I went back to Edith's. The Pitt Rivers also has a collection of photographs, thankfully annotated unlike the ones I'd seen in Bloomsbury. I knew about these from a letter from Edith to Beatrice Blackwood of the Pitt Rivers Museum. The two women had corresponded reasonably frequently, though I couldn't tell quite how friendly they were. I did know that it was Beatrice who had been due to ED's for tea on 15 November 1944. The appointment had not been kept – Edith had died earlier that day.

ED had written to her in July 1944

Dear Miss Blackwood – I have just finished sorting out my lantern slides for the Anthrop Inst and find I have some duplicates of various Balkan subjects ... So next time you come here I propose to give them to you for the Pitt Rivers to add to those you already have.

Or will risk sending them by post later on when thing are not in such a mess, as just now with all this evacuation rush and the doodle bug scare. It is a great nuisance. I hope you have not come in for any of it. I feel myself that it is not so bad by a long way as the

bombing at the beginning of the war. But people's nerves have worn thin.

Somehow these images of early twentieth century Kosovo had made it to Oxford, dodging the doodle bugs. With them were photographs in albums, each one wrapped with a calico ribbon like a gift.

I was excited to see pictures of 'Miss Durham's Montenegrin guide (and wife) playing the *gusla*'. This, I assumed, was Radovan, who features in the diaries and letters I'd been reading. I had liked what I had read of him – how he had hung around until everyone else had left ED alone to sleep and had then checked the bars on the windows and the locks on the door, and had waited outside ED's door until she had double-locked it. His is always the voice of caution – it was because of him that ED didn't accept the tantalising offer made to her by the Turkish officer at Deçan to go to Gjakova. On reading ED's letter where she describes this offer, I had willed her to accept, as it would have taken her further into Kosovo and for longer, but ED says 'I saw in Radovan's eyes that he strongly disapproved. I thought that if it was found out up country that he was a Montenegrin he might suffer for it and I could not help him. His orders were to bring me safely back to the Voyvode at Andrijevic or go to prison if he came back without me. I thanked the officer and said it was time I returned to Andrijevic.' On their way out of Kosovo when another of ED's escorts was spinning stones down the 1000ft hillside ('His joy was to roll rocks down especially flat ones which he balanced on the edge and sent spinning into the depths and he laughed loudly as they hopped and span. People inclined to giddiness would not have enjoyed it'), she notes that nevertheless 'even Radovan the serious found it amusing'. In the photo with his wife he doesn't look like he found very much amusing, although to be fair he was squinting into the sun.

When I had finished turning all the pages of the albums, Elin offered to take me into the galleries of the museum, currently closed for renovations. It was a treat – the museum is probably my favourite anywhere in the UK, with its ruthless categorisations (one case has a label 'birds and bits of birds, and uses they've been put to.' Fishing flies are displayed alongside Papua New Guinean headdresses. The case labeled 'body modification' includes the tiny shoes of a Chinese girl whose feet had been bound, rings for extending the necks of Burmese women, and a Wonderbra.) Now all these were shrouded in protective cloths while a group with what Elin called a 'restoration hoover' cleaned the dust off the oars and spears that had been hanging from the ceiling. It felt like an appropriate image for a day spent bringing things from the past to light, a day lived in multiple time zones.

On the bus back to London I thought about that younger me, setting out on her journey to become a teacher, falling in love with the fellow student, setting off to the Balkans. And I thought about the younger ED, a century before, sharing these journeys. I lost track of time.

I got out at Victoria and watched the bus pull away as I gathered my bags and coat around me. Something was wrong; something was gone. Patting down my pockets, the absence became clear. I really had lost track of time: what was missing was my diary. It never was returned to me.

9 Love life

'A Maltsor [man of the mountains], stripped to the waist, leaned over the pot to stir it. The firelight played on his muscles, and the sweat glittered on his hairy breast.'

Everything I had read about and by Edith, like this description in *The Struggle for Scutari* of dinner in the munitions depot, had given me a picture of her as a woman very much alive to the senses. I remembered her appreciative note in a letter from Albania in 1914,

> **the Dutch officers – notably one Malingoot … who is
> built like a Greek statue, pervaded the hotel clad only
> in bathing dress and rode in and out the hall – in that
> costume – on a pony.**

This was a woman who wasn't squeamish, virginal or Victorian about appreciating physical attractions.

And yet. She never married. Of course, nor had I, but as everyone except my grandmother acknowledged, I might as well have. Spinsterhood seemed quite a family trait – neither of Edith's intellectual sisters, Florence or Hermia, married either so there were role models or at least partners in challenging traditional expectations. But I wondered who Edith had shared intimacy, or adventures, with.

Maybe she made her own pact, that to have some of the freedoms she craved she was better off negotiating with a sick mother than a bearded husband. Or maybe she wasn't considered good marriage material – in *High Albania* she narrates an exchange between her guide and his companions,

'One suggested that a 'writing woman' would be a good sort to marry, but Marko said that kind would not fetch wood and water, which damped the enthusiasm.'

Not just moustachioed Marko but his Hampstead equivalents might have worried that taking on Edith was more than they were up to.

In *Through the Lands of the Serb* she enjoys the story of some of the offers that did come her way,

> 'Art married?' 'No,' Great excitement and much whispering. 'Wait, wait,' says a woman, and she shouts 'Milosh! Milosh!' at the top of her voice. Milosh edges his way through the crowd. He is a tall, sun-tanned thing of about eighteen years, with the eyes of a startled stag. His mother stands on tiptoe and whispers in his ear that this is a chance not to be lightly thrown away. A broad smile spreads over Milosh's face. He looks coy, and twiddles his fingers. 'Ask her! Ask her!' say the ladies encouragingly. 'Ask her!' say the men. Milosh plucks up courage, thumps his chest and blurts out 'Wilt thou have me?' 'No, thank you,' I say, laughing, and Milosh retires amid the jeers of his friends, but really much relieved.

The Shakespearean diction (I guessed it was ED's precise, not to say pedantic, way of rendering the familiar form of 'you' from Serbian through its last known use in English) adds quaintness to the story. Straight-talking, strangely endearing Edith is suddenly presented as *Much Ado*'s Beatrice. All the more, I wanted to find out about her Benedick. Edith continues the story,

> 'Milos thou are not beautiful enough' say the men, and they suggest one Gavro as being more likely to please. Gavro takes Milosh's place with great alacrity, and the same ceremony is repeated. The crowd enjoys itself vastly, and tries to fit me out with a really handsome

specimen. I glance round, and my eye is momentarily caught by a very goodly youth. 'No! No! He's mine, he's mine!' cries a woman, who seized him by the arm, and he is hastily withdrawn from competition amid shouts of laughter 'I have no money,' says one youth frankly, 'but thou hast perhaps enough.' 'And he is good and beautiful,' say his friends. For they are all cheerfully aware that their faces are their only fortunes. There is a barbaric simplicity and a lack of any attempt at romance about the proposed arrangements which is exquisitely funny, for they are far too honest to pretend that I possess any attractions beyond my supposed wealth. I have often wondered what the crowd would do if I accepted someone temporarily but have never dared try. Five offers in twenty minutes is about my highest record.

But none of the offers – at home or abroad – were taken up. Maybe she was gay – I had heard suggestions of that, but then there are always suggestions, particularly for a woman who didn't marry and who went on to achievements unusual for her sex. No-one had any evidence of an intimate relationship between her and anyone of either gender, and I found myself wanting to set her up with someone. Even the rumour of someone would do for me – enough for me to be able to imagine her with some company and caring.

There's no better place to find rumour than an embassy party. My experience is that these events are never thronged with elegant guests reaching to take one of a pyramid of Italian chocolates and whispering carefully poised bon mots, but they are full of people saying very indiscreet things.

The Kosovan Embassy in London was newly opened. Kosovo had only just declared independence, and one of the early tasks of a country inventing itself is to set up embassies abroad: Berlin,

Washington, Brussels and London were selected as among the first cities to receive Kosovan ambassadors. Someone was sent to London to find an appropriate suite in an office block; political party machinery graunched into action in Pristina, and we received an email to say that an ambassador had been announced. Rob recognised the name of a man he had met a few times when we were living in Kosovo.

'Can you get in touch with him?' I begged. I wanted to have access to every bit of Kosovo being sent over to London. Like Edith, this was a means of communicating with the place I cared about. Rob obediently drafted an email of congratulation on Mr Hamiti's appointment, with Albanian flourishes. Not much later we received an invitation to the party to celebrate the presentation of the Ambassador's credentials to the Queen.

My first thought wasn't of Ferrero Rocher. Instead my mouth was tingling with anticipation of a different treat, because this would be my chance to speak Albanian again. There would be people who I could talk to about the things I cared about. There would be people who knew the names of the people I knew. At this party, my fellow guests would all know who Edith was.

We turned up at the restaurant chosen for the party. I had heard about this place before – set just off Charing Cross Road, it's a bistro serving modern international food with excellent chips and handsome waiters. They have a faint air of exoticism but you can't place it – this is no Albanian themed restaurant with folkloric pictures – until you hear them talking to each other. The restaurant is owned and run by Kosovar Albanians, and in the 1990s this was the place that the Albanian community in the UK came to pay their 'Homeland calling' tax. While schools and hospitals in Kosovo were closed to Albanians under the Milošević regime, the Homeland Calling tax funded unofficial education and healthcare in private houses. Without this clandestine, efficient system, many of my friends from Kosovo would not have survived. This restaurant was a part of Kosovo's story of victory through endurance.

That night it was full of an assorted bunch of Kosovar Brits and Brits half in love with Kosovo. There was the British social worker who had set up the charity to work with unaccompanied underage Kosovars who had arrived in great numbers during the 'nineties to seek asylum. There were some of her former charges too – the successful South Bank architect and his beautiful girlfriend. There was an MP who told me he had become fascinated by the Kosovo case when he got talking to bar staff at his local pub in London years back and discovered where they had all come from. There were the people you see in every diaspora community – shady characters, or people who have now come out from the shade and are flashing their new-found money around. They mingled with journalists – British and Kosovar – academics, women in flat shoes from the Foreign Office, and between them was all a hubbub of conversation – in Albanian. I stood at the side for a while, recognising some faces from book jackets, but more happily recognising the nouns, the accents, the strange code that I had learned to crack. Emboldened, I went up to someone nearby.

'*Unë jam Elizabeth.*'

They smiled. 'You speak Albanian?' and I was in. You could watch the Kosovan network in action as I was passed, pressed from one hand to another. Some people had heard of projects I was involved in, mutual friends were discovered, someone had even seen me on television – watched in satellite from Hackney as I'd run a charity auction in Pristina a few months before. I was home.

And as the room came to my aid, everyone agreed on one thing: I must meet Bejtullah. He knew all about Miss Durham. Yes, it was he who had edited the book I had read of her published articles. And yes, he was just there in the corner.

'*Unë jam Elizabeth. Po hulumtoj një libër për Edith Durham.*' It was my password. He patted a chair next to him and we started talking.

'So what do you want to know?' Bejtullah asked me. It was a trick question, surely. I began, not by answering the question, but by telling him some of the things I already knew. The museums I'd visited, the research I'd done. I presented my credentials. But ultimately, there was no way of hiding the fact that my current preoccupation wasn't with Edith's filigree collection or with her minute anthropological descriptions. 'But did she have a lover?' I blurted out.

I wondered briefly whether Bejtullah would be shocked. This was a national hero for his people; was I being disrespectful to ask about her sex life so soon? But Bejtullah is too good a researcher to be fazed by such things.

'Well,' he confided, leaning his mouth nearer to my ear. 'They do say that she had an affair with Nevinson.'

Nevinson? I had never heard the name. I couldn't even be sure whether it was male or female. But the twenty-first century researcher doesn't need to ask for details. Even when you're looking for 100 year-old bits of gossip, there is always Google.

Henry Wood Nevinson was born in 1856, seven years before ED. He studied at Christ Church, Oxford, like my own beloved, and went on to be a journalist of radical ideas. In particular, he was a supporter of women's suffrage (I thought of Edith's acerbic comments on those 'maniacs' in a letter I'd read at the RAI, dating from 1908, and her comment written in Albania,

the Labour Party should come out here for a bit and then it would know when it was well-off. So should the Suffragettes – the best would be to sell them to harems to pay for the window breaking.

There is an account in the biography, *War, Journalism and the Shaping of the Twentieth Century: The Life and Times of Henry W.*

Nevinson, of him attending a meeting at the Albert Hall where the Suffragettes kept up constant interruptions of cabinet ministers. A fellow journalist wrote of the incident, 'Nevinson's blood boiled when he saw one of the stewards clench his fist and give a knock-out blow on the chin to one of the militant women. Other women were being roughly handled. Nevinson jumped from the stage box, and fought half a dozen stewards at once until they over-powered him and flung him out.'

So a man of action, even if it was in a cause that Edith didn't approve of. Yes, I could see she might go for that. Other women clearly had – Henry had a wife (from 1884) at the same time as having not one but two lovers – Nannie Dryhurst from 1892 and Evelyn Sharp from 1901. He broke up with Nannie in 1912 – over an argument about women's suffrage. Ah, maybe not so much Edith's type.

But his biographer wrote, 'He was cultured and courteous yet rebellious. He travelled to faraway and dangerous places. A touch of shyness, an ability to listen to others and an appreciation of women's rights and of intelligent women ensured that many found him irresistible.'

It was plausible. But as I read Nevinson's biography I learned it was more than that. According to the biography, after 1911, 'To his surprise, Edith sent him love letters ... in amongst denunciations of Turks ... was 'I am yours to take – or leave.' Henry was bemused, admitting that he found this 'very strange, causeless and incredible'. In his book, *Fire for Life*, he describes the glamour that attached to him by his connection with her – if she was the Kralitza, Queen of the mountain tribes, then he was the Kral. He writes of their work together for the Macedonian Relief Fund,

The Kral and Kralitza spent the days in the counting house, counting out the money, tearing up various

kinds of cloth for garments, apportioning tarred felt for roofing.

Along with the tearing up of clothing, there is a cosy domesticity to the description, and he describes the house in whose outhouses they stored timber 'furnished with a strange assortment of Persian china, Afghan weapons and typical French cartoons' and you can imagine the two Britons playing house, playing at being King and Queen together in their ragged court of starving refugees.

By 1913 they were travelling together through the south of Albania, as Nevinson recalls in his memoirs,

sometimes putting up for the night with a landowning Bey, sometimes with an Archbishop, sometimes with a rigid Mohammedan, who shut Miss Durham up in his harem, among other women, and sometimes sleeping under the fir trees or beside a spreading and marshy river, when night overtook us.

The biography noted that throughout their travels she is called Miss Durham in his diaries (though, interestingly, in his published memoirs she is Edith Durham). 'Yet her letters called him 'Sweet love' and admitted how much she loved him. Their parting had been as 'terrible as death''.

Oh, I was wincing. So was this unrequited love? Oh, Edith.

Nevinson's biographer continued, 'Edith told Henry that he was 'the only person' who ever credited her with 'feelings'.'

I willed him to treat her gently, kindly, be deserving of her.

I read on. Soon Edith was 'suggesting that they meet in Rome. In June ... Henry explored the city with her.'

It was a seductive image. My own last visit to Rome had been one November and I had left Kosovo shivering in power cuts and snow. On arrival in Italy I had felt the outside air on my cheek without wincing. I had checked into a hotel at the top of the Spanish Steps and while I waited for Rob to arrive from a work meeting I ran a bath, with hot water and scented steam that made me dizzy. At home in Pristina our boiler had broken. When Rob arrived I dressed and we went out to dinner, eating artichokes al fresco in the mild evening. The rest of the weekend was a riot of ice cream and underwear shopping, going into stationers selling hand-marbled papers, just to touch, to rub between finger and thumb. Was it ridiculous to imagine Edith and Henry doing anything of the sort? I didn't care. In my imagination, she was strolling the Piazza del Campo dei Fiori, talking excitedly to an intelligent man who was looking down at her as if he loved her. She felt the pressure of his arm against hers. For one June evening she didn't care about his wife, his mistress, his suffragette lover. She noted his hands, she felt his body heat; and she felt her own answering warmth.

So now I could picture her with someone. I wanted to know more, and the person who seemed likely to be able to tell me was Angela V. John, Nevinson's biographer. I wrote to her, an enthusiastic message with a hint of teenage gossiping – 'you'll never guess what: your guy and my girl …'. She sent a message back almost by return, as enthusiastic as I had been, and kindly gave me careful details of where I could find Nevinson's diaries in the Bodleian.

So it was back to Oxford. The first stop was the reader registration office where a kindly librarian explained the process of applying for a new reader's pass. As a former student it was easier for me but at the desk behind me, another potential new reader like myself was having the procedure explained; as it was his first time at the Bodleian he was required to read the pledge which every Oxford undergraduate has to read too, swearing not to 'remove from the Library, or to mark, deface, or injure in any way, any volume, document, or other object belonging to it or in its custody; not to bring into the Library or kindle therein any fire or flame'. The librarian had a laminated version of the pledge in various languages, but the man behind me elected to read it in Latin. There is something rather intimidating about Oxford's libraries.

'Errr?' The librarian tried to get my attention and handed me the university record book for the year I graduated. 'Please can you find your name here,' she asked, and I started thumbing through the lists. It was a strange sensation, seeing names I hadn't thought of in nearly twenty years. And then I came to the list – the exact text in the exact font which had been stapled up outside the exam schools in 1994. With a similar rush of adrenaline I started scanning the list. Well, I was on there, and yes, I'd passed. Not with a first, but a respectable 2:1. I had a similar sense of anti-climax, of the what-might-have-beens, and I wondered what my twenty-year-old self would have thought to see me now, back in the library, researching the love life of a long-dead woman.

That was all it took, and I had permission to read the diaries. In another building I took my table among the monkishly silent readers, with their manuscripts laid out on cushions in front of them, the pages held down with strings of little clay beads, like rosaries.

Nevinson's diary had a red leather spine and a marbled cover. It was as neat as ED's, with a regular script where all the double 'ss'es were rather ostentatiously written 'fs'. Much of the content was familiar from Angela's biography, but some of the emphasis only came through from reading sentences in the original context. The notes gave glimpses of a developing relationship – Miss Durham reciting 'a fine Montenegrin ballad',

We [Nevinson and ED] walked out towards the big plane tree. The moon one day past full. Then drinks and long converse, partly about her difficulty in drawing at the scientific Kensington museum. Fine story of the putrid snake.

I couldn't decide what point was being made; it's Nevinson who included the detail of the moonlight; was the putrid snake his own puncturing of romance, or ED's?

A few days later they went out to visit some destroyed villages. 'Then left Miss Durham who went back alone to Scutari and I think we were both sorry to part'. Back in Scutari together a few days later Nevinson comments about world affairs, 'The Morocco crisis very serious. Feel I ought not to be shut up here, and yet am content'. It seems unlikely that the roof felting and allocations of cloth for shirts is what was making him content, and no-one else features in his diary, so it seems that a growing fondness for Edith must explain the comment.

The details he chooses to record of her build a growing intimate, not to say romantic picture – 'walked with Miss D in steamy air after heavy rain to some low hills', ED reciting more ballads (this time Serbian on Kosovo), sitting 'long' watching 'one of the grandest sunsets of time', him giving 'Miss D' his sleeping rug while they 'conversed long'; 'talked on Byron and literature with Miss D at night'.

There's something of a gap year flavour to their voluntary work romance ('Tore up the shirting and stuff for jackets in lengths of 2.5 metres and arranged them in packets with Miss D. She was exquisite in desire to please and help') in a strange land; yet she was in her late forties, he in his early fifties. From his diaries it is clear that there was flirting, but who was flirting with whom? It was she who recited the ballads; it was he who mentioned the moonlight. Was it a reciprocal feeling?

He wrote,

she is quite superb in courage and wit, and the essential feminine lies under it, not so deeply hidden as people think. We went to the plane tree and found the river flowing deep where it had been dry.

Nevinson was an accomplished prose writer; the 'deep' river's flow is not an unconscious metaphor. Did it even conceal some physical contact beyond the meeting and teasing of minds that he'd described up till now.

He is quite clear in other diary entries about the limits to their relationship. He writes of their stay at a priest's house,

> house simply stank, but the little grey-eyed and bewildered priest did his best. Miss D and I changed our sweaty things and discussed the situation with him… Got rid of Marko from the room to save ourselves from his snoring, and Miss D and I slept in our clothes on beds in opposite corners and with perfect innocence. I slept little but watched the stars through the bare windows.
>
> Up with first light and washed at a stream outside without disturbing Miss D. It is a strange feeling one has to a woman with whom one has spent an innocent night in the same room. She only said I didn't snore. I said she hardly breathed.

After his return to England, leaving ED in Shkodra, he notes in his diary each time that he wrote to her, the visit to her sister to 'take news of Miss D', the books he ordered for her (and his own reading of her *High Albania*). On receiving one of her letters he narrates its content and then 'walked alone in rain … Telegraphed to Miss Durham'. In the light of all this, the passionate letters that Angela John had told me about (which are never actually attributed to ED in Nevinson's diaries, where he is carefully gentlemanly, writing 'a strange letter came from far away' or 'a letter said', 'one wrote to my battered carcase') don't seem quite so surprising, though the style is still incongruous: one letter read 'If I could but hold you in my arms for one little half hour, I could make you understand all that is in my soul. How I long for you'. But then perhaps we are all incongruous in our love letters, just as we are in our dressing gowns. That letter continues more plausibly, and giving some insights into how their relationship could work

You are such a good comrade. I miss your quick
responsive mind and your wholesome sense of humour.
Almost more than the touch of your dear arms and the
sound of your voice. Now I've no one to laugh with.
And I felt so safe with you. You took care of me as I've
never been taken care of. You know a side of me that
no one else knows or will ever know. I want you more
every day.

In Nevinson's review of his year on 31 December 1911 he notes as one of the year's achievements, 'a glorious 7 weeks in Albania and Montengro. Met Miss Durham and won her friendship.' He doesn't mention breaking her heart.

But in January, another letter came,

you were so good to me. When you arrived I was
feeling quite beaten and done – and you came and
straightened all out, and did the heavy work I wasn't
up to and came to my room and brought me tea and
waited on me and encouraged me. It was like paradise
… When someone takes your head between his hands
it is like a benediction.

In March she wrote again, casting their time in Shkodra together once more in romantic terms. Where Nevinson had majored on moonlight, she talks about 'flashlight' – a more spiritual illumination

In the midst of all the rabble and confusion and
unreason in you came – sane and full of delicate
humour and hope … we recognised one another and
that means that all of a flash – in a little minute – we
saw deeply into one another's souls. Those flashlight
moments – they used to be called revelation – how

**incomprehensible they are, and how they change the
colour of all the world. What I saw then makes it
impossible for me ever to hate you.**

Nevinson at last concedes to his diary a positive response, from
vanity if nothing else, to the love he seems to have won from such
an extraordinary woman,

**And here am I, an elderly man who has failed in most
things, and won high success in none, and am regarded
as rather a nuisance, a crank, a savage, and probably
a bore. What is it then that this strange hard creature
loves?**

It seems likely that their relationship did remain at the level
of a great, exciting, tantalising meeting of minds (perhaps with
an occasional stumbling together that would account for the
references to touching of arms and holding of heads). At least,
Nevinson's apparently immense libido and appreciation of
women didn't seem to have extended to Edith. Once back in
London his diary mentions meetings with a number of women in
the course of his work, particularly among the suffragettes, and it
is striking how often he gives physical descriptions of their faces
or clothes. I realised that he had made not a single reference in
his diary to what Edith looked like.

In a letter in March, Edith seems to be philosophical about
the impossibility of their relationship, 'Life is nothing but a long
string of renunciations.' She was in the land of the sworn virgin,
an Albanian custom which allows a woman to become – legally,
socially, indeed in every way but physically – a man. A girl
announces that from this day on she is to be a man, and she will
then start dressing like a man, acting like a man, being treated like
a man, and enjoying all the rights of a man. She can spit, swear,
fart, inherit property – all the usual benefits of Y chromosomes.
The one thing she can't do – ever – is have sex.

For some individuals, and for some families in Kosovo and northern Albania, the commitment to celibacy is considered a price worth paying. The tradition is dying out now, as women gain the legal right to inherit property and the education to fight for it, but there are still families where no son is born, and a daughter is chosen to 'become' a 'man'.

There must have been some resonances for ED in the tradition, which she mentions in her writing (in the *Journal of the Royal Anthropological Institute* a few years later she published an article on *High Albania* and its customs in 1908 where she said 'they also seemed to have an idea that as I am unmarried I belonged to the sworn virgin class'). Nevinson's diary mentions Edith telling him about the tradition too. She, like those women of Albania, knew of the advantages it could bring. Maybe only at the age of 48 did she become fully aware of just what she had renounced.

10 God, winter, summer, rain, snow, good morning, good evening, good appetite, goodbye, goodnight

For most of her travels, unlike during Nevinson's brief stay with her in Albania, Edith didn't have native English speakers to talk to. I wondered how she'd got on in Albanian, remembering my own humbling efforts when I was first in Albanian lands. It's not an easy language to pick up – perched alone on its branch of the Indo-European tree, with a word for thank you ('faleminderit'), one I thought I should memorise early on, which is the longest word to express gratitude that I have come across.

A week into our life in Kosovo and with our baggage, including cooking equipment, still not arrived, I had taken myself to a cafe for some lunch. The waiter came and I tried to order. He didn't have a clue what I wanted. I was tired, hungry and unimaginative in my communication strategies. He went away, hopefully to prepare me some food, but I realised I had no guarantee of that, and no way of checking. In a wave of self-pity, culture shock and exhaustion, I had found myself weeping silently at the small formica table. The waiter returned. So we couldn't understand each other, but he could see I was upset; he spoke to me – incomprehensible syllables of what I presumed were consolation. I tried to explain, to wave it away, to articulate a few of the sounds in the unending 'faleminderit', but with each hopeless attempt my eyes welled up more. The kindly man went away and returned shortly afterwards with a cup of Turkish coffee which he placed on the table before me. It was so thoughtful of him; I tried to thank him. *Falend... Falem...*

But (unlike Edith, whose diaries I had found infused with the stuff) I can't drink Turkish coffee. I actually gag at the dark, bitterness of it. I tried to lift the cup to my mouth, but the smell was so strong, so foreign, yet again so inexplicable, that it only brought more tears to my eyes. How could I possibly survive in this country, with its flavours that made me retch and its unpronounceable nouns stuck in my mouth? I looked up and saw the waiter watching me. This was hopeless.

He saw my distress and, clearly running through his lexicon of unspoken sympathy, reached into his pocket and offered me a cigarette. Hopeless again.

That afternoon I had realised that in the next month I was either going to have to learn to smoke or learn to speak Albanian.

It was an adventure for tongue, teeth and tired brain, but the positive reinforcement was worth it. It is so rare for a foreigner to speak Albanian that even my most inexpert 'faleminderit' was greeted with applause. The response, and my excellent teacher, had inspired me to work hard at it, and I was as proud of my Albanian as of anything else I'd achieved while we lived in Kosovo. I was rewarded with the feeling that I was being made a member of an exclusive club.

I wondered how my membership transferred to the London chapter of this restricted society, working hard to seek out fellow speakers here. I ended up finding work as an interpreter for London hospitals. I would receive warning that an Albanian speaker had been admitted, or had an outpatient appointment, and then I would set off on the underground with my dictionary, looking up the words for 'kidney stone', 'lymph node', 'glandular fever' as appropriate. Usually the patients were stout elderly women from villages in rural Kosovo. Frequently the words they used for kidney stone, lymph node, or glandular fever were different from my dictionary translations anyway. They used the Turkish that had been common when they were children, learning their way around their bodies, or they used dialect words, euphemisms, pointing. I thought of Edith in the disease-stricken districts where she had ridden to distribute quinine, and the grandmothers of these grandmothers who sat with me now, who must have pointed, pleaded in the same way with her as they did with the NHS doctors. So what had Edith done about learning Albanian?

On further research I discovered that she was modest about it, and maybe even a little defensive. Despite her proud boast to the eugenicist Ruggles Gates (perhaps in order to disprove some of his unattractive racial theories) that 'I have always been able to settle into the ways of any land I was in ... and oddly enough wherever I go I am rarely taken for English' she admitted in a letter written right at the end of her life, to a Dr Morant, that

I am slow at learning languages ... By the time I started work in Albania I had the greatest difficulty in tackling Albanian, especially as at that time there were three different alphabets & only Italian & German dictionaries which each used quite different orthography. I struggled at it when I had time. But life was so exhausting that tho I picked up a certain amount for daily use I never got a real hold of the language ... You see so much of my strength was used up in relief work, feeding starving villages after the Balkan wars, getting houses re-roofed, distributing seed corn, looking after wounded. Often ten or 12 hours in the saddle and sleeping on ground with saddle under my head. Far too exhausted to remember words and grammar.

Her English grammar almost breaks down at the memory of it.

In her book, *Through the Lands of the Serb* she makes a different excuse, with the claims of independence 'unless a route is so complicated that a guide is absolutely necessary, I infinitely prefer worrying it out alone; and as for languages, everyone knows that one wants food, drink and sleep.' With the memory of my generous, uncomprehending waiter in my mind, I begged to differ.

Forty years previously, early in her Balkan adventures, she was perhaps more honest, in a letter to 'Uncle Ashley' at the RAI. 'Have been slaving all day and every day at the language 7 or 8 hrs a day. It is shocking how slowly I learn.'

The RAI reference made me wonder, and as I researched further in the Institute's archives I discovered that there was actually a record of her dictionary being preserved there. I knew how I felt about my own dictionary, with its cover lost, and its corners soft from thumbing. I had carried that dictionary not only on tube trains on the way to other people's London hospital appointments, but everywhere with me in Kosovo, obsessively checking the words on hoardings, graffiti, packaging. It had been my travelling companion and comforter; I once told a Kosovan friend how I felt naked if I set out from home without it, and he said he knew what I meant; he was the same about his gun. So I would like to go back to the RAI and hold Edith's own protector in my hands.

In fact, the references to her 'dictionary' in the catalogue turned out to have been inaccurate, and what I found on my visit to the archives was something even more personal than my well-used book. This was no published document but an exercise book filled by ED herself with the words she had come across. It was a far more intimate way of following her language learning. She had first grouped her vocabulary ('animals and birds', 'common objects and geographical terms') and then listed it alphabetically in the subsequent pages, each divided into two columns – one for English to Albanian and the second for translation the other way. On other pages she had scribbled phonetic translations that also showed me the key words and phrases she had learned. It was a powerful reminder of what is really important in human society and in nature; I wished I'd had her notebook with me in that lonely cafe. It might have bemused the waiter, but I would have felt we had made human contact if, in between my tears, I had been able to blurt out Edith's strange incantation of key nouns and phrases:

God, winter, summer, rain, snow, good morning, good evening, good appetite, goodbye, goodnight.

11 God's workshop

Thanks to the internet, my own Albanian was still being used every day, even when I didn't have hospital translating to do. The members of the filigree co-operative in Prizren kept in touch with me by MSN Messenger with messages which were formal and respectful; traditional Albanian rituals that seemed out of place with the inane grins of MSN's smileys and online abbreviations. 'Good morning, Mrs Elizabeth,' the message would appear on my screen, with its accompanying MSN ber-ber-boing noise. 'How are you? How is your family? Your health?' They suggested I should come and visit them in Prizren, and I ached to do so. I played with my silver ring, moving it up and down my finger like a bride having second thoughts. And I typed them my answer,

'I am well thank you. And how are you? Are you tired? How is your family? Thank you from my heart for your invitation. I miss you. I would come to Prizren with great willingness, but for the moment I am staying in England.'

I told them about my ideas for an exhibition and they wanted to know more about the possible exhibits. Were there more than the items held by the Bankfield, the British Museum and the Pitt Rivers? What about the amulets that she had written about buying? Where were they now?

Obediently, I researched further, and discovered a letter written by ED to her friend at the Pitt Rivers, Beatrice Blackwood, where she Edith had explained that

Sir W Ridgeway... asked me to lecture at the Fitzwilliam. He took me in hand and commissioned me

> **to buy amulets for him and used to send me questions**
> **to find the answer to re tribes – marriage – funerals etc.**
> **I used to tell him I would hunt the hares if he would**
> **cook them.**

The 'hares' of good luck charms Edith brought back from Kosovo for Sir William Ridgeway had stayed in Cambridge, held by the University's Museum of Archaeology and Anthropology. Their catalogue noted that they included some glass and metalwork earrings labelled by ED as coming from Prizren.

I caught the train from London, and as I sat in the jolting carriage I wondered how Edith would have taken her treasures to Sir William. Perhaps she had even set off from King's Cross in late 1908 with a Gladstone bag full of amulets from Kosovo, where mine, in late 2008 was heavy with a laptop loaded with digital photos.

Shortly after arriving at the 'Arch and Anth', I set off again with Wonu, one of the museum staff who was to accompany me on the bus ride out to their storehouse. All but one of the ED items (the one I found later, in a dark corner of a display cabinet) were in storage rather than on display, and like the British Museum in London, in Cambridge the museum keeps its warehouse on cheaper land, well away from the city centre. During the journey there, Wonu and I chatted. She was despondent about the storage – it was badly needed, given that only three percent of the museum's collection was on display at any one time, but rain had come through the roof earlier in the year and she had had to put out buckets to stop the place flooding. I thought of the journeys made by Edith's treasures, wrapped carefully against damage, bumping in the *stremas*, the carriages, the steamboats, across Europe. I thought of their journey through time, too – surviving the blitz, mould, rust. Surely twenty-first century Cambridgeshire wouldn't fail these objects that a hundred years of travel had kept safe? I hoped the amulets would protect the place.

We were nearing our bus-stop and I was getting excited about seeing the exhibits that I had read catalogue listings for. Now we had entered the university land where the store building was; we passed other University departments' outbuildings – the Bill Gates building for IT research and the University Farm. I increasingly got the feeling that the three-dimensional objects I was heading for were part of a wider world of real learning, to which the books of the university in the historic city centre were just an index.

When we got off the bus, I was disappointed at our destination – a large hangar with enormous rusting garage doors. Outside the doors was an ordinary dining chair which for any visitor from the Balkans gave a sad look to the place. I had passed such incongruous chairs outside front doors before; they are not placed there to catch the sun – this is no sidewalk culture of old ladies gossiping as they shell peas. In Kosovo an empty chair outside the front door means just one thing; that there has been a death. Sometimes the chair is covered with a hand towel; sometimes a photograph of the recently departed will be propped up on it, but most starkly the chairs are left there with no further explanation. You do not even know who it is who has passed.

Perhaps the chair here was appropriate. After all, museums are all about the dead. And museum storehouses even more so than museums themselves. This was anthropology's dustiest attic.

And like so many dusty attics, it was a rummager's delight. I came in past an old washing machine, an upturned table, wondering just what jumble sale of the Empire I had walked into. But once inside the main area some order could be seen. A corn dolly hung with a small label noting it with 'JG Frazer'. This hangar held the Golden Bough itself. Elsewhere, wooden boxes stacked to the high ceiling had a rough catalogue chalked on them: 'knives, forks and spoons', 'lamps', 'locks, foreign', 'keys, France'. It was as if someone were moving house. 'Victorian personal ornaments', 'bone', 'shackles', 'organic remains'... as if someone rather frightening were moving house.

Next to these were more wooden boxes, with a different taxonomy. They had more enigmatic stickers – 'Yemen. Heavy', 'Babylon', 'Jericho. Basketry and wood'. This is what God's workshop would have looked like on the second day.

At one end of the worktop, near the sink, was a small resealable plastic bag. It was carefully labelled, 'God dolly, Somerset.' I looked at it thoughtfully, with the reverence and intelligence one reserves for exhibits. Nearer the sink was another, identical plastic bag. I leaned over attentively to see what this held, and read the handwritten label, 'red bush'; it held the curator's teabags. I couldn't decide whether this gave me more respect for the curator's coffee break or less respect for anthropological collectors' fieldwork.

One wall was bristling with spears, though they seemed rather domestic, ranged in height order in neat wall brackets, like spanners in my dad's garage. They were tagged, though I didn't go up close to read exactly which battles, which foes they had been plucked from; whose blood it might be browning in the grooves of their serrated tips.

Another wall was made up of metal cubbyholes. Some held pots, stacked like an Easter egg display, with calico ribbon around each one to hold a label, only adding to the impression of a chocolatier's window. From others of the metal holes extended oversized weaponry, each with a tag dangling from the end, reinforcing the morgue-ish atmosphere of the place.

But one oversized object had been considered too long even to store like this. Along the top of a set of substantial metal shelves, strange-shaped sections of fine wood were stacked like steaks. It was – or had been – a canoe. Beached here in Cambridge, and chopped to fit, it was like whale meat carved into hunks that would fit in the freezer. It made me feel sad.

Wonu took me to see the area where the textiles collections were hung. The clothes were carefully shrouded in suit-protectors – as if we were in a surreal Moss Bros. Wonu showed them to me; the native American cape, the headdresses, and the Inuit suit made from seal intestine, and I itched to try them on.

I did get a chance to try something on – though it wasn't made of seal intestine. Wonu went to find me the items I'd identified in the catalogue and she passed me some gloves to wear so that I could handle the amulets. No purple latex here – these gloves were genteel white cotton, like debutantes'.

She returned and put in front of me the boxes of Edith's collections. In my fine white gloves, I opened the first box, feeling a great moment of theatre.

Inside was a cockspur amulet. In her notebook during her time in Pristina, Edith had mentioned a 'fowl's claw' charm. This must be it. Fowl indeed – the yellowing spur was curling as if in malice – but then maybe the more disgusting it was, the more likely it seemed that it would see off evil? And anyway, I didn't care. This – a tiny scrap of offal – was my connection with Edith. It was her legacy to us all, and it was a small bit of Pristina in the middle of the English Fens.

There were other boxes too which I realised with a thrill must also date from ED's Pristina visit. In her notebook she had written

Bazar partly covered, bad roof all to pieces. One man with whom I spoke was Vlah from Monastir. Bought of him 3 amulets – one hedgehog's foot, 1 wolf's tooth and 1 fowl's claw at 6d each also pair of earrings at 1/6.

The Vlachs are a people generally now equated with modern-day Romanians. Though their descendants may still live in Pristina, they have changed their ethnicity – there is no-one in today's Kosovo who calls themselves Vlach and their grandsons probably call themselves Serbs. But then nor had I ever seen a hedgehog's foot for sale in today's Kosovo. A hundred years can change a lot – for minority ethnic groups, and for hedgehogs. In fact, the hedgehog changed its name even sooner than the Vlachs did, because by the time ED's notebook was published as *High Albania*, she had obviously realised that she was muddling up her small nocturnal mammals, and it was recorded that at this bazaar she had bought a *mole*'s foot amulet, and she excluded mention of the others. I wondered whether this had anything to do with the price. Maybe Sir William wouldn't have been so impressed with something that had cost sixpence?

But here was the yellowed wolf's tooth amulet. I had seen something similar in cases at the Ethnological Museum in Pristina. Now I was able to pick it up, and cup the magic in the palm of my white glove. I thought of the creaking floor of the Ethnological Museum – of Bekim and Alisa and the excitement of a museum just opened, a history just reaching climax, of Kosovo in the build-up to independence. It really was a kind of magic to be touching this wolf's fang right here and now.

And at the bottom of the pile I found the earrings too, along with a gewgaw cockerel brooch (I wondered at ED's taste – or whether this, too, had been said to have had some power to ward off evil, and was another of Sir William's hares). They were labelled in her elegant handwriting as bought in Prizren. It was crude filigree, and I photographed it for Faik and his colleagues.

When I returned home I sent the digital photo to the co-operative in Prizren. Ber-ber-boing; their response was polite but unimpressed. How was my health? My family? As I knew, they could make much finer work than that. I should go back to Kosovo and they would like to present me with something.

I should go back.

12 The many faces of Marko Shantoya

In fact, I planned a trip not to Kosovo but to Albania. It was a journey I had to make if I wanted to really understand how she'd travelled. Since the Bankfield Museum had put her moccasins behind glass I couldn't literally walk in step with her, but I heard that the stick she had used to steer those steps was still owned by the family who had guided her. Marko Shantoya (grandson of Edith's Marko Shantoya) kept it in his house in Shkodra, northern Albania.

Edith and I were on our way. I knew she would be a fabulous travelling companion – I loved her spare style in dealing with physical discomfort; she was going to be a great ally as we battled with Balkan accommodation. This was the woman who had written of her stay in Peja,

**Next morning I found I had not only the Vladika
[bishop]'s room but his sheets, which were grey and
inhabited. Providentially I suffer little that way. I made
a great slaughter and improved the situation.**

I would love to be able to be so swashbuckling in the face of bedbugs. Of course, with her there would be no whinging allowed. I remembered her writing,

**I was the only one of the party who did not require
sun protection and gave my umbrella to Radovan who
was on foot and hot. I found my tam o'shanter quite
sufficient and was surprised at my companions.**

I wondered how far I should take this idea of following in her footsteps, and idly googled for a tam o'shanter that I might be able to take with me. I don't know quite what I was expecting, but the only ones available to buy online came complete with 'hilarious' orange wig for Burns night or Hogmanay pranks. The Albanians always spoke highly of the Scots, drawing parallels between the clan system, the codes of hospitality, the bravery of their warriors. Friends had told me about watching *Braveheart* in the 1990s, at the cinema in Pristina, with Serbian subtitles, and how every Albanian had left the cinema at the end of the film with tears in their eyes, dreams of freedom in their breast, and a Mel Gibson swagger in their step. But I still wasn't sure that Mad Jock's tam o' shanter wig would be welcomed in the Accursed Mountains.

With Edith at my elbow, I worried there would be little time for frivolity. Reading her notes I had mainly felt gritty and slightly nauseous. She described sleeping in her clothes, days without washing, rising at 4.30 and being forced to take *raki* and coffee and no other breakfast before hours of riding in sun. I wondered, to be honest, whether I could hack it. I tried to reassure myself – I was younger than she had been, and I had microfibre and Factor 40 on my side.

I looked at the *Medical Handbook of Travel* published by Edmund Hobhouse in 1899, the kind of volume Edith might have consulted as she got her bags together in Hampstead to start on the train journey London-Paris and then on to Italy from where she could catch a steamer across the Adriatic. The book contained a daunting paragraph on the dangers of trains in Dr Stuart Tidey's chapter, 'Travel in Europe'. Apparently continental trains run on coal 'of inferior quality and the engines emit dense volumes of smoke, charged with soot and grit.' You could therefore either get smut-spotted or close the window to prevent this, but 're-breathe breathed air, possibly charged with all sorts of horrors in the shape of microscopic organisms left by ... travelling predecessors ... The better alternative is to submit to the begriming process, which at least has the merit of being aseptic, and provide yourself with a wet sponge in an indiarubber bag to sponge your face and hands, and with an atomiser containing paroline with a little menthol and eucalyptus to spray into your mouth and nostrils from time to time'. I didn't even know what paroline was, and I didn't like the idea of spraying it up my nose. I wondered whether Edith would have worried about such things, but decided that by that stage probably nothing would stop her on her onward journey.

I could lament my homesickness for Kosovo, my boredom in England, but I wouldn't try to claim that description by Edith of herself before her visit to Kosovo, 'completely exhausted by constant attendance on an invalid relative, the future stretched before me as endless years of grey monotony, and escape seemed hopeless.' Maybe she had built up a better appetite for paroline snorting and hours of riding in sunshine than I; I imagined her moving dutifully to and from her mother's bedroom on trivial errands, gently up and down the shallow steps in that fine wooden staircase at Ellerdale Road as the imported mahogany creaked in frustration beneath her. And at the end of the day, the calendar consulted – one day less till she would be up on horseback, mistress of her time, moving fast away from the querulous calls from the sickroom. She earned her travels.

But there was no point getting into a squabble as to who most deserved a trip to the Balkans, especially when the person I was quibbling with had been dead for 65 years. She would take me to new places; she would give me new perspectives, but ultimately I would have to make this my own trip. She would have encouraged me in this, I was sure – I remembered her comment in a letter to her sister,

I have just been commissioned to write a short article on Balkan travel for a new magazine called 'Exploration'... I must say people who can't travel without being told how had better not travel.

So that was the deal she was offering – she wouldn't tell me how to travel, I would have to make my own way. But I looked forward to stealing a sideways look to see how she was doing it, and maybe receiving a sisterly nudge in the right direction when my attitude slipped.

I went to Shkodra, taking the bus and stunning ferry over (artificial) Lake Komani. I had a gentle churning of adrenaline on the journey, and tapped my foot in time to the traditional Albanian songs playing on the radio,

Jam Shqiptar
Jam malësor
Bab e gjysh
Me pushkë në dorë

('I am Albanian, I am a highlander; father and grandfather with a gun in hand'). Being in Albania felt familiar but not the same as being in Kosovo – the language was subtly different, with borrowings from the Italians just across the water (whose country had for generations supplied not only television programmes but also a colonial government) not from the Serbs. The last hundred years of history have been utterly different – Albania got independence while Kosovo's Albanians seethed under Slavic rule, and although there were terrors for the citizens of Albania under Enver Hoxha's increasingly paranoid and vicious regime, these were terrors inflicted by Albanian on Albanian rather than the oppression by others which strengthened solidarity – and conservatism – in Albanian society in Kosovo. In Albania, an international presence had come as an occupying power; for the Albanians of Kosovo, the international community were seen in 1999 as saviours. As a British woman travelling now between Kosovo and Albania that makes a great difference in the way you are received.

We passed infeasibly laden donkeys (I'd never seen a donkey in Kosovo, where the villages were dying, and so much land lay

Lake Komani

fallow) and I looked out at the landscapes that took the same basic inheritance that Kosovo had had, and overlaid different nuances of language, of history over it, like the faces of two brothers who'd made different things of their lives.

Soon we came out of the rural roads into a fair-sized city. Edith had spent much of the period from 1910 to 1913 based in Scutari, modern day Shkodra (not the part of Istanbul where Florence Nightingale was based – though given the humanitarian and aid work ED did here the associations are appropriate) and it was here that Nevinson had visited. I looked around me as I had learned to do in London, imagining which of the buildings I could see would have been familiar to Edith. I had some directions for how to find Edith's walking stick, from Antonia Young. She had given me an address for Marko but more usefully, in a town which had changed its road names too frequently for anyone to keep up, she told me that I should visit the Tradita restaurant in town because the owner there was sure to be able to tell me the way to Marko's house. Where Edith had used Marko 'Shan' Shantoya as her dragoman for the wild mountains, I was to use Gjon as mine to reach a walking stick.

I found the stone Tradita restaurant easily. It describes itself as a museum-restaurant and it shines with old wood, painted wedding chests and rooms strung with traditional woven sashes into whimsical jungle walkways. Headless mannequins sport traditional costume from the surrounding mountains (different from the woven woollens I was familiar with in Kosovo) and the walls bristle with rams' skulls (for good luck – except for the ram) and spindles, the floors strewn with old rugs and runners like an anthropological jumble sale. The lord of this strange manor is Gjon, who looks like an exhibit himself – shaven headed as a mannequin (though without the 'perçin' tuft of hair that ED had described as being left by Albanian fighting men so that if they were killed in battle and their skull carried off as a trophy,

at least they could be carried in a dignified way without their enemies' fingers up their noses) in an Elizabethan-style white smock tied round with traditional woven belt. I mentioned AyDIT DourHAM and he welcomed me in, settled me down with a glass of juniper-flavoured *herdhicë* on the house, and asked me whether I was tired and how my family was.

He told me about his love for history, and his country, lamenting 'I look in the mirror and I see an old Illyrian. I look around me and see how diluted our line is.' He was a little mad, but part of the monomania we shared was for ED and he listened with genuine interest to my research. He himself was the only person in the world to have set up any memorial to her – he told me proudly of the plaque he had placed at the high point of the mountains which form Shkodra's breathtaking backdrop, with a bas-relief portrait of her and the inscription, 'E Durham, Kralica e Malesorëve' – the untranslatable phrase which was the Albanians' title for Edith, 'Queen of the Mountain People' or, in her own version, 'Queen of the Mountain Men' (which makes her sound like something from The Hobbit) or 'Queen of the Highlanders' (which makes her sound like something from Rob Roy).

And yet to my surprise he didn't know about the walking stick. But this just made him all the more keen to help me find it. He looked at the address Antonia had written for me, and shrugged. He was born in Shkodra but he didn't recognise the road name. Before I'd even finished my drink he was out of his chair

'Let's go. We'll find it if we ask people.'

We set off into the burning heat, like the day Edith had described in Shkodra, 'roasting. The heavy blue sky closed down like a lid, and the land was white with dust'. Shkodra's wide boulevards meant there was less shade from buildings, but it's a city with some pride and town planning, where trees had been planted to shade pedestrians pounding the streets in search of a walking stick. On a cooler day it would have been a pleasure to walk around – up to the castle, which rose above the town, or into some of the intellectuals' coffee shops and bookshops (one we passed called Libraria Edit Durham) but in this weather it was best to conserve our energy and focus on the task in hand.

'I know someone who will know where this guy lives,' Gjon assured me. After we'd walked several dusty streets we found ourselves at a door where Gjon rang the bell.

There was no answer.

'OK, let's try the post office', Gjon suggested. I trailed behind him down more dusty streets, wondering just how conspicuous we looked – the chap in traditional dress and his foreign friend. At the post office I showed the scrap of paper where I'd written Marko Shantoya's address, but the postman's response was the same as Gjon's had been.

'Well, do you know someone called Marko Shantoya?' asked Gjon.

'Ah, it's Marko Shantoya you want? Why didn't you say so?'

I breathed out with a smile. The postman gave us directions and Gjon and I set off again, retracing some of our steps but finally coming to a new part of town. We found the cafe the postman had used as a landmark, turned left, looked for house numbers, and rang the bell.

It was answered by an old man, and with a beaming smile I greeted him. 'Good day. Are you tired? Are you by any chance Marko Shantoya?'

Yes, yes he was.

'I've come because I'm writing a book about Edith Durham.'
He looked blank.

'I understand that your grandfather was the guide for Edith Durham? Your grandfather, Marko Shantoya.'

His expression settled into comprehension,

'Ah, I am Marko Shantoya. But I'm not *that* Marko Shantoya. But I can tell you where he lives.'

My enthusiasm for the information he gave us was slightly dimmed after what had been several hours of wrong turns and strange streets. Gjon, too, was starting to look uncomfortable.

'I'm sorry, Mrs Elizabeth, but I have to get back to the restaurant ...'

It seemed unlikely I could find the place without him but he had been so kind with his time I didn't want to make it difficult for him to leave. But the man who was – and was not – Marko Shantoya stepped in.

'Of course you can go and we will take her.'

Quite according to the laws of the traditional code of Albanian civil law, the *Kanun*, I was therefore formally transferred from the protection of one man to another and I said a grateful farewell to Gjon. Meanwhile, Mr Shantoya called inside the house, and a teenage boy appeared. Getting his instructions, he put on his shoes and gestured for me to follow him to find a walking stick.

It was another dusty road, another door – in fact not far from where we had started our quest – and with the teenager grinning supportively, I once more rang a bell to ask for Marko Shantoya.

Another young boy answered and I explained what I was there for. Oh yes, this was Marko Shantoya's house. The boy, in fact, was also called Marko Shantoya, named after his grandfather and his great great grandfather. It was one Marko Shantoya too many for me today and I rather weakly asked whether his grandfather was at home.

Marko (the third of that name today) came to greet me, and invited me inside. At the door I went to take off my shoes but Marko flapped urgently at me with his hands,

'No, no. We're not Muslim,' he said. I hadn't known there was considered to be a religious dimension to the taking off of shoes, but I realised I had never been inside an Catholic Albanian's house before, and anxious not to cause offence, I stepped for the first time in an Albanian's home with my shoes on.

I explained why I was here, and after Marko had told me a bit about his family I asked whether I could take a picture of him.

'Not in this shirt,' he looked shocked. 'I'll go and change'.

He left me alone in the room and I looked around me at the neat suburban Albanian living space – all ruched nylon chair covers and hand-knitted cushions. Some traditional handcrafts were pinned on the wall; bags and waistcoats spatched into uncomfortable positions for display, and mixed up with plastic nicknacks and a large framed black and white photograph of a young man with a fine moustache. I wondered at all of them.

While I was looking, a woman arrived in a startling leopard skin print dress. This was Marko's wife. She looked me quite deliberately up and down, and then her gaze focused on my shoes. I could see she wasn't impressed. Embarrassed, I said, 'I did try to take them off but Mr Shantoya said I shouldn't worry.' She was clearly unhappy and when I walked to the door to take them off and leave them at the lintel she didn't stop me. That felt better, and I walked back into the room barefoot.

Soon Marko joined us. The first thing he said to me was, 'Why did you take your shoes off?'

Surely he knew what his wife was like? I smiled.

'Why did you change your shirt?' and he smiled back at me and we negotiated the position he should stand in for his photograph. While he got ready I asked about the much older photograph on the wall.

'That's Marko Shantoya' he said. The fourth Marko Shantoya, but also the first. This was Marko who had been Edith's guide – at whose home she had stayed, who had accompanied her up hill and down dale. This was the reason I had come.

It wasn't what I had expected him to look like, based on the description I'd read by Nevinson of a man 'rather fat and sleepy and given to garlic but loves Miss D like a spaniel' but I realised I may not have aimed off sufficiently for Nevinson's jealousy. This man seemed rather dashing; he seemed watchful and intelligent – indeed the perfect dragoman.

'Can you tell me about him and Edith Durham?' I asked Marko.

Marko's wife answered for him. 'Here's the letter,' she interrupted. I recognised the contradictions in her role from all the museum curators I'd met on my quest, required to be both pimp and prison warder in regulating and encouraging other people's engagement with the objects in their care. She passed me a few sheets of rough paper with familiar writing. It was a character reference dated Shkodra 1912.

It is with much pleasure that I recommend my guide and dragoman Marko Shantoya. For 8 months in 1908 he served me excellently in long and difficult journeys in the mountains. Since then I have employed him in 1910, in 1911 and in 1912. He is faithful and very reliable and is well acquainted with the country. He is also a very good cook and his knowledge of German,

Italian, Turkish and Albanian make him a valuable interpreter. His knowledge also of local story and customs make him an interesting guide and travelling companion. I boarded for many weeks at his house and I can cordially recommend it for cleanliness and good cooking and attentions. ME Durham

Marko explained that the house they had lived in then had been destroyed. And then he told me about the walking stick. It had come on the occasion of his own birth with a message via an English officer from Edith to the little baby, now standing as a shrunken 70 year old before me. The message, he said, had read 'I hope it will bring him as much pleasure as I had when I walked with it across *High Albania* with his grandfather'.

Marko's wife had left the room, but she returned soon.

'And this,' she said superfluously, 'is the walking stick!'

In her hand she held a fine, straight wooden stick, slightly battered around the point; I thought of Shala's crags, the stumbling stones of the Accursed Mountains, how ED had recorded that she had 'scrambled and slithered, waded through wet beech leaves, slid mud slopes and climbed rocks' on her way into Kosovo. The knob was ivory or bone carved into what might once have been a lion, now smoothed into an amorphous intricate shape as the scrambling, slithering and sliding had taken its toll on the grip as well as the steadying point.

They let me hold it – the cool bone of the end under my fingers like a handshake with a dead woman.

13 The Cause

I wanted to make connections between the world of Mrs Shantoya's twenty-first century leopard-skin print dress, and the women in hand-woven aprons of Edith's visit. The walking stick lay like a fragile bridge between the two worlds and I was thinking about the exhibition that could explain them. Now I knew what could be displayed. Could it be done? Could I find money for it?

I started to read Edith's account of her time in Shkodra, and the doubts about the exhibition, which had begun when I found out about museums' conditions for loans, started curdling and coagulating further. Edith had been in Shkodra at a time of war, and her book, *The Struggle for Scutari*, has a very different backdrop from the picaresque adventures of *High Albania* and *Through the Lands of the Serb*. I knew it as the cradle of her relationship with Nevinson, but it was also the birthplace of a different Edith. I had met the intrigued traveller, the Hampstead watercolourist on tour; a game chronicler of unknown lands and collector of trinkets destined for the museums of British university towns. But in 'Scutari' the opportunity had come for her to put her energies to more immediate use. *The Struggle for Scutari* narrates how the pluck which had manifested itself previously in being doughty in the face of sunburn on the long walks between monasteries was now shown in a more serious – deadly serious – context of war, aid to refugees and the medical and humanitarian disasters that unfold in their wake.

The transformation seems to have been unexpected. She began by taking some of her money to give to the governor of Podgorica who was in charge of maize distribution.

Scarcely had I given him a pound or two, however, when one after another Albanians, Montenegrins, and foreign correspondents came and begged a few minutes private conversation, and besought me not to trust Stanko with a penny … All friends of the insurgents begged me to keep the money myself, and give it straight to the needy. The foreign correspondents undertook to collect money through their respective papers, on this understanding.

Before she knew it, she was not just a private donor, but an implementing partner in a refugee relief operation. Washing out from her prose is the exhaustion and exhilaration of being part of something so desperately needed. At one point she was helped in the work by Martinaj, an Albanian professor – 'Together we tramped the slums of the town, and scrambled down the cliffs and into the caves along the river banks'. It's the kind of rough travelling she had been doing since at least 1901 but now it had a purpose. And she was becoming an established authority on the situation for other outsiders – she writes that 'Correspondents swarmed in. Most of them rushed to me for information'.

Her operation was grass-roots, hands-on –

'Money for relief work was coming in fairly well. The toil of administering it, however, was very severe, for it was not large enough to permit of hiring assistants or of taking a special room … For lack of other accommodation, the wretched, filthy people swarmed into my bedroom daily. Though I removed the only rug and drenched the floor with carbolic, it was all of a hop with fleas; and at night the rank stink of the bale of raw hide for sandals half choked me'

but nevertheless she writes evocatively of the time she spent,

At night we sat under the mulberry-trees in front
of the Hotel Europa, a crowd of officers, officials,
patriots, correspondents, and scalliwags, all in a patch
of brilliant light from the glaring, spluttering acetylene
lamp. Out of the darkness creaked and groaned the
ungreased wheels of the ox-carts; they filed slowly past,
stacked high with ammunition, and disappeared into
the night, to crawl secretly up to Kolashin and other
border posts. The crowd roared applause.

And

At night I dined with the Commandant and a lot of the
insurgents in the Commandant's quarters, which were
also the ammunition depot .... A fire on the ground
gave a flickering ruddy light, and a dim lamp showed
the military telegraph, which ticked incessantly. In
the gloom at the end stacks and stacks of ammunition
boxes reached from floor to roof. Rifles were piled
about ...

We sat on empty ammunition boxes round the fire.
A great many insurgents trailed in. Some, deadly tired,
threw themselves on the ground, barefoot, soaked with
rain and half naked, and slept like dogs. A few squatted
around and nursed brand-new Turkish rifles they had
captured in fight.

Half a sheep was stewing in the caldron over the fire.
We sat round silently, poking slivers of ammunition
boxes under it to keep up the blaze ... there was no
ventilation save the row of loopholes for rifles. The air
was stifling.

At dinner I was almost always the only woman
in a crowd of officials, officers, a varied assortment
of correspondents of all nations, spies, and Balkan

> adventurers. As the weather grew hotter and hotter,
> their tempers grew shorter and shorter... Sometimes we
> verged on war at the dinner-table.
>
> The nights were sweltering. My room and all the
> hotel swarmed with blackbeetles, which ran over one at
> night and drank the sweat, and laid eggs in my clothes.
> The corridor stank of orderlies.

Her stamina only just lasted the gruelling conditions – she describes attacks of lumbago and rheumatism which meant she had to work lying down and refugees came to her while Martinaj dealt out on her directions. Teresa Buxton, a British volunteer who worked with her in 1913, described her 'short hair, no stays, very plain and stout – a filthy tam o'shanter and dirty dark-green flannel blouse'. Her energy was sapped and her standards were slipping.

But despite the obvious discomforts, the vivid descriptions suggest senses alive. And there were the responsibilities and satisfaction of handling large sums of money: she describes how Charles Crane of Chicago, the wealthy son of an unlikely sounding 'plumbing parts mogul', came to visit her and on leaving handed her a little bag which she later found to contain eighty pounds in gold (worth perhaps £25,000 in today's money. In fact, this was just the beginning of a series of donations from Crane to ED's work). The next morning she bought 200kg of bread and set off to a village she had just heard of in need. The act of turning gold into bread, of being the one who – despite the blackbeetles – loads up that bread onto donkeys and hands it to the hungry, must have offered a purpose which hunting Dr Ridgeway's 'hares' in the form of obscure amulets might not have provided.

Even if I could raise the money for the Edith Durham exhibition in Kosovo – the cost of a business class ticket for all those museum curators to accompany each of their expensively packed amulets and earrings – I was starting to doubt whether I should. I thought of Charles Crane's little bag of gold, containing certainly no more than I would need for the exhibition. I thought of Edith's donkeys laden with the bread which that money bought, to be given to the hungry. Would she have approved of my plan?

Now there were no more wars raging in the Balkans, but there were still displaced people, Roma families living in makeshift accommodation, children without shoes, old men going to bed hungry. There was devastation of a different kind in Kosovo's environment where filthy pollution and environmental degradation went unremarked and untackled by a weak civil society. What should I do with Charles Crane's little bag of gold, even if I could get my hands on it, or its twenty-first century equivalent? Maybe the best way to honour Edith's memory was to leave her earrings just where they were in a museum store in Middle England and to use my energies to help the people of Kosovo with some of their more immediate needs.

For some time Rob and I had been talking about starting a charity in Kosovo – at least some loose umbrella organisation for some of the projects we were interested in. If we could manage to pull off the twinning project for the Ethnological Museum, if I wanted to find out more about the needs of the Roma community, and do something to help them, if we really cared about Kosovo's environment then we would need some organisation to do it through – a bank account and all the trappings of seriousness that a former socialist country loves (in particular, a rubber stamp, oh a stamp). I knew that Edith had continued her work in and beyond Albania from 1918 through the London-based Anglo-Albanian Society, whose secretary she was. Maybe this could offer me a model.

The Society's president was diplomat, MP and spy Aubrey Herbert (the half-brother to Tutankhamun's Carnarvon), and a man who was twice offered the crown of Albania. Described as 'The man who was Greenmantle' in allusion to John Buchan's character (and apparently the inspiration for 'the Honourable Herbert' in Louis de Bernieres' *Birds without wings*), his papers were reported to be easily accessible to the public at the Somerset Heritage Centre, and I decided I would go there, looking for a new light on the post-Albanian Edith, and maybe a blueprint for organising efforts to support Balkan people.

On arrival I was introduced to the Heritage Centre's gloving procedures, which took the routines I had got used to in the Pitt Rivers and elsewhere to a new level of sophistication; the receptionist asked me whether I'd brought my own, and in the absence of a personal pair of cotton gloves I grimly submitted to the latex gloves in a box at reception. It was like going bowling and not having your own shoes.

I found a table with space, and the papers from Aubrey Herbert's archive that I had ordered up were brought to me and I placed each fragile sheet on the cushion supplied, as if for an indulged lapdog.

I was tumbled straight into the inbox of an extraordinary man a century ago. There were acknowledgements for contributions to the boys reading room, a request for policy responses from the Farmers Tariff Union, a terrible poem called 'A soliloquy of youth and age', an invitation from Sarah Bernhardt, a request for contribution to the hedging and thatching prize fund, and for a subscription to the whist league, next to a bill from a theatrical wig maker and costumier. As with ED's archives, I was struck by how beautiful the writing was, and how terrible the typing. Notes were written on the letterheads from London clubs and Oxford colleges, and on grubby bits of paper from working men asking for, or thanking for, posts of work. One letter exhorted, 'Brother, you are desired to attend the MASONIC duties of your lodge'; another in an awkward pencil script was painfully touching and brought early twentieth century England closer to the Kosovo I was familiar with today. It was sent from the nearby town of Crewkerne,

> **Dear Sir, please excuse the liberty I am taking in writing to you, but I am writing to ask you if you could help me a little I have lost my little Baby aged 5 months and I am without any means to bury her. I have 5 children very young the Eldest is not 8 year yet and we had a lot of sickness lately. My wife has been ill and it has been a great expense to me. I have always given you my vote and I did belong to the Working Committee but could not attend regularly through my wife being ill.**

As an MP, Herbert had been involved in many of the causes of the day – there were rumblings of suffrage and the Irish question, and what seemed to be speech cards, written in large bold script (Herbert had always been visually-impaired),

> **dizzy. Heir; Greek fort. Conclusion of Peace. Map; Macedonia. Compensate Greece. Area. Venizelos. Stubborn vanity. Mortal peril.**
> **Indian bitterness; Sentiment; Dreadnoughts.**
> **Two associations. Brotherhood of Man.**

Too often in the accounts given of significant men or women (like Aubrey Herbert or Edith) or in the accounts we give of ourselves, we focus on the impressive and important, the polished delivery rather than the bullet point notes and the scurf of correspondence, bills and social obligations, and memos to the milkman despite which achievements are made. By diving into a life through its wastepaper basket I gained a greater, not lesser, sense of how Aubrey Herbert had focused his energies and made his priorities.

In amongst the not-so-ephemeral ephemera were the footprints of others I recognised who had come before me on the quest for Herbert. A reservation slip which had fallen in between the letters, like a Coke can dropped anachronistically on an archaeological dig, turned out to have the name of Bejtullah, whom I'd met at that Embassy event, whispering of ED's relationship with Nevinson. He was always one step ahead of me, like an Albanian version of the Scarlet Pimpernel. It was Bejtullah who later told me how it was that Herbert had taken up the Albanian cause – travelling in Turkey, he was stopped by two officers in the Turkish army who threatened to kill him. An Albanian lieutenant from Kosovo, also in the Turkish army of the time, saved his life and from that point he committed to helping the Albanian people, in gratitude.

Another old friend was here, some familiar writing that leapt out at me like glimpsing a well-known face in a crowd: there were letters from Edith. From Shkodra, she thanked Herbert for his donation of money, and 'for the cherries' (I was intrigued – in August Kosovo was stained red with cherries, and I couldn't believe it was worth it to anyone for fruit to be imported from England to Albania). The letters from her show how tireless her work was and give some idea of her diary. In 1916 she quips 'I have been running my own Foreign Office on behalf of Albania very hard.' She reports having

> sent off a lot of pamphlets and have got some
> sympathetic replies. Two long letters from Lord
> Fitzmaurice and a cheque for £5! Manchester Guardian
> gave us a short leader yesterday. The Herald (Labour)
> has promised a notice. Labour Leader published
> a letter asking for recognition of Albania's rights
> ...The American Embassy is very much on our side.
> They asked for more of the pamphlets and sent up a
> Professor Coolidge to interview me ... That nice young
> Captain Barnes of the RAF has turned up again and

is coming to see me next week. He is going in some
secretarial capacity to the Peace Congress too ...

I have had a War Office man to see me and am to
have another shortly and probably the American
military attaché.

I have sent pamphlets and a note to all the members
of the Council of the League of Nations society. B'p of
Oxford sent sympathetic reply.

Am sending now to a lot of the House of Lords and
am leaving the Commons till election results are known
but have sent to the uncontested.

In 1917 she was 'reading a paper down at Hammersmith
on Albania next week. A hole and corner place but I hope by
continually throwing seed in these corners some of it may sprout.'

There was also a letter from her that year which seems to be
in response to a request from Herbert for a list of people whose
opinion would be 'valuable on the reconstruction of the Balkan
States'. (There are eighteen names – including Nevinson's – but,
as she concludes, 'I have not named a good pro-Greek because
I am not personally acquainted with anyone who can abide a
Greek. But one can no doubt be found.')

Letters from others showed the breadth of Herbert's concerns
for Albania. One was part of a correspondence he had initiated
to see whether a British sea line could be established to
transport passengers and goods between England and Albania
(his correspondent was skeptical), and other papers were rough
statements of accounts for a concert in aid of Albanian Relief at
Steinway Hall on 11 February 1914. I noted

1.1.0 Lady Gwendolen Herbert
2.0.0 Lady Victoria Herbert
2.2.0 The Hon AUBREY HERBERT
3.3.0 The Countess Dowager of Carnarvon

and a total of 48.4.11 – a few thousand pounds in today's money. The cause wasn't receiving overwhelming support.

The papers recorded other attempts to raise money through a dinner, ED's lectures, and a letter to the Lord Mayor. So this was what it meant to run a charity overseas. I wondered whether the egg-laying blackbeetles were really so bad.

There were frequent references to ED's meetings with Herbert including at Pall Mall's Travellers Club and Anglo-Albanian Society meetings at the House of Commons. There was also a 1920 letter thanking Herbert for the convalescence ED had clearly had at the Carnarvon home in Portofino; 'Had I not been at Altachiara when I was so ill I don't know what would have become of me' and warning him to care for his own health ('Don't get to work too soon. A few days makes little difference to the work in hand and may make all the difference to you. You are much too valuable to too many people and causes.').

In fact, the warnings were not well heeded. By 1923, at the age of 43, Herbert's always poor sight had deteriorated to the point where he had become completely blind. He was advised that having all his teeth extracted would restore his sight but the dental operation resulted in blood poisoning.

From this bungle he died – a loss to many people, including his wife and children, and to thousands of Albanians who had never met him. The papers following his death show that his family continued his interests in Albania, with more fundraising accounts, including generous donations from ED herself – in 1924, £760, which is the equivalent of tens of thousands of pounds today. ED's correspondence with Lady Carnarvon about the fund was full of donors and dollars – Rockefeller had sent $10 000 to the American Minister in Albania for relief work, and the American Red Cross had followed up with $5,000. In 1924 ED was again writing to the family, now to Aubrey's half-sister, Lady Victoria Herbert.

With infinite labour I have got together, including
some collected by Mr Parr the Consul £1,615. The
Parrs write that £3,000 is the minimum that will do
real good. Mr Eyres our Minister at Durazzo writes that
things are terrible. People dying every day of want and
that in the Dibra district (where the Serbs pillaged the
oxen so that ploughing was impossible) the land has
steadily gone down in cultivation and that some 16 000
persons have perished. Two successive droughts put the
finishing touch to their misery.

He asks for £20,000 as the sum to save all the
starvation areas. Both he and the Parrs think we are
doing nothing and that £1600 is a mere driblet.

I have sent personal and persuasive letters to everyone
I can think of who knew Albania and Col Herbert's
work for it, and to all I can get the names of who
are at all connected with the Near East. It has meant
hundreds of letters. Even then the sum obtained is
small for the bulk of it is £1,000 from the Imperial War
Relief fund and £125 is Save the Children. This leaves
£475 from private donors. My own circle of friends is
anything but wealthy.

Can you not manage to collect a little? I want very
much to get £2,000 but really do not see my way to do
so.

I have someone collecting shillings for the Fund but
£2 or £5 is the most I can hope for from that.

Sincerely yours

The letters to the Newspapers produced very little. I
sent to 18 papers and reaped about £40

I felt dispirited and exhausted just reading of ED's letter-
writing marathon, and remembering the woman who had taken
bread in her saddlebags up to a destroyed village. The contrast

was striking between the two modes of aid she tried – the years of hands-on aid in the field with the 'smell of orderlies', and the decades following that of letter writing and cajoling shillings from reluctant Britons who didn't know and didn't care about stricken Albanians.

On the train back from Taunton I had an important moment of clarity: I didn't want to spend the rest of my life giving illustrated talks in Hammersmith if I could spend it disinfecting the floors of Albanian hotels with carbolic. I wanted to go back to Kosovo.

14 The 1903 journey. Rugova

The African proverb says 'while you're praying, move your feet'. I was hoping so badly that Rob could get a job back in Kosovo, but it wouldn't harm to start moving my own feet. By Skype and email, from our home in England I started working with some other NGOs in Kosovo to set up a project that would take me back, if only for a summer camp. We planned two weeks of activities for young people – Albanian, Bosnian and Roma/ Ashkali/ Egyptian – learning together about the environment and planning environmental protection projects back in their communities. Together with the Environmentally Responsible Action (ERA) group and the Balkans Peace Park Project we planned nature trails and videos about the threat of illegal logging, poster-making competitions giving the earnest facts about turning off the light when you leave a room, a night hike and the experience of being out under canvas. We wanted to offer a chance for urban Kosovan kids to understand how 'the environment' can look and smell and sound, miles away from concrete, in the hope that then they might be more interested in protecting it. For many children with their brave new backpacks, as for Edith, it was their first night in Kosovo away from home. The camp would be held in the Rugova valley, Edith's entry point to Kosovo in 1903:

> We ... slid mud slopes ... always winding along the
> valley, pretty high above the torrent that tore along
> below. We got some smoky milk at a most wretched

cottage the entrance of which stank frightfully as they
had nailed up raw ox-hides to dry just inside the door.

She had been coming over the mountains from Montenegro;
more than 100 years later I took British Airways to Pristina.
Indeed, even if I'd wanted to follow Edith's route I wouldn't
currently be able to, as that border crossing between what is now
Montenegro and present-day Kosovo is closed. Of course, in 1903
the land was without borders and united – under the common
oppressor of the Ottoman Empire.

I went up the Rugova valley from within Kosovo, making
Edith's journey in reverse.

It was a dizzying fortnight from the moment I first cricked
my neck to stare up the limestone Rugova gorge. The peaks
towered above the car, and below us the water raced. We were in
a 4x4, safe and plump as an airbag – and difficult to manoeuvre
round the narrow bends. The verge between the road and the
river below – the literal, littoral margin of error – was eroded or
non-existent. A small polished granite plaque with two fresh faces
etched on it commemorated two brothers killed at the roadside.
I'd got used to these in Kosovo – mostly the etchings showed
young men in Kosovo Liberation Army uniform. With a civilian's
awe and sudden sense of safety I asked Kushtrim from ERA, who
was travelling with us, about the plaque. 'What happened? Were
they in the KLA?'

'No, it was a car accident.' I looked down at the riverbed below
us and felt even dizzier.

We reached the village after another half hour of driving.
There were houses spaced out between haystacks and fields plush
with corn, where leafy undergrowth hid pumpkins like forgotten
footballs. I looked at it with new eyes, imagining what the scene
might have looked like to someone just over the mountains,
someone a century ago. I felt it was impossible to get into her
head – would these things have seemed exotic? Primitive? Or

maybe more familiar to her than to me? Rural life in the United Kingdom in 1903 was no doubt more similar to rural life in Kosovo at that time than the experiences in the two countries are today.

Kushtrim took us to the furthest house of the ten or so I could see studding the landscape, where I was introduced to Mustafa and Fete. Things got dizzier – first we were offered thick Turkish coffee (Balkan health statistics are still united under a common oppressor) and then there was *raki* – the drink I find gives even a nice chat in a pleasant sitting room the vertiginous instability of a drive around hairpin bends above a boiling river. I was getting out of my depth, deprived of solid, familiar things. And there were going to be two weeks like this.

There was other dizziness to come – when the children who attended the summer camp lit an overenthusiastic campfire one evening and we watched it singe the leaves of a tall tree nearby

and wondered where it might go from there; when one of the older teenagers, a tall, quiet boy whom no-one noticed, didn't report for our closing circle ritual after supper one evening, and half the volunteers had to fan out across the valley calling the kid's name and hearing it bounce back in empty echoes from the other side. I felt rising panic, and the helplessness of being a foreigner here. What was he thinking? Where could he have gone? And why?

I thought of Edith riding this valley, and noting that in the dark she had 'a rather narrow squeak in one place but was pulled thro cleverly by one of the pack men.' Perhaps Emerson was needing us right now to 'pull him thro".

But Emerson returned – strolling casually back into camp and explaining that he had been looking at the river. And the campfire was easily damped down with the help of Kushtrim and Mustafa. I had had it explained to me that Kushtrim's name came from the call made from mountain to mountain when an Albanian tribe is marshalling for a fight. Literally it translates as 'Who [is] brave?' – the question hollered between the peaks, as we had been doing rather more discreetly in our search for Emerson. I was grateful for the callers, the full lungs of the men of these mountains, and grateful for Kushtrim's bravery. The longer I stayed in the valley the more I came to appreciate that it offered not only scares but resources for managing the frights that it threw at me.

When Emerson was back and contrite, and with the kids in a sleeping bag apiece, I left the camp and walked off into the silence. After the clamour of voices: Bosnian, Albanian, English, Canadian, Irish, Estonian, Finnish – the babel of kids and volunteers we had brought together to make this camp happen – the night felt very dark and still. I could hear my breathing as I walked. Like yoga practice, I let it calm me, and felt the adrenaline start to ebb away.

Perhaps this was why Emerson had gone off. The river was invisible now, just a pulse in the background, but I realised I was probably looking at it as he had said he had wandered away to do. I thought about the unknowable people beyond the dark – the children we were working with, and their unfathomable thoughts, the villagers, the boys who had died in the car crash, and all the others who had died in uniform. I thought about unknowable Edith and her journey through this land – hers and my own scrambling and slithering among and with the help of Mustafas and Kushtrims and Edith's dependable packmen.

Maybe they had been there all the time. Maybe they had been there every night, but it was only then, that evening, as I stopped and stilled, that I saw the fireflies. They danced in front of my eyes like darkness winking; like drunkenness, like will o' the wisps, like something flickering through time. I should have expected them – Edith had seen them here too and I had read her letter to her sister about her walk through Rugova,

I cannot tell you how weird it was. The moon came out. It was all black under the trees, the torrent roared below and sparkled in the moonlight and a quantity of fire flies flitted about.

Not so unknowable then. Me and Emerson and Edith, at different times – Emerson and I separated only by hours, Edith and I by over a century – all silent and spellbound, arrived in the darkness of Rugova.

Edith & I; on the trail of an Edwardian traveller in Kosovo

15 Patriarchy at Peć

Moving my feet – up to the mountains and down to the river – turned out to have been propitious. Rob received a phone call offering him a new job, back in Pristina.

We were going back to live in Kosovo! To walk a city haunted by stray cats and streets acrid with roasting coffee and brown coal, where people looked each other in the eye as they passed, expecting to see friends they recognised. Where the neighbourhoods throb with the muezzin's wail every day, and all summer with endless distorted music over wedding loudspeakers, and old men might still sit against a wall at dusk while rooks wheel and shimmer in the sky above them.

Back, to beyond Pristina's streets, to landscapes of blond streaked cornfields and egg-shaped haystacks, where hedgerows bloom and plums tinge a tree blue and above them, even into summer time, the cool mountains tower with patches of snow that bathe your eyes just to look at them, and where you know you can forage tiny mountain strawberries. Where markets bulge with tomatoes that still have the spice of the stalk on them, and driving home you see women setting tables under the trees for long, large family meals.

And also, as we worked hard to remind ourselves – we were going forward. In a torrent like the white water of Rugova, you can't step into the same river twice. We were coming back with purpose, with a charity for me to run here, now busier, with new volunteers having joined us, with ideas for supporting heritage projects, taking the kids' ideas on environmental protection forward, and with one significant new friend to visit here.

'Peć very soon now,' said the Zaptieh [Turkish policeman], 'ride lady ride. Thou walked like a soldier but by God thou must be tired. The way is better now.' … At last after 16 and a half hours on the road we clattered over a stony breakwater by the riverside to the big gates of the monastery which is surrounded by a high wall. … The Zaptieh banged the big knocker, the gates were opened, I slid off my beast and we entered. I could see surrounding buildings and a fountain and a group of several men sitting on the ground, one in monastic dress.

In between fundraising and fieldwork, now that I had the chance, what I wanted to do to deepen my relationship with Edith was to visit all the places she had been in Kosovo. This monastery felt like a significant first step. Albanians would tell me that for embarking on an important new phase of a project I should make sure I used my right foot to enter.

In fact, I forgot to think about that as I approached the forbidding monastery. It is a Serbian religious site – indeed, *the* Serbian religious site, being the seat of the Patriarch of the Serbian Orthodox church – and as such carefully protected by the international military presence in Kosovo. Memories are still raw of the burning of Muslim *tekkes* by Serb forces in 1999, of retaliatory attacks by Albanians on Serbian churches in the riots of 2004. So arriving at this place of worship you are greeted by a chicane of concrete barriers, barbed wire, a kiosk draped in camouflage, and a pair of lean sultry Italian soldiers, two of the 1,900 members of the Italian contingent within the Kosovo Force (KFOR) of many thousands across Kosovo.

Not that a foreign military presence was anything new in Kosovo – in Edith's day the monastery wasn't guarded, but she wrote on her visit that 'soldiers are everywhere' and that there were 30,000 Turkish troops in Peja alone. Now the Turkish soldiers in KFOR were focused more around Prizren, and this army's aims of peace and security for religious sites was serving a different political purpose from the 1903 occupation, but the effect of strutting young men in uniform at every turn may have been the same. Edith saw Italians in Peja too – but in a different kind of uniform: the Franciscans at the Catholic church a few miles away.

Their great great great grandsons (or more likely, given celibacy etc, their great great great great nephews) who were now back in Kosovo as part of the *carabinieri* lifted their fancy sunglasses to look at us better. 'Passports?' they asked.

'O, si, si,' I si-si-simpered, and handed mine over. It's not a bad photo of me, but they seemed unimpressed as they checked the documents, and took them back to their kiosk. They waved us through, and I smiled a little more seriously at them this time, feeling Edith's hand on my shoulder.

Edith describes the 'Iguman', the head of the monastery, as 'a friend indeed and ... most kind to me' but on my visit the silent nuns loitering in the gloom of the chapels here could hardly raise a smile. I wondered how they got on with those Italian guards. Did the soldiers take their glasses off to talk to them?

Edith had had plenty of chat –

On my arrival ... everyone was so astonished and excited to see me that it was trying. They gave me a chair, a rickety wooden thing, and I sat in the chill moonlight stiff and tired and said how many brothers and sisters I had etc etc in answer to questions.

I knew the routine, though I was always a disappointment. How many brothers? None. Oh, a slight frown of pity for my parents without an heir. Well, how many sisters? One. Just one? Edith would have done better – two brothers (there had originally been three, from the census records, but Arthur must have been dead by the time of her visit to Peja) and five sisters. Another example of early twentieth century Kosovo being closer to early twentieth century Britain than the countries are today.

Unhindered by small talk, we made our way directly to the three joined churches which make up the Patriarchate site. The first was built in the thirteenth century, and they all had the smell of something very old, and dark. In the gloom, you can make out frescoes, eyes staring at you from gaunt faces. The chapels are haunted by their paintings, by their past.

As well as the pictures of former Serbian rulers, there are Bible scenes, familiar set pieces, with mournful jowls: the nativity, apostles, Christ Pantocrator. This is a building created from institutional memory, where reading and looking, remembering and imagining, prayers and visions are indistinguishable from one another. The church's past takes a physical shape around you, and as you walk under arches, into small chapels of dead, still air, you realise that here you are a player in a vast, centuries-old theatre, taking your place among kings and saints and shepherds, and other British women who came here before you.

Edith looked at the books held in the church's treasury –

The books I handled had lost their title pages but were, I believe printed in Venice and had lovely headings. I duly admired and they explained to me that the church had formerly possessed a good many books but that a bad Starshina had sold a number, probably for less than they were worth.

She seemed rather overwhelmed –

The darkness prevented photography, nor could any photograph give an idea of the place because it is all colour ... enormous mass of detail ... the whole effect is extraordinarily barbaric. The walls entirely in Byzantine style and strong colour. ...A curious throne under a canopy with dingledangles on it is that on which

Stephan Detchanje was crowned. The whole style of art is something Eastern, exotic, quite foreign.

It was stiflingly so and, despite managing a little grin at Edith's irreverent 'dingledangles' description, I wanted to get out. I left the chapel into the echoing spaces of the narthex. The door was open to the grassed area outside, and my spirits lifted at real sunlight, after the theatrical effect of candles. There was a small dusty counter where a weary nun scowled. I went over so she could scowl at me at closer range while I idly looked at the cheap postcards displayed next to her. Despite the distorted palette and something sticky obscuring one corner, it was clear that one of the images showed a very powerful Madonna and child. I hadn't seen this painting and in broken Serbian I asked the nun in which chapel I could find it. She shrugged.

I paid for the postcard, and went back into the first of the chapels, carrying the card in front of me and scrutinising each wall, square metre by square metre, and checking back against the fuzzy reproduction image. I felt like a cop in a missing persons operation. My chances of success were about as good – this chapel's wall paintings make up a church calendar, with 365 pictures, one for each day of the year. None of them was a Madonna and child. I tried the other two chapels too, without success. Returning to the nun who hovered over the counter, I asked again where it might be. She shrugged again, and I left.

The neat gardens of the Patriarchate complex welcomed me into fresh air. Herbaceous borders made splashes of colour, and we sat for a while in the sunshine amid the old stone. The Patriarchate felt a little more bourgeois than what I had expected from ED's notes – she had described their horse 'turned loose to find what it could in the monastery enclosure but as that was fed over by geese there was hardly a half inch of grass on it.' Today there were no geese, and no horse. Every so often a frowning nun would emerge from one of the buildings and busy across to one of the others, but the rest of the time it was utterly still. We could hear the Bistrica river roaring past outside, and look up at the bulk of the 'Accursed' Mountains. Edith had sat here too – she had done a fine drawing of the churches from a similar spot – and she described the busyness of the place,

I hung around the monastery all day and was not at all tired as all was new and strange and plenty of fresh people came in and out ... All day Turkish officers and 'tommies' too swarmed in to see the church. The poor Iguman was quite tired with going round with them and they all had to have coffee and other refreshments.

During our visit, other than the nuns, we were the only people there.

We left, collecting our passports without comment from the Italian soldiers. Edith had had rather more trouble with hers, which had similarly been taken off her by the Zaptieh, and sent to the police bureau. She dispatched her guide to fetch it, but he came back empty-handed. He returned several times, and the Iguman sent someone too, but they got no response. Even the next day the passport didn't arrive at the appointed time.

So many passports changing hands across the centuries – Italian men fingering the personal details of visiting Brits, the Turks and Serbs trying to negotiate for the return of people's identities, poor little Kosovo transferred from one international presence to another – men of God, men of Empire, men of arms. I thought of those books that Edith had seen – printed in Venice, stored by Serbs in Kosovo, then sold on. So much had come to Kosovo from abroad, passed through the place, and on to other countries, sold on from Kosovo 'probably for less than they were worth'. If Kosovo had ever thought to establish an alumni association, it would have connections across the world – Arizona national guardsmen, EU bureaucrats, Turkish imperialists, Serbian churchmen, missionaries, do-gooders, curious travellers. And at the end of it, what had it been left with? I needed my faith to be restored – and this church with its surly nuns guarded by the international military presence wasn't doing it for me.

Peja is renowned throughout Kosovo for having the most beautiful girls, and there were good-looking women, or less attractive ones well looked-after, stalking the streets here with smiles. Heading into the town we got a sense of a confident, functioning provincial community. A group of secondary school leavers were having a cheesy photo taken against the landmark building in the main square, public works were underway in the newly pedestrianised area, and there was a noticeboard with the twin masks of comedy and tragedy on top of it, which suggested the presence of a theatre – whether now or in the past. As men passed each other in the streets they stopped and said hello, asked after family members; people seemed purposeful and connected to each other. I saw a shop selling the multicoloured saddles, made from patches of bright leather, that I had noticed on uncomfortable-looking horses on the main road down here, and another shop selling old handcrafts. I treated myself to a woven table runner in dark purples and black, and another in exotic reds, as well as an embroidered cushion cover. The shopkeeper and I bartered as if it was a game we liked playing, and at the end he threw in a pair of woven slippers for free. I liked Peja.

Not Edith:

**It is a fairly large town and filthy and awful with a
frowsy squalor that one cannot imagine ... The shops
all little booths like at Scutari but nothing pretty or
of interest in them ... The pavement of course vile**

... Crowds of filthy ragged people and dirty Nizams
[Turkish soldiers].

I would agree with her on one thing, though – the packs of dogs which were still in evidence. She wrote,

the street dogs in swarms made me understand why
the Easterns call dogs unclean animals. Great wolfish
looking beasts a mass of scabs and scars from fighting,
or covered with mange, hairless, horrible.

Not a natural animal-lover, I had almost been won over by London foxes in the years before I moved to Kosovo, and when I had sat down one homesick day in Pristina to write a list of things I missed about the UK, I was surprised to discover the foxes featuring. Kosovo's dogs were no substitute – where urban foxes slink around street furniture and lose themselves in shadows so that you can't even be sure that you really saw them, Kosovo dogs pad boldly and sometimes fatally stupidly down the middle of the road, tongues and teats or testes on proud display. Kosovo's stray dogs had kept me awake at night with pack fighting; London's foxes only with fierce sex in my garden. And while I'd heard grumbles and anxieties about the germs carried by foxes, in Kosovo, children had died from being savaged by packs of strays. The problem had been so bad that KFOR soldiers had been called to act. Notices were posted in the papers for the few pet owners in the city to keep their dog safely at home on a certain night. Then a lorry patrolled the streets collecting all dogs who were left at large. They were taken to a big park outside the city, and killed, and when footage was subsequently released of the apparent glee with which some of the squaddies had carried out their gruesome task, a minor Abu Ghraib-style scandal unfolded.

We dodged the dogs and made our way to the main hotel in town, the Hotel Dukagjini. It's owned by one of Kosovo's most successful businessmen, Ekrem Luka, as rich as his surname would suggest: his company owns not only the hotel but a radio and TV station, an insurance company, a publishing business and bookshop, and a mobile phone company. The hotel is an ancient Communist-era structure, recently refurbished with glass tables and funky lighting, trying to draw your attention away from its 'seventies heavy dark wood – like a flashy designer silk tie worn with a brown polyester suit. The guidebook told me how the hotel's history has mirrored the city's – it is now privatised, having been a Socially Owned Enterprise in Communist Yugoslavia; under Milošević, Serb paramilitaries had converted it into a casino, and then for several years after the war in 1999, it housed the Italian *carabinieri*. Edith commented about the Turkish troops, 'the town has to feed them' – in twenty-first century Kosovo they only had to house them, but maybe the loss of the paramilitaries' casino was worth it.

In the hotel restaurant we ate pizza which tasted like they had sprinkled tea instead of oregano on top (Edith had had 'good soup and meat done up in little balls and wrapped in vine leaves'). But our room wasn't bad; the bathroom had running water – hot and cold – and soap called Fax. The door to the balcony wouldn't shut properly, so I had dreams of businessmen, or worse, arriving in the middle of my slumbers, but I did better than ED – she had been given the best room at the Patriarchate but it had been here that she had written of having to kill the bedbugs in the bishop's sheets she'd been given and that,

> I was only just dressed when the Iguman [head of the monastery] knocked at the door and asked to come in. I admitted him, all smiles and friendliness. He had himself brought the washing apparatus. My hopes of a clean at once disappeared. There was a pretty thing with a spout like a teapot and an ornamented tray with a stand in the middle with a cake of pink soap on it.

**Also a muslin towel with embroidered ends. I feebly
made an effort and asked them to leave it with me but
the Iguman was far too polite and said he would wait.**

In the published version of ED's visit, which is almost identical
in many places to what she wrote to her sister at the time, she
omits the lingering churchman and the pink soap. Perhaps the
Edwardian reading public wasn't quite ready to think about how
unaccompanied lady travellers kept themselves clean.

The next day Edith went in search of her passport so she
could move on. It still hadn't arrived, so she went in person to
the police station,

**up a broken wooden staircase onto a large landing
crowded with awful filthy people waiting for passports
etc, begging for food, all a buzz with flies, a perfect
Hell. Now and then an official came in and bellowed
in Turkish. We were asked to sit on the rail which
protected the top of the staircase. I was streaming
with perspiration and pulled out my handkerchief and
with it a hard crust of yesterday's bread. At once a man
snatched it up and swallowed it like a dog does. It was
most terrible but I dared not offer them money or show
any. The Iguman stayed with me. I couldn't have stayed
alone.**

With such experiences fresh in my mind I set off for my own
business meeting in Peja, visiting a local TV station to explore
whether they might offer funding for the project we were trying
to run with local kids as environmental activists.

Enthusiastically, I explained why our project was so important
for Kosovo's development – not only because of the drifts of litter
you see around the town, and the illegal logging threatening the
green-grey mountains that tower above the city, but because of
the need for Kosovo's kids to see themselves as agents of change.
We knew from our Rugova camp that kids said they cared

about these things, but the most polluting element of Kosovo's environment, in my opinion, was the belief that it was impossible to change anything, even the things you cared about. I explained how a TV programme could follow these young people as they developed their own environmental projects (some wanted to plant saplings, others had suggested a litter pick-up, or installing litter bins, one group wanted to plant a community garden) – it would be great TV. The head of children's programming heard me out until I'd finished.

'Hmm...' she said, 'I can't see where the product placement would be'.

So she didn't consider young people a product worth placing? Didn't consider their stunning mountain location a product worth placing?

'I want to help you, really I do,' she said. 'Here, take this business card.' It had the name of the owner of a local supermarket chain. 'Maybe they could let you have some of the food that's gone out of date to feed the kids while they're working on the project. That would save you some money, and then they might pay us for their products to be placed when we're filming.'

I had an extremely nasty taste in my mouth – nastier even than the taste of rotten free food, as I left the office for some fresh air. The streets of Peja were still thronged with kindly people, but some of their structures stank. Edith's uncompromising comments rang in my ears, and I decided that now it was time to leave Peja and its 'frowsy squalor'.

Photograph taken by Neil Robinson in Kosovo in 1956.
Reproduced by kind permission of Judith Robinson

17 Deçan

When, one Saturday morning, I was interviewed on BBC Radio 4 about my work with the Ethnological Museum in Pristina, it led to interesting anthropological insights on how my friends and friends-of-friends spent their weekend downtime. 'I was just washing up when …' or 'I was taking the children to trombone lessons and …' people sent messages to explain how the radio and my unfamiliarly familiar voice had broken in on their weekend. One woman who got in touch was, like me with Edith, interested in tracking British travellers through Kosovo's past. Judith Robinson's late husband, Neil, born when Edith was 68, had stayed in Deçan for a month in 1956 as a member of a Cambridge Universty student field trip. As the official photographer for the trip he had been loaned an early Kodak colour camera, with which he had recorded not only the botanical specimens which were the focus of their study, but also the people and buildings they had seen in the area round their camp. Although I had never met the family before, his widow emailed me to say that when she heard me on the radio she had wondered about Neil's box of photographs in a cupboard. I imagined her going to them, sifting through the images of shepherd boys, women knitting, men burning lime, girls selling cherries; frozen relics of a way of life that no longer existed, in a country she had never visited, and the fragile remains of the memories and experiences which had made up the man she loved. When she contacted me to ask whether I thought the Ethnological Museum would be interested in the pictures, I immediately wanted our charity to be part of this reunion –

bringing together the images with the country they had become, but also bringing together this woman in her sixties with a part of her late husband's history.

We got in touch with the British Embassy in Pristina, hoping they would also be able to see the human story, and the ethnological importance, in bringing the pictures home. Through poverty and war there is precious little record of the Kosovo of the past, which is the reason that Edith's accounts of her travels are so valuable. There are few first-hand accounts, especially those without political agenda, of the people and lives in Kosovo over the past one hundred years, and there are few photographs of Kosovo in the nineteen fifties, and certainly none like Neil Robinson's strikingly innovative colour images; for most people living here, the 1950s in Deçan was a black and white business. The Embassy got it: they offered to pay the costs of printing and mounting thirty-five of the photographs for an exhibition, and for a reception at the Ethnological Museum on the opening night. The ambassador also offered to host Judith and her daughters at his Residence if they wanted to come to the opening of the exhibition.

I arranged a video call with Judith, trying to piece together from the pixellated image on screen what this woman was really thinking about her offer. Did she trust me? Did she trust Kosovo to care for the bundle of history she was proposing to bring back? Was she willing to open up the memories of a husband who'd died three years before?

It seems the answer was yes.

Judith was a solicitor by profession and her caution and precision were evident in her quiet questions during our conversation. It was the same precision which had led her late husband to note by each photograph the location where it was taken and how many feet above sea level it was, a pedantry he shared with Edith and which meant nothing to me, who was divided from them not only by their scientific enthusiasm but by their units of measurement. But Judith had an interest in adventure too – perhaps like the instincts which had led Neil to investigate the mysterious hinterland of Yugoslavia on his student field trip in the 'fifties. Judith said she'd like her daughters to come to Kosovo with her, and when I met them – Astri, Elva and Iona; unusual, vowel-rich names you'd concoct to use up your Scrabble tiles – I discovered a similar mixture. The international entomologist, the archaeologist and the psychologist shared delight in scrambling over uncharted territory – whether of the mind or the ant or the Bronze Age – and likewise a delight in pinning it down in exact phrase. With their uncompromising certainty about the way things should be done, they reminded me of someone. We discussed their itinerary and Judith explained that what they would really like to do would be to return to the site of Neil's camp in Deçan.

I told Judith about my project, returning to the places visited by Edith; the trip she was suggesting sounded a perfect opportunity for us both to go back in time. Staying overnight in the area we could visit both the Serbian monastery at Deçan which Edith had visited and go up the valley to the site of Neil's botanical research, and a spring where Edith had paddled. Neil's Kosovo and Edith's were separated by only 53 years – less time than the gap between Neil's visit and our own, for example; just as I sensed that the flight to Kosovo was becoming a stepping stone for Judith back into her late husband's past, my new acquaintance with Neil became a stepping stone for my journey back to Edith. The peasant lifestyle they both recorded seemed strikingly similar, though the land had shifted from Ottoman to Yugoslav rule in the intervening half-century.

Judith sent me Neil's report on his visit, and I compared it to Edith's account of her travels around the same area. Neither were impressed with the administration of their time – Edith made the trip to Deçan on a special dispensation, escorted by two Ottoman police officers, a school teacher and a theology student, while she was still waiting for the police authorities to return her passport for her onward journey into Montenegro. On Neil's visit the police showed themselves as even less helpful – he recorded in his travel notes the case of an Albanian with a gaping shoulder wound to whom his team had given a lift into town to see a doctor, but to their horror the Serbian People's Militia put him in jail when he arrived, and released him only through 'persuasion amounting to corruption'.

Administrative shortcomings extended to education – while on her journey around Deçan, ED was asked by an Ottoman officer what she thought of the Albanians. She answered 'I think they are brave and they have intelligence but they know nothing, they are wild and they live like animals.' Through her translator, Yakoub, she received the following reply,

> The officer says it is quite true they have great intelligence. What is so needed is schools, many schools. That they may learn. Now there will be schools and all will be informed. The officer says there must be schools.

She notes,

> I agreed. It occurred to me that having had Albania for 500 years the Turkish government might have thought of this before but having no control over Yakoub's editing I merely said vaguely that schools were good.

Fifty-three years later, Neil recorded 'We were surprised to find that some of the boys knew a few phrases of French. One boy could speak enough to explain that they were taught this at school in Deçan during the winter. We also found that some of the children could read a little, so the efforts of the Serbs to educate them were evidently having some results.' But I thought of the family I knew, living near Deçan, whose seven-year-old daughter had dutifully recited to me the English poem she had been 'taught' at school. It had taken me some time to understand what she was saying, 'Bel zar reen-geeng/ Bel zar reen-geeng/ Cummalonto school now...' Despite her assiduous *cumming alon'* to school on the *reenging* of the *belz* for a year now, it was quite clear that she had no idea what she was saying in my language.

When Judith and her daughters landed in Kosovo I picked them up at the airport to go straight to Deçan, via Peja where we 'collected' Edith. We travelled in two cars, one driven by Afrim, a taxi driver from Pristina. The route Edith had taken on horseback we lumbered along in convoy, seeing the same landscape she'd described, though she noted that at the time of her visit

> the people are hardly able to cultivate it on account of being raided. The ride was a very pretty one, the land is rich and fertile ... Such crops as there were, were splendid. The hedgerows quite English and splendid grass meadows.

Soon we arrived at the Serbian orthodox monastery, a jewel set in monastic farmlands which produced the delicious honey, cheese, *raki* brandy, and excellent blood-red wine that I'd tasted in Pristina. It's a UNESCO World Heritage Site, and from the road before we reached the gates, we could see it nestling in its green valley, and could tell that it's a gem of a building. The ideal of World Heritage, a belief that some places 'belong' to all of us, is powerful, and of all the places in Kosovo – certainly more so than the Peć Patriarchate, which is also supposedly a piece of World Heritage, despite its gloomy nuns and political wrangling – Deçan feels like it has earned the title. When Edith visited, she noted that 'Twenty Nizams [Turkish soldiers] are quartered in the monastery and it is also guarded by Albanian Zaptiehs of its own; most wild looking Mahomedans who are nevertheless very faithful', and this inter-faith commitment to defending the site even in more recent history meant it was never threatened during the excesses of the 1998-9 war nor the riots of 2004 which shamefully saw 27 Serbian Orthodox churches or monasteries destroyed by Albanian mobs. Many of my Albanian friends have fond memories of childhood picnics in the grounds of this monastery, and I have been assured, by Serbs and Albanians alike, of the power of the relics there to ensure fertility. However, when I asked him, Afrim, our taxi driver, said he hadn't ever visited. When we'd parked outside the imposing gates (familiar to me from a sketch made by ED which is among her papers at the RAI; familiar to Judith, no doubt, from the photograph Neil had taken), I suggested to him that he should come with us. He was unsure.

To be honest, I was unsure too. I'd heard of entry being refused to Albanians at Serbian religious sites and, as Edith had written a century before (in *The Burden of the Balkans*, published a few years after her trip to Deçan), 'Churches are the most powerful political engines in the Balkan Peninsula, and the raw primæval passions of the Balkans find their bitterest expression under the cloak of religion'. The last thing I wanted was to give fuel to such engines. I thought about the injured Albanian whom Neil's friend had given a lift to in 1956, not realising he was driving him straight to jail. But this was World Heritage, for God's sake. And Afrim was a lone Albanian in the company of five earnest English travellers – could he really be construed as a threat of inter-ethnic violence? My own blood was up and I casually handed over his passport together with the Robinsons' and mine to the twenty-first century equivalent of Edith's *Nizams* – more Italian KFOR – and was relieved when all were passed back without comment. Our group went through.

The monastery is built in three colours of marble, which was glowing in the soft light of late afternoon. Around the door are ornate carvings (which Edith described briefly as 'Byzantine curly-wurlies') and opening the door, the glow intensified, though this time with the gold of candlelight and the haloes of hundreds of frescoed saints and kings. Together with the smell of incense the experience was dizzying. Edith sketched here 'for the sake of the Byzantine costume' but I don't have her skill. Of our party, each of us went to our private devotions; I walked around in an atheist's equivalent of prayer, checking against my guidebook, looking up, staring meditatively. Then I thought God spoke to me.

'Can I help you?'

In fact, it wasn't God, though it looked just like him – the same robes and long beard, the solemnity and a kind, intelligent deep voice (though I had never troubled to think what accent God would have? Native English speaker? RP?). This was one of the monks. I explained (much as I might have done to God) that we were just looking really, but he offered some historical information and explained the subject of some of the frescoes. In a low voice I called over to Judith and her daughters and to Afrim and as the monk explained to the other women in English I started translating from the English into Albanian for the benefit of our driver. To my amazement, the monk turned to Afrim and addressed him directly in Albanian. This wasn't what we had expected of the Serbian church – the institution with their patriarchate here, uncompromising in their resistance to Kosovan independence, their stance premised on the slogan 'Kosovo is Serbia'.

When the monk's helpful explanations were over, (the taxi driver shifting a little uncomfortably, though he managed to thank the monk in polite Serbian at the end, just as he would have learned at school) I complimented him on his languages. He smiled briefly,

'We learn Albanian so we can speak to the community'. Yes, this is what World Heritage should be like.

I could see some of the benefits for the church too – there was a small party of tourists other than us, and a little gift shop selling icons, sweet-smelling beeswax candles, rosemary and lavender oil, tincture of St John's wort with extravagant claims for what it could cure, a luxurious herbal face mask I treated myself to, and the produce of the monastery lands. When Edith had visited she was told it was 'fifteen years since an English has been there and scarcely any other Europeans'. I don't know whether my vision of tourist as peacebuilder and harbinger of prosperity is naive but I spent liberally. And the facemask turned out to be fantastic.

Edith got to spend the night at the monastery but having read her account

**a room that was fairly comfortable but no opportunity
of washing at all. The theology student washed me
with a quarter of a pint of water and a sort of salver. At
supper they cleaned my spoon on the pillow case**

I had arranged other accommodation for the Robinsons and myself.

We were to stay in a typical refurbished *kulla* fortified stone house in the village where the conscientious non-English speaking seven-year-old and her family lived. The house is an imposing stone building that would have been a new-build at the time when Edith visited the area. She saw houses of this kind, saying that they are 'more like blockhouses than anything else and have hardly any windows much larger than loopholes'. The design is unique to Kosovo and Northern Albania, with its roots in the blood feuds which kept families holed up for years at a time, too scared to allow out any of their males in case retribution was taken – in accordance with traditional Albanian law, as defined in the Kanun of Lekë Dukagjini – for a crime committed by some distant member of the family. The houses they stayed in were built to be easily defensible, with stone walls facing outwards, punctured only by small arches that a rifle could be fired through. In Kosovo, blood feuds are now almost entirely a thing of the past, leaving the *kullas* derelict or destroyed. A

Swedish NGO had restored this one, as part of its efforts to preserve parts of Kosovo's history and vernacular architecture.

Although probably neither Edith nor Lekë Dukagjini would have understood, as one of our projects to support cultural heritage we had even once organised a yoga weekend within these mellowed walls, scattered round with woven rugs and carpets. This evening, the Robinson girls and I all sat casually in a comfortable cross-legged position around a huge low table spread with large trays of food made by a catering group of local women. They served our English visitors as if they were royalty – these people who had travelled across Europe because they believed it was important for Albanians to have the photographs which reminded them of their country's history. For supper Rob had travelled down after work to join us and we had invited Arberita, an ethnologist from the museum in Pristina whose family was from the Deçan area. Also in our party, just as in Edith's, was a school teacher. Rexhep was also an amateur local historian and in his sixties, so he was old enough – we calculated as we broke the huge round cornbread together – to have been one of the boys in Neil's photographs. He gave a none-too-brief summary of Deçan's past, asked the polite and ritual questions of the Robinsons – about the married girls' families, their journey. I could see they were struggling to stay awake after a day of travel, but Rexhep knew the rules of Kosovan hospitality. He presented the visitors from England with a copy of his monograph about local history, and inscribed it with respect.

The next morning we made an early start to see if we could find the exact spot where some of Neil's photographs had been taken. First, though, we stopped at a women's handcraft and antiques centre in the town. The Robinsons had read about the wool spinning in the area and were interested to see some weaving. One of Neil's most powerful photographs was of an old woman in traditional *marhama* white starched embroidered headscarf knitting at the doorway to her house. She knits the traditional Albanian way that women here had tried – unsuccessfully – to teach me, with the wool looped around her neck. Sunlight comes through the doorway to catch the white cloth of her blouse like a Vermeer. Neil wrote of the scene that she was

> **knitting a pair of socks, one of which lies on her knee. Clothing made this way contained all the natural oils of the sheep fleece, and this probably accounted for the characteristic animal smell of the Shiptars [*shqiptar* is the Albanian word for an Albanian. In fact, this version, *shiptar*, is the word Serbs use pejoratively for an Albanian, though Neil had no doubt faithfully written down what he had been told, presumably by Serb sources], which was discouraging until we grew accustomed to it, but may have been no reflection on their personal cleanliness. We found that even the white felt caps which we bought emitted the penetrating aroma of sheep, but when almost all a man's clothes were made of this type of wool it became quite formidable.**

I had sent Neil's report to the ethnologists at the museum, and sitting in the car with pretty, soignée Arberita with her fine features, her stylish clothes bought for her by her husband in Germany, and her handbag filled with scented wet wipes and perfume atomiser, I felt it must have been uncomfortable reading not only for me.

The women's handcraft and antique shop was full of wool (though I failed to notice its smell), and Elva and I each succumbed to a small woven rug, and the owner presented us each with a gift 'for respect'. We were also able to see some traditional *opinga* rawhide slippers which Neil had written of in meticulous detail –

> **The Shiptars' footwear is worthy of comment because, like the rest of his dress, it was his own particular make.**

The shoes were made out of string, and one piece of leather: the sole, which was flat, without any built up heel. The uppers were of woven string with transverse strands running across the foot into a vertical braid around the sides. Simplicity to the point of discomfort was the keynote of the Shiptar economy.

It was this item of Edith's wardrobe which I'd seen on display in Halifax. It was another reminder of the closeness not only in time, but in lifestyle, of Neil's Kosovo experience to Edith's. I had read about these *opinga*, and seen them at the Ethnological Museum, but through the unblistering plastic strides of progress there is no longer anyone in Kosovo who wears them.

From the handcrafts shop we turned off the road into the track that leads up the Deçan gorge. It felt like we had with us all the resources we should need to find the site of some of Neil's photographs – his report, scanned versions of the photographs, and our resident experts. Through the windows of the car I was aware of each of us parsing the landscape with our own private grammar. Rob was remembering maps; Iona had heard Rexhep's talk about ancient fortifications and the remains of a defensive wall which he promised to show her in the valley we were driving through. She was looking up at the rock face, and through the transient foliage to the enduring skeleton of stone below, calculating where a fort would be best placed. Elva was preparing phials of pure alcohol in which ants could be preserved (I asked whether she always had them with her and she explained that in circumstances where she was travelling by air with hand baggage only, she would ask for a vodka on the plane and would use that to preserve specimens) and explaining the habitats where different ant genera might be found. 'Could there be a genus unique to this valley?' I asked.

'It's possible but not likely,' she said, though her gaze was flickering into the undergrowth we passed through.

Meanwhile, Astri was filling me in about her father, the missing member of our party. As well as the pictures of him on expedition in his early twenties, Judith had sent me a photograph of him taken shortly before he died. I guessed he had been at a wedding as he was in a formal suit with a buttonhole. He was turned to the camera with a wide smile. Everyone smiles at weddings, but I got the impression that this was a comfortable way for his face to sit. I liked him instinctively, and – as no doubt everyone in the car did – I felt his absence.

In the front of our two cars were Rexhep and Judith, each – like me – only half-focused on the present-day Deçan gorge. Rexhep, the amateur local historian, was an archivist of memories and each turn of the road was a new search term in his vast mental database. 'This road was only built in the 1950s' he said ('so new when Neil was here' said Judith; 'so in Edith's day it was just a track' I thought; Rob wondered 'did the old road follow exactly the same path?'; 'so the habitat would have been quite different' mused Elva. For Iona, still mentally hewing rock, millennia back, it was an irrelevance.) Judith had print-outs of the scanned photographs in a file with her, but she seemed to know them thoroughly without reference to the file. I saw her mentally holding them up to each new vista in front of her, comparing until she could get a match. I guessed there was another process going on too, holding up a fictional third image – the image she had constructed in North West England, far away from Kosovo and from Neil, of the land she was going to be visiting. I wondered how close a match she had for that, too.

Rexhep had been painstakingly studying the images at supper the night before, and had told us he could tell the turn in the road where one shot had been taken. Before long he called out to stop and we parked up and got out. I was dubious – it was certainly a turn in the road, and the river was flowing in the right orientation, but how on earth could we be sure? The scientists of the party clustered round the photograph, shifted to one side to try to get a view, squinted. The rock formations matched exactly, even down to a patch of discoloration in one place which was echoed in the photo. But ... I spoke aloud the curiosity that the more precise members of our party must have seen straight away. 'The river's not quite in the right place.' Not by much, but the course cut through the rock, and the silting up of the bend, with the young trees that had grown up in place had changed the shape of this particular corner of the landscape.

In our own ways, and with our own specialist knowledge, we were all aware of the theoretical power of time – the little deaths and disillusions, the decay and erosions, the gaps it opened up between present and past, those with us and those missing. But to be presented so baldly with the power of geological forces was a shock. In a small voice, Judith said, 'I suppose it was more than half a century ago that he was here...'

They took a photograph, though, and I took a picture of them taking it and I wished more than ever that Neil Robinson, the smiling man with the buttonhole, could have been with us and with his three bright, curious daughters, and his widow on her private pilgrimage.

We carried on up the valley to see if we could find the location of the camp, and so that Iona and Rexhep could hunt out the remains of the fortification he had promised her. I was on my own little pilgrimage – to the site of one of my favourite ED anecdotes. She describes the walk to a mineral spring in the valley on the wrong side of the river. They had detoured quite a way to reach it by bridge, but on the way back

> Yakoub remarked it as a great pity to go all the way back to the bridge in the sun when the monastery was so near. If the lady would only take her boots off we could cross the river. The theology student

was doubtful. He asked me if I had ever done such a thing. I said I had. They were delighted. So was I as I was longing for a foot bath. It was over my knees in midstream and horribly slippery but I got thro and felt much the better for the wash. They expected me then to go thro brambles and a quickset hedge bare foot and when I said I couldn't they most discreetly climbed the hedge themselves and left me to dress in private for which I was duly grateful.

The details of the quickset hedge and the private dressing are omitted in the published version of the event, but the little story is still a refreshing splash of human interest and sensual detail in Edith's hard-riding, Turkish-coffee-and-nationalism-fuelled accounts of her journeys through the Kosovo of 1903. It's nice to see her enjoying herself – and maybe that's the impression it made even on those who were there at the time. Her narrative continues to their return to the monastery orchard where she lay in the shade with her escorts. One of them, Yakoub,

said suddenly, "I would not be a king, I would not be a king if I could. A king lives in a prison. Everyone wishes to kill him. He is not free. I would be like you. I would have enough money to live and I would see the world. I would go everywhere. You are everything and everyone services you and you are a woman. Truly it is wonderful. With us the women serve the men. That is better. Here (he counted) you have 5 men all to serve you. I would be like you if I could. Thou maiden that everyone serves."

Edith had done her share of serving, looking after her mother in Hampstead. And if she'd stayed in north London she wouldn't have had two police officers, a school teacher and a theology student to escort her about the country and paddle with her through mineral springs. As Paul Theroux describes it, travel 'holds the magical possibility of reinvention; ... you can pretend ... to be different from the person you are ... rebirth'.

I knew from my own experience how your social credit goes up the further you go from home, and Judith and her daughters had begun experiencing the air-miles effect at dinner the previous evening and in the shop today. It's a seductive experience, unsettling and beguiling, and the only way I have found to deal with it is to promise myself that I will show greater respect to the visitors to my own country whenever I next get back there. In the Albanians' wooing of the woman they were later to name 'The Queen of the Mountain People', I think this moment is significant. As an unmarried woman in Edwardian England, ED could never expect to be addressed as 'thou maiden that everyone serves.' In Deçan she got a taste of being a princess, if not yet a queen. She makes no comment at all on the conversation; her next sentence is simply 'we went back to the monastery'.

I wondered about that, too. Did she identify her monastic, 'maiden' status as a source of her powers? Certainly, if she had been travelling through Kosovo with a husband or lover as protector she would have been unlikely to have had the same reception, and as a single man she would have excited more suspicion. Her status was uniquely linked to being not only a foreigner from a far away land, but also a woman, and most importantly of all, an unmarried woman.

However, her account of her stay at Deçan continues to the next morning when she goes out to do that drawing of the monastery gate. A young Turkish officer came out and there is some coy suggestion of flirtation – 'I believe he would have let me photo him but I didn't like to ask' and instead her translator suggests that he sits for a portrait.

He sat admirably and if I had not had so many spectators I could have done him well. As it was they told him it was done long before it really was and

all were enchanted with the result. The Turk I think
had seldom if ever talked to a foreign lady and found
my unveiled face quite embarrassing. At any rate he
turned his eyes discreetly downwards whenever he
spoke to me. He preferred to sit a little behind me and
speak sideways over my shoulder. In trying hard to
understand him I once looked him hard in the eyes and
he turned his head away at once most modestly. He had
to go to look after his men and said 'au revoir mamzelle'
and retired. After a bit I was told he would like to talk
with me in my room so we all arranged ourselves on the
divans and he duly turned up. Yakoub stood attention
and translated. It was sufficiently droll. Turkish is a
flowery tongue. The lieutenant talked glibly with many
bows and smiles used his hands to gesticulate with very
freely all the time. He had very good hands by the way

she wrote in a letter, which forms the basis of her published
account in *Through the Lands of the Serb*. In the published version
there is just one tiny but intriguing addition to the story. She
notes the lieutenant's good hands and adds 'and neat joints'. Why
add this biomechanical detail? It seems a distancing mechanism,
something to distract from the fleshly and suggest that her interest
was purely structural, not sensual – the return of the virginal to a
woman briefly tempted into the slippery boulders and unveiled
faces of discourse with a good-looking foreigner? She seems to
have had a light hand fetish, as these are not the only hands she
comments on, though the others belong to a sixty-five year old
man she met in Albania and who told her about the surgery he
carried out for village people, telling her 'you must have good
hands and good fingers', beside which she adds in brackets 'his
own were very fine'.

I was thinking about far too many things all at once, and
meanwhile, Rob was driving us ever upward through the Deçan

valley. I needed to keep my eyes open because it should be somewhere around here that we'd find the spring Edith had walked to and drunk from before she went paddling and admiring young soldiers' fingers.

I was definitely thirsty, so it was a very welcome sight: the car stopped by the side of the road, with a woman ferrying out empty Coca Cola bottles from its boot; just what you'd do if you knew where a mineral spring was to be found. We pulled up next to it and Rexhep confirmed that this was a spring. It had been piped now so the water gushed and chortled out of a small metal fountain, but the effect was the same. We all doused ourselves, and I cast a quick glance at the slippery stony riverbed next to us, imagining pairs of sore feet and strong ankles wading luxuriously through the coolth, pale as ghosts.

Judith found the site of the camp where her husband had stayed, and after some adventuring (Iona also found the defensive wall she'd been promised) we returned swiftly to Pristina for the opening of the exhibition of the original photographs. There were about 100 people attending and Judith made a moving speech ('these photographs belong here, with you; take good care of them') and was interviewed for television and newspapers in an overwhelming evening. People moved around the old spaces of the Ethnological Museum and the past came to life.

It was only after Judith and her daughters had returned to England that I reread some of the documents she had sent me about Neil's expedition. I saw his polite note at the end of one report, 'I wish to acknowledge my gratitude to the Administrators of the H. E. Durham Fund, whose grant enabled me to take part in the Expedition.' After the day we had spent in the company of a Durham, even the name seemed too much of a coincidence, but then I remembered that ED's brother was Herbert E Durham. Indeed, he is mentioned by her in the letter narrating her travels back from this visit to Deçan. The reference is in the context of a conversation with Yakoub who, on hearing that Edith's brother is a doctor, wants to know Herbert's opinion on what can be done for couples who, like Yakoub and his wife, have not been able to have children.

I got in touch with Neil Robinson's college, King's, and they sent me details of the HE Durham by whom the fund was bequeathed. From his obituary it seemed that this man and Edith would have had much in common – the same sharp curiosity and wanderlust (the obituary describes HE Durham as a pioneer in tropical medicine and he was a member of the incongruous sounding London Beri-Beri expedition), forthright opinions (according to the obituary he was a 'man of strong personal likes and dislikes who never for a moment wavered in his loyalty to old friends'), and some artistic interests – where HE's penmanship was amateur to ED's Royal Academy exhibiting (the obituary says fulsomely that 'coloured drawings in the notebooks and interleaved textbooks of his undergraduate days are witness of his artistic talent') he outdid her in photography, as he had been a medallist of the Royal Photographic Society.

But were they related? I delved some more. And to my delight I dug up biographer's gold. He – HE – was indeed Herbert E Durham, the sibling closest in age to Edith after the death of their brother Arthur in 1893. I imagined them trading beri-beri tales with Balkan stories, and wondered whether he had liked her *çifteli* musician photograph as much as I had. What must the Durham household have been like? The anthropologist swapping ideas with the pioneer in tropical medicine over the tea tray? It reminded me of a family I'd just met.

Herbert had outlived Edith by less than a year, and on his death he left a bequest for the general purpose of the 'assistance of work in the University for the advancement and dissemination of our knowledge of the life of man and other animals in health or in disease'. Initially the bequest had required that male students should be its beneficiaries (given the behaviour of his sisters, one could hardly imagine that Herbert would be unaware of the interest there would be from women scientists and students in the topics he'd specified; maybe, with memories of the 3:6 male: female ratio of his brothers and sisters, he'd considered that their male peers were the ones in need of extra support). There was no mention of the Balkans in the terms of the bequest – it was just a delicious coincidence that unknowingly, Judith and I had been on the track of two visits to Kosovo both with their roots in the same family.

18 Edith hitches a lift with the Bible Society

While ED was admiring the Lieutenant's hands in Deçan, he had offered to arrange for her to continue her journey as she had initially planned, to nearby Gjakova, even though she was without her passport. In the end, and with reluctance, Edith turned down his offer because she worried whether her Montenegrin guide, Radovan, would be safe, as the agreement she had made on leaving Montenegro was that Radovan was to return with her or go to prison if he arrived alone. She and Radovan therefore went back to Peja where, eventually, her passport was returned to her and they were able to continue their journey, out of modern-day Kosovo and home.

Once back in England, she wrote passionately about Turkish rule in the Balkans; in the *Monthly Review* she wrote that the Turk's 'greatest admirer must admit that as an administrator and as a trainer and teacher of subject races he has failed dismally'. It's an interesting line of criticism to take, and obviously draws directly on those experiences in Peja and conversations in Deçan. The argument strikes me for its modernity and mildness – it is a technical criticism (much like the reproach often made of more recent administrators in Kosovo, such as the United Nations Mission in Kosovo, UNMIK, which was set up as a condition of the end of the NATO bombing campaign to push Milošević's military and paramilitary forces and their ethnic cleansing out of Kosovo) predicated on an expectation that empires would 'train and teach' ('build capacity' in modern development parlance).

I learned from an article ED published in the journal, *Geography*, that she had returned to the Balkans, though not to Kosovo, in 1904, travelling round Albania with an employee of the British and Foreign Bible Society and with stocks of revolutionary Albanian-language bibles. Was this a new Edith? There had been a complete lack of any spiritual or religious interest in what I'd read of her writing until then; and not even any record of baptisms in her family. But in fact the account reinforced my picture of a woman more interested in horse-drawn adventure and Albanian emancipation than in evangelism.

> For many weeks we rode and walked through Albania. There were no made roads then. We forded rivers where the horses almost swam, and plunged through marshes where the horses were bogged and had to be hauled and dug out. We visited all the chief towns. Wherever there was an Albanian Governor we were welcome to sell all the books we could. At Berati, where there was a Turk, we were arrested and brought before him. He said he had no objection to Christianity. We might sell as many gospels in French as we pleased, but not in Albanian; and he confiscated them all. It did not matter, as we had a store awaiting us ahead. It was an inspiring journey. Moslems as well as Christians hastened to buy books in their own language. 'Now,' said a young gendarme, 'I can teach my young brother to read.'

While I was still researching, one of those things happened – like the Durham family legacies which turned out to have inspired both me and Judith on our journey to Deçan – which sometimes make English society seem as small and navigable as Kosovo. I was back in London for Christmas and invited to a party where one of the other guests introduced himself as the Arts Development Officer of the Bible Society. I chatted to him about Kosovo and about Edith but he already knew much of what I told him. He'd been to Kosovo himself and he'd heard of Edith. He told me I should get in touch with an Albanian colleague who was working on a new translation of the Bible into Albanian – a modern-day collaborator in Edith's Bible Society enterprise.

On my next visit to the UK, I travelled to Swindon to meet Oldi Morava, the Bible Society's Albanian translator. I had hoped he could tell me something about Edith's travels with the peddler of Bibles; in fact, he knew very little about the history, but the time we spent together gave me new perspectives on Edith's world and my own.

I've worked as a translator on a professional basis – not only the unlovely medical interpreting work I'd undertaken in London but two books have been published in my translation. I'd worked for a translation company in Kosovo which had a government contract, meaning that I take responsibility for some of the English versions of Kosovo's laws, diplomatic communiqués and plenty of press releases. But talking to Oldi I realised that translation can be more important than that: a matter of life and death – indeed, of eternal life and death. Of course Bible translation has never been a neutral activity: the first complete translations of the Bible in England, from Latin to a language that congregations could understand, were fuel for the social and religious turmoil of the Reformation. You can understand how the same extension of access to holy scripture in early twentieth century Albania was a cause for concern among those Turkish officials who arrested Edith and her Bible Society friend.

But even once the principle of translation has been agreed, the process is going to be fraught. Oldi and I spoke in Albanian together and it was only when I heard in this new context the usual phrase, 'Është fjalë për …' meaning 'it's a question of …' or 'the issue is …' but hinging on the word 'fjalë' which literally means 'word' that I realised that *words* are inevitably *questions* or *issues*.

For a start, Albanian has two dialects – Tosk and Gheg. Tosk is almost identical with the form of Albanian officially adopted as the standard in 1972, in a decision that was tactful – and tactical – given the Tosk-speaking southern heritage of Albania's paranoid dictator at the time, Enver Hoxha. Gheg is what is spoken in Kosovo and northern Albania, except by the upwardly mobile. Just as I have a telephone voice, slightly plummier, more careful with my vocabulary, many of my Gheg friends can slip into an artificial Tosk, complete with hypercorrections and self-consciousness, when they feel it's needed. I hate to hear it, because to me it sounds like a lack of pride in their mother tongue, but I was born into a family speaking Standard English in Received Pronunciation, so I probably have no right to comment, in any dialect. My own Albanian is laughably Gheg – perhaps as odd for Albanians to hear as it would be for me to come across an Albanian academic speaking Geordie. The two dialects are – except at their extremes – comprehensible to one another, with Gheg-speakers finding Tosk easier to understand than the other way around, because Tosk is what is generally heard on the great democratising force of television. Some of the differences are across the board – the Gheg N for the Tosk R, or the vexed issue of the infinitive about which linguists like my language teacher conceive long-standing feuds ('I told him that if he thinks it's possible to construct an infinitive combining the Gheg 'me' with the Tosk 'të' then I have nothing more to say to him'). But the question for missionaries is which one would Jesus speak?

Jesus, the young revolutionary = Gheg

Jesus, the founder of a world religion = Tosk.

Jesus, man of the people = Gheg

Jesus, respected teacher = Tosk.

Do you want your Jesus to sound like the spokesman for a province still held unfairly under international administration (Gheg) or like Enver Hoxha (Tosk). Of course, I'm putting the options unfairly but it's these connotations that are at stake. A few decades before Edith's bible-touting tour, an Albanian called Konstantin Kristoforidhi translated the bible – into both Gheg and Tosk.

The modern approach of the Bible Society is to rely on no single Kristoforidhi. Oldi is just one of those working on the new translation. The Old Testament is translated from the Hebrew (Oldi has a Masters in Hebrew from Oxford) and the New Testament from the Ancient Greek. Oldi and his collaborators, based in different countries, meet a few times a year for a week to compare translations. As Oldi points out, these are not just discussions of angels and pinheads – from the Hebrew, for example, it is possible to translate both 'Në fillim Zoti krijoi qiellin e tokën' and 'Kur Zoti filloi të krijojë qiellin e tokën' (roughly 'In the beginning God created heaven and earth' and 'When God began to create heaven and earth'). The difference in dogmatic terms is huge – as vast as the universe – since the latter makes it possible that creation was not *ex nihili*.

Oldi's passion for his work is evident and he gives me a glimpse of the reasons for it. He says he comes from a Muslim family but 'I didn't hear anything about God from my parents. I remember being given a red egg [an Orthodox tradition] one Easter but not the reason.'

I imagine that unexplained red egg rolling around Oldi's childhood and the childhoods of others in those lost generations when Bibles were burned – when so many books were burned – in Hoxha's Albania. I'd been given a red egg too on a journey back from Albania one Easter time. I was told to keep it in my kitchen cupboard to ensure prosperity, and I did so – just in case. Oldi's red egg took a long time to take effect, but finally after the fall of communism and the arrival of missionaries, at age 11 Oldi remembers being given his first book of children's Bible stories. He says, 'I'd never read those stories before – not Genesis,

Moses, Noah'. I remembered my own childhood Bible story book, bright with illustrations of swarthy men with great bone structure and jewel-bright capes and huge adventures (whales, parting of the seas, miracles). Unlike Oldi, I hadn't led the life of a believer as a result of my childhood reading, but my imaginative and cultural life was inconceivable without those images, and the language built on them – the references running through Shakespeare, poetry, art galleries, village names, traditional food, idiom. That's what Edith was taking in her panniers through river and marsh: access to a world culture, a shared frame of reference. She was a small, plucky force for globalisation. And of course the stories aren't value-free. The nineteen-seventies version I had from my liberal parents majored on Good Samaritans, standing up for what you believe even in the lions' den, and a Christ child whose birth was announced not to idiot politicians but to working men (though to be fair the shepherds shown in those pictures had freshly laundered robes and none of the dirt under their fingernails or 'penetrating aroma of sheep' that Neil Robinson and anyone else who spends time with real shepherds would recognise). If any Christian cargo is to be found in Edith's books and saddlebags, it is these.

In the same year as her Bible touting tour in Albania, Edith ran the process of cultural connection in the opposite direction, bringing out from her saddlebags the account of the travels she'd made through Kosovo the previous year, with a dedication to her mother. *Through the Lands of the Serb* was described by the *Times Literary Supplement* as an 'interesting, witty and attractive volume … delightful in every way'. The English-speaking world was hearing about Kosovo first-hand for the first time.

19 Quicker and cheaper than riding

All I knew about ED's movements in the next few years were from the accession notes I'd copied from the catalogue at the Pitt Rivers Museum – in 1905 Montenegrin travels resulting in a *gusle* stringed instrument bought at Njegus, a clasp knife in Niksic ('part of a bride's outfit' – the mind boggles at the feistiness of the Niksic brides), a Prizren-made flintlock pistol bought elsewhere in Montenegro, and a gilt button bought in Dubrovnik. In 1906 she was evidently in Bosnia, bringing back a double flageolet from Banja Luka, a salad spoon inlaid with wire from Sarajevo and some silver filigree earrings elsewhere in Bosnia the same year along with a sketch of hay stacked on trees. There is something poignant about being reduced to our souvenirs like this – the frippery of jewellery and a single gilt button, the frustrating memories held in musical instruments you don't know how to play, and the bridal clasp knife owned by an unmarried woman. I wondered whether she had ever worn the earrings. I had an image of her sitting room in Hampstead cluttered with these things and rather like the storerooms of the Arch and Anth I'd visited in Cambridge.

She wrote from her travels to her sister, Nellie, about why she had taken a new house in London for herself that, among other reasons, 'your house was all bunged up with my things'. I could imagine poor Nellie's home bristling with flageolets and flintlocks from places she knew nothing of.

While Edith's travels took her around the Balkans beyond Kosovo, I was busy perfecting my travelling style, in preparation for her return. When she wasn't on horseback or on foot, following pack ponies over terrain considered too dangerous for riding, she reported having navigated the Balkans in a 'tilted cart' she called a *strema*. She gives plenty of description of it in her letters to her sister – it is 'a cart covered with a tilt and drawn by two horses as it comes cheaper and quicker than riding. It skins the flesh off your bones nearly till you get used to hanging on and fixing yourself up with straw etc'. In her notebook she writes of another *strema* journey – 'Only a little hay at bottom as protection. Braced feet against one side and back against other. Plunged thro' Djakova in dark. Jolting something hideous.' In the published narration of that particular Gjakova journey in 1908 she repeats the description from the notebook and surprisingly adds another detail too – 'Marko and I bumped together like dried peas in a pod.'

When I visited the archives at the Pitt Rivers Museum I saw one of ED's photographs of a *strema*. Perhaps the photograph was for purely ethnographic purposes, but I wondered whether she'd made that record in the same way you might try to commit to memory the features of a travelling companion you were fond of. I think she may have enjoyed *strema* travel more than she admitted: what with the bumping around with Marko, and the huddling up in hay, the *strema* seemed to me to be a rather fine way to get around, and certainly superior to the other transport that I have used in Kosovo. Usually I get around by taxi or by bus. The taxis generally offer better conversation but they come dangling egregious air freshener and jangling Albanian popular music (usually wedding dance music played on the *surl*, an instrument described charitably as being like a clarinet but which usually sounds like a duck). The buses have the same music, though they replace the air freshener with cigarette smoke. Sometimes they show one of Kosovo's more idiotic sit coms (the one with the three old guys who shout at each other) and sometimes the passengers laugh. Sometimes they don't laugh, and whether they do or not it seems extraordinarily sad. With the exception of Greyhounds across America I've never been able to see a bus as romantic.

So I envied Edith her *strema* travel – all that bracing and plunging and jolting, in the open air – and wished such adventures were available to me. I'd never seen a *strema* on the road in Kosovo, but there was a possibility of something similar: the *motokultivator*. It's not quite like anything Edith would have seen but from the first time one of these twenty-first century peasant bad boys roared up at me out of the darkness on a Kosovan country road, I conceived a dangerous passion for a ride.

The *motokultivator* can be best imagined if you think of a small tractor without any housing. It's the most basic form of self-propulsion possible – an engine mounted on wheels. At the front there is either one or two seats that have been taken from a wrecked car. The driver operates a long steering column (these strange primitive hybrids have been nicknamed Kosovan Harleys), and behind him is a flatbed trailer used for transporting goods or families or lucky English travelling ladies.

I didn't know how one could go about getting a lift on such a beast – I'd never seen one at rest with its driver to be able to enquire. But the idea grew, every time I saw one. They were always driven by men, with their legs splayed, langourous Harley-style, even if the machine they were taming had more of a putter than a roar to it.

I thought my chances might increase when our charity started working with the Roma, Ashkali and Egyptian community in a suburb of Pristina called Fushë Kosovë. The status of this community has hardly changed since Edith encountered the 'gypsies' she describes in shamefully racist terms alongside description of their baboon, in *Through the Lands of the Serb*.

Elsewhere she describes meeting others from this community, with perhaps a little more admiration – the men working

> half-stripped, a-ripple with tough muscle, under little shanties made of sticks and flattened-out petroleum cans. How the land got on before the petroleum can was introduced it is hard to imagine. In the hands of the gipsies it is the raw material from which almost everything is made

The community was still poor, and fashioned from flattened petroleum cans, and the kind of work with which families got by was frequently what you might need *motokultivator* transport for: shifting building materials or junk or garbage; scrap metal collection; selling on job-lots of sudden surplus vegetables at market. On my daily visits to the community I would often look out through the windscreen of my taxi from Pristina – my view interrupted by the lurching of some falsely scented fruit air freshener – and see these princes of the road roaring past.

We were working to set up some projects to support economic development – microfinance initiatives where we trained a group of women, for example, to make soap from olive oil, packaged in cute handmade cloth bags and set up a small business selling their produce. It is not an innovative approach to fighting poverty today, but it must have been rather more groundbreaking when Edith wrote to the *Guardian* in 1931

> There has been no rain in Albania since April and in that small country, dependent entirely on its maize and wheat crop, such conditions spell famine. A great part of the peasantry, especially the refugees, from Yugo-Slavia are without funds to buy at even normal world prices. If they cannot harvest their own grain they must starve. It is no moment to appeal for charitable funds, but there is one method by which these people can be helped to obtain money to tide them over the cruel

winter that lies before them. The peasant women are beautiful cotton and wool weavers. Their work can be obtained from a depot in London, the Albanian Shop, 5 Westbourne Street, Sloane Square. Should any of your readers be wanting cheap washing wool rugs, cotton material for furnishing or clothes, cushions, tray cloths or runners, by buying at this depot they would be helping to save many Albanian peasant households from a winter of starvation, while at the same time they would be benefiting our own cotton trade as the cottons used for weaving are nearly all obtained from Manchester.

I had been working on our own 'Trade not aid' project for some months – enough, I felt, to have built up a bit of trust in the community, maybe even a bit of credit – when I tried for a ride. I was at the market – a term that suggests rich piles of fresh produce and good natured bustle and haggling, and which doesn't really evoke the mean, dirty piles of goods salvaged from dumpsters and laid out on cloths on the muddy asphalt. The only thing ripening in the sun here were old trainers. Men with bad teeth stared at you as you passed there, and even as I'd started knowing some of them by name, so that they would mutter 'good day, are you tired,' at me in the approved greeting, they would still follow it up with a suspicious stare.

As I did almost every day, after I'd locked up our centre, I walked through the market and asked of the casual crowd waiting and staring, 'taxi for Pristina?'

Usually there was someone who'd give you a lift in their car for a reasonable price, but today it turned out that none of the guys standing staring was a driver.

Seriously? No-one? They all shook their heads, almost sorrowfully. To one side was a *motokultivator* with a few bags of peppers piled on its flatbed. Its owner was sat in the driving seat with a cigarette. This was my chance!

'Taxi to Pristina?' I asked. He shook his head.

'But ...' I wanted to argue. It didn't make sense; I would pay him a fair price – more than he'd get for those peppers.

But who knows what his reasons were. Pride? Prejudice? Or maybe he didn't have his papers in order and didn't want to risk a trip into town where he was more likely to be stopped. And there was no point pushing it – if you're going to be jolted around on poor roads, you don't want to be jolted by someone who resents you being there.

I started the long walk to the bus stop a mile away.

The rejection rankled. I was annoyed to be cooped up in the diesel fug of the regular bus when I could have the wind in my hair and be bouncing amid a cargo of peppers. And I worried about why the driver had refused me. He didn't like me? He didn't trust me? He didn't think it was suitable for me to be travelling like that? Like any pleasure forbidden it only increased its desirability.

I watched more carefully the men who drove these rough unseemly machines, and I watched the women they sometimes had bundled in the cart behind them – old women in headscarves, shapeless as sacks of peppers. Or younger women with fine bone structure who turned their face from the wind so their hair was combed out behind them as they travelled, and their eyes seemed set on the horizon like social realist sculptures. I noted how they sat – the elderly with legs straight out in front of them like rag dolls, or the young crouched over the low sides of the trailer, gripping the wooden slats while they looked down at the speeding tarmac below, caught out and grinning when a pothole or a speedbump threw them off balance.

One day I would travel like that.

It was a day with the same pattern of locking up the centre, and walking down to the market. The same used shoes lined up on a rug by the side of the road for sale, next to tiny cairns of potatoes, a jumble of sharp and glinting metal pieces rescued from the dump. The same men stared, asked whether I was tired. Some greeted me by name.

'Taxi for Pristina?' There were no offers. There wasn't even the *motokultivator* standing to one side this time. I set off towards the bus stop again.

Five minutes from the market I heard the engine behind me, and I turned to see a *motokultivator* heading my way. They're not fast and the road was empty so we had plenty of time to see each other. This was a good chance! I waved at him.

The driver drew level with me and I shouted over the noise of the engine 'to Pristina?' He shook his head.

Why? It didn't make sense.

'Why?' I asked. 'I'll pay you. Like I do with the taxis. And I'm running late. Please?'

He shook his head.

OK, I had my pride too. I started walking again.

It was only a few steps later that he called to me; his *motokultivator* was still stopped in the middle of the road. He shouted out a price that was ridiculously high – more than a car would have charged. I tried to haggle and then I caught myself. Did I really care? I know Edith would have got a good price, would have been stubborn about the principle of not overpaying. But Edith hadn't had a meeting in Pristina to make in twenty minutes during rush hour.

So we had a deal. I had the money and I'd never remember the price, only the experience.

Ah, but to get to the experience, you first have to mount the trailer, I discovered. I'd never seen this done – all those statuesque women riding my dream had been in situ by the time I'd seen them. Edith would have had Marko to help her up but my driver didn't seem very interested in helping out. He sat at the front with his engine running like a meter, and craned his neck round occasionally to see how I was getting on. I tried lifting my leg high enough to step onto the trailer. Nope, wasn't going to work. I put my bags down inside the trailer and tried the diagonal leg-swinging technique, but you still have to pivot on something. Ouch. In the end I went for the run-up and tip-yourself-in approach. No-one had been watching.

And then we were off. It was a wider trailer than Edith's *strema* cart had been so I couldn't brace myself as she described. I tried different positions and however I sat, I felt like I was enacting the drama of centuries. There was what I thought of as Pioneer pose, staring forward, or Endurance – crouched and still, impervious to the lurching that tried to unbalance me. Occasionally I let my enjoyment of the journey show in a smile as I tried out Picnicking Villager pose, eyes flickering around the road and traffic as if they were a rare treat, though this was harder to carry off on your own.

Not that I was sure I was entirely on my own. Sometimes after a bad jolt I thought I heard a well-bred oath uttered just beneath the sound of the straining engine ahead of me, and there was someone I glimpsed like the double vision you get briefly when you're bumped down onto hard metal. In my extended apprenticeship Edith had shared lots of things with me, but never before today had she so explicitly taught me how to travel.

20 The 1908 journey. Gjakova souvenirs

When ED came back to Albania, and then to modern-day Kosovo, in 1908, she was a different person. With the death of her mother in 1906 she was now an orphan. The death had come at the end of a long illness, preceded by years of childbearing (nine children born within ten years). For Edith it must have meant many things – a freedom from the duties of being the eldest child with the responsibilities of caring for a mother, but also perhaps the loss of a confidante and companion? I'd found only three references to her mother throughout her writing. One in a letter to Marie Stopes on the subject of birth control noted that 'My own poor mother would have rejoiced to know that success had been achieved. She poor dear was worn out by frequent childbearing and was convinced that the status of women would never really be improved until they had the power to regulate childbirth'. The comment offered a sense of feistiness to the mother of this feisty daughter that made me feel better for her, and that offered the possibility that the two women might have had some interesting conversation in the sick-bed hours when ED wasn't off on her travels.

The second reference was even more interesting, though tantalising in what it did not reveal. It comes in another letter to Marie Stopes and explains that the family's involvement in the movement for birth control had reduced by the end of the 1890s when ED's mother's cousin 'who took such an active part in the movement, went abroad at the end of the 90s. My mother's health had completely broken down and she took no further part in any public movements.' It's the word 'further' that intrigues me, as I never did find any mention of what part Mary Durham might have played even before the 1890s, but it gave the possibility of another dimension to poor Mrs Durham, hitherto known only for her children and her illness.

The final reference to her is the dedication of *Through the Lands of the Serb*, though that could speak as much of duty or guilt as of affection. It could also be a straightforward attribution of responsibility – if it hadn't been for Mary Durham, her need for nursing which first sent Edith to the point of breakdown and necessitated her travel for recuperation, but also her permission for ED to continue those travels even after 1901, then the book really would never have been written.

So for this trip to Kosovo, following her mother's death, Edith could feel mistress of her time. She perhaps also felt more mistress of her subject: she was now a successful author, and had even – the previous year – been elected to the Royal Anthropological Institute. Her journey to such an election was quite a transformation: Antonia Young had showed me a copy of a 1943 letter from ED to Beatrice Blackwood, curator at the Pitt Rivers Museum, where she'd written,

How I wish I had ever had the chance of studying under any of these great anthropologists. The ridiculous thing about me is that until I was asked to read a paper at the Anthrop. I had hardly ever heard of Anthropology – let alone read anything about it … I had never even heard of Frazer [author of The Golden Bough].

But now the anthropologist was back in her old hunting ground, and she had unfinished business. After her thwarted attempt to reach Gjakova in 1903, on this visit she intended to

visit the town. Her delight in arriving finally at her destination
is obvious from the record in her notebook –

> Came to top of pass Cafa Prushit and saw Djakova on
> plain below with a long descent of rolling hill between
> us and it – roofs and mosque minarets arising from
> trees, like all Turkish towns beautiful at a distance. It
> seemed impossible I was really coming to Djakova –
> remembering the efforts of 5 years ago. The pleasing
> sensation of having arrived wiped away temporarily
> the fatigue of the long day in the saddle and two bad
> nights.

When she published the account as *High Albania* she added in even more detail about the oriental charm of the city, with all the nostalgia of two years away from it. The town had 'red roofs glowing among green trees, slim white minarets twinkling delicate like lilies'. To her slightly spiteful modifier of her description of the town as beautiful 'at a distance', she added a more balanced comment, 'And when it is civilised and black factory-chimneys arise in place of white minarets, it will be lovely neither within nor without. You cannot have everything.'

Gjakova does indeed now have black factory-chimneys – alongside its minarets – but I still have a soft spot for the town. It may be where Edith travelled to as her family was shrinking, but for me it is technically the town where my family grew. Our friends, Alisa and Burim (he from nearby Klina, she from Gjakova), had beautiful baby Adena in 2009, and as is Albanian custom, they didn't cut her hair until they could gather the family for the occasion. As is also custom, they would appoint a *kumbar* and *ndrikulla* to make the ceremonial first cut of a lock of hair threaded through their wedding ring. From the day of that ceremony, the *kumbar* (a man) and *ndrikulla* (a woman) would be counted as family – invited to family gatherings, responsible for blood feuds (Alisa is an artist and also museum curator, Burim a sculptor, and they weren't the blood feuding type, as far as we could see) with their family not allowed to marry into Alisa and Burim's family for twelve generations. The role is unrelated to religion (Alisa and Burim are nominally Muslim though neither of them has ever been in a mosque nor given much evidence of other religious observance) and seems likely to predate the coming of Islam, at least. But it is deeply Albanian – and as Vaso Pashko wrote in the nineteenth century, 'The religion of Albanians is Albanianism'. Alisa emailed Rob and me. Would we agree to be Adena's *kumbar* and *ndrikulla*?

It was a double honour – both a recognition of friendship with Alisa and Burim, and a symbol of some assimilation into our adopted home. Of course we sent back enthusiastic and grateful acceptance of the invitation, and a date was set for a dinner where the haircutting would take place, in the presence of Alisa and Burim's assembled family. We read up about our responsibilities, turning to Edith for advice. In *High Albania* she explains that we should give Adena 'several napoleons,' and receive 'some fine garments or fancy knitted socks.' We compromised on the napoleons with some silver filigree and set off with our gift and memorised instructions with some nervousness. Alisa and Burim were smiling encouragingly, but there were three generations of their families sat around the table, watching us and smiling less. I suddenly understood that Alisa and Burim's quixotic decision – to invite this foreign couple with their odd accented Albanian, their inexplicable enthusiasms for Kosovo, but their obvious connections to a country on the other side of Europe – into the family might not be met with universal delight by their uncles, sisters-in-law, nephews. I had thought we were being invited to a celebration of Adena, but as the minutes passed I realised increasingly that we were present at an interview of Rob and me and our suitability for this role.

It began to feel even bigger than that – a metaphor for our relationship with Kosovo. We worked hard at our language, digging out idiomatic expressions and cutting grammatical corners just like Kosovars did; trying not to let Alisa and Burim down. We were subjected to questions in the usual Kosovan style – How was our health? Were we tired? How were our families? Were our parents still alive? How many brothers and sisters? (oh dear, I felt our compact families and my parents' lack of a son chalked up as a debit once again) Were we renting in Pristina or had we bought? We had met some of the family before at various occasions – exhibitions of Burim and Alisa's work, a weekend spent in Gjakova where we'd stayed with her parents – but it wasn't always easy to remember whom, or how they were related to the others. We edged our way around our questions carefully and smiled achingly, despite the uncle who never smiled back.

Presumably we passed; at least no voice of protest was raised when the time came for the hair cutting. To my relief, it was made clear that it would be the *kumbar* who did the actual cutting of the hair. Adena was a wriggly one-year old, and waving a pair of scissors near her precious head, while under the critical gaze of her grandparents was not for the faint-hearted. I held her arms in a tight grip that I hope seemed all that you would want of an *ndrikulla* – loving, supportive, practical, competent, safety-conscious – as Rob made the prescribed snip of her golden curls and tapped her head to North, South, East and West with a blessing. Everyone clapped – even the unsmiling uncle – and Alisa and Burim handed us the 'fine garments' (a nightie for me and a shirt for Rob). We were officially family.

So for me, coming to Gjakova should feel like coming home. In fact, I see Alisa's family more in Pristina than in their home town, and the journeys that bring me to the town are usually less social. My work as an educational consultant accounts for some of the trips I've made – to see the descendants of the schoolmaster, cousin of Marko 'Shan' Shantoya, who turned up at the priests' house where Edith was to stay. The schoolmaster invited them to pay a call on him which, after a twelve-hour journey, including stumbling in some rigid *opinga* sandals which hadn't yet been broken in, was clearly not what Edith had in mind. However, aggressive hospitality is a familiar danger of Balkan travel, and she knew what she had to do.

Edith's notebook that I'd read at the RAI records simply 'Plastered with dust and sweat I begged to be allowed to wash hands first. Shan said I was quite clean' but in the text prepared for publication two years later she adds some more specific details,

I was plastered with dust and sweat – had not washed for three days, let alone had my clothes or even my footgear off ... Marko insisted that I was perfectly clean and looked beautiful.

There are so few additions made to what she wrote in the field that any new text is noteworthy. So I'm intrigued about these sentences. The 'dust and sweat' and unappealing details of personal hygiene on the one hand make Edith seem more heroic, less interested in the pleasures of the flesh; is Marko's recorded compliment simply to counterbalance that impression, lest the Edwardian reader consider her drifted too far from decency? Or is it gentle poking of fun at Marko, the kind of man who could consider a woman in such a state beautiful? Or is it a brief blush of sentimentality, for the man she was obviously fond of?

Despite the rigours of travel, once ED reached the schoolteacher's house she seems from her writing to have perked up. Shan's recently-married niece was back for her first visit to her family 'and in full Prizren bride dress. Quite wonderful. Hair parted across back of head. Two plaits one upwards and one down in a pigtail'. She goes on into elaborate detail of coiffure, with sketches – part anthropologist, part bimbo.

It was still all too much of a good thing –

I was too tired. The usual spirit drinking had to take place and here was the usual spread of bits of hard egg, grapes, melons. As usual all started snack eating. Most painful process when one is tired and wants real food. Awfully hot in room. Could not get off with less than three glasses of spirits. Struggled to talk Italian with the bride, the schoolmaster, his wife, everyone and aired my Albanian with aching limbs, splitting head and empty

stomach. The virtue of hospitality is carried in Albania
to impossible lengths. Why they could not have waited
till the next day is incomprehensible to the western
mind.

The next day she walked out to investigate Gjakova and wasn't
much taken with what she found.

Streets impossibly filthy and stinking. All muck from
privies and refuse from streets chucked out into any
open spot and left to fester. The carcase of a dead horse
rotted in the sun, while the hooded crows – the only
scavengers – tore at its gaunt ribs. No windows looking
on street. Only blank mud walls – awful kaldrom
[cobbles] with mud puddles at side or beds of dust –
scorching weather. Bazaar in usual style.

Her dismissive treatment of the bazaar is a shame, given the
attention received by the bazaar since. Perhaps to someone who
had visited Ottoman bazaars elsewhere, Gjakova's shops were
nothing more than 'usual'. And perhaps Edith was just tired when
she wrote it, because after she had been in Gjakova a few days she
was at least working up some enthusiasm for the musical pipes
she bought there, one of which I'd known about because it had
later been bequeathed to the Pitt Rivers Museum.

Certainly, in the late twentieth century, and with most of the
sewage cleaned up, the bazaar was a thriving and noteworthy
centre of Albanian commerce – and perhaps this was its undoing.
I was presented with a wonderful book of photographs of the
old Gjakova market by the professor at a private university in
Pristina where I worked for a term. The earliest photographs must
date from the time of ED's visit and show the pipes like the one
that she was wheedled – or whistled – into. They show cobbles
and shutters, embroidery of 'galloons, gowns, waistcoats and
tight woolen trousers', bookbinders, saddle-makers, clog-makers,

confectioners, piles of stock for sale – eels, wax, snuff, scarves, slippers, figs and salt.

But on the night of 23 March 1999 all that was swept away in an explosion of destruction, racial hatred and cultural erasure. About fifty Serbs in military dress were seen by residents walking towards the old town. Each of them was carrying a five-litre can of petrol. The burning of buildings which followed, together with more targeted demolition – for example of the jewellery shop where there were believed to be hidden safes, or the library or tower of the mosque – destroyed the old town. Later that spring violence returned to the old town when 2,500 residents were rounded up by Serb forces. The women and children were released after 24 hours, but most of the men never returned.

Alisa's studio was burned too, and when she returned there she found her LPs charred and melted from the heat in a vicious violent distortion of beautiful songs. She's never told me how she felt when she walked in to see the destruction, but she's told me how she reacted in the months that followed, using the twisted vinyl as the inspiration for a series of African-style masks she exhibited as 'Gramofytyra' or 'Gramofaces'.

She's an exceptional example of positivity and creativity in the face of small-minded destruction, and after the war ended, there was a need for many like her. The burned stump of a bazaar was a visual symbol for the Gjakovars and the international administrators trying to support Kosovo back on its feet. It's therefore easy to understand that it was one of the early wounds to be bound with European Agency for Reconstruction money. Using photographs (maybe the very same images in the book which the professor had given me) and memories, a reconstruction was planned to build the bazaar as it had been.

Of course this approach to architectural heritage is not uncontroversial – there are those who would say that this just creates a Disneyland of history, and that buildings should be preserved in ways that keeps the records of their history. But would you say that to a burns victim? That her scars are part of her history and no plastic surgery should be carried out? Would the charred remains of the paramilitary violence really be something that would revitalise the old commercial heart of the city?

The resulting bazaar still has a patina of artificiality – all the shops, with their archaic shutters, are as old (as new) as one another, rather than the wood softened into varying shades of sepia that I'd seen in the photographs. More significantly, not all of the traders have returned. Many of the shops lie empty, the shutters battened down even on market day, in mute tribute to Gjakova's dead and the limits to the powers even of the kindly Europeans to make it better. Many of those that are open don't have traditional craftsmen working within them anymore – when the Serbs herded those old men out, or torched their shops, they put an end to the filigree, the sandal-makers, the feltmakers. Generations of artisan skill came to an end in the flames of that March night, and those of the sons who survived were reluctant to carry on.

That's not true for all the workshops. Perhaps ironically, the coffin makers still hammer and saw. That's one thing the war didn't put an end to. More inspiringly, other carpenters – in particular making cradles and wedding chests – also continue their trade. The cradles are distinctive – as brightly painted as houseboats, with bold crude flowers in orange and green, with red curlicues and elaborate borders. On the ends is painted the Arabic imprecation 'Mashallah' or the Albanian equivalent, meaning 'good luck' but written 'me fat' as if it's a pidgin English description of the chubby incumbent.

The wedding chests are just as striking – vast great trunks that would be taken by the bride to her new home, and contain all the handcrafts she has spent her maidenhood preparing for married life. Traditionally the contents would be layered – the top layer would be garments and accessories for her wedding day, followed by baby clothes and clothes for herself as she grew older. The bottom layer would be her shroud.

I was disinclined to fill a chest like this (being almost equally disinclined towards weddings, babies and death) but the chests are stunning, and the first time Alisa brought me to Gjakova I bought one. As Edith knew, there are advantages to being a strange foreign woman in the Balkans – you don't have to wait until you get married to acquire a Niksic bridal clasp knife, nor a Gjakovar wedding chest. With some help from Alisa and a friendly bus driver, we got the chest back to Pristina.

In fact, although I didn't realise it at the time, even back in 2006 when I bought it, the Gjakovar chest was a part of my commitment to Kosovo – a plighting of a troth. Unlike Edith's pipe souvenir, my wedding chest is an item that would be prohibitively expensive to ship back to England, so even when we left Kosovo two and a half years later, the chest stayed, at the house of a friend of a friend. When we'd moved back we were reunited and I'd like to swear, as one might to a lover, that never again shall we be parted.

'Edith wrote in her notes that it was "in oak wood on
hillside,"' I shouted at Sabri, our driver, over the roaring and
bumping of the car and the thumping of the stereo. We were
somewhere near Devič monastery, deep in the lush enfolding
hills of early summer in Drenica. But just how near we were,
we really couldn't tell. Our map, borrowed from a KFOR
friend, marked the monastery in large red letters. As a part of
the minority population's cultural heritage that the international
forces had been specifically tasked with protecting, it was an
important landmark on the map. Unfortunately, without any
other reference points named on the map, this one label was
almost useless to us. But travelling with Edith paid off again; in
a century, villages may change their names and monasteries may
be burned down and rebuilt, but hillsides and oak woods endure.
I looked carefully at the leaf shapes on the branches rattling at
the car windows. 'Yes, this is oak wood. I think we're going in
the right direction along this slope.'

Within minutes we had confirmation that the monastery must
be near, in the form of Hesco barriers flanking a bridge. Hesco
is a brilliant military invention – flat-pack grids of wire which
can be assembled into cubes and lined with tough bags and then
filled with earth in situ to form an easily transportable, modular,
light-weight but extremely robust barrier. Where there's Hesco,
there's been war; where there's Hesco there's still tension and fear.

It's not the sign of the monastery that Edith encountered when
she travelled the same route – by the time she got to today's

Hesco-ed bridge she notes being in a 'stream of pilgrims'. The pilgrims were travelling to celebrate the Feast of the Assumption and she writes later that there were 2,000 of them for the festival she attended. Her account is a Chaucerian tale of a 'seething mass', 'people running hither and thither with steaming trays', 'very merry party', 'cheery and gay', 'bales of parti-coloured luggage', 'drum, ceaseless pompom, folk dancing and singing, glare of campfires', 'coffee and cognac', and 'gipsy bands'.

Despite our stereo, the valley seemed particularly silent in contrast with ED's account which I'd had open in front of me in the car. We stopped to check with a monosyllabic Albanian boy swinging a stick as he minded a cow, and when we finally arrived at the monastery gates we were halted by razorwire and a solitary Kosovan police officer.

In fact, despite the razorwire and the Hesco, the Kosovan police officer is a sign of hope; I had read in my research prior to this trip that it was only one month before that the Kosovan Police Service had taken over responsibility from KFOR for guarding this Serbian religious site. The police officer was (or at least spoke) Albanian (I remembered that the head of the monastery on Edith's visit had been Albanian); the reluctant acceptance by the Serbian church that he and his colleagues would protect them, and that there was no need for anyone's French, Italian, or American big brother to patrol, was one more building block in the restoration programme mending the ugly holes in the ancient fabric of this monastery. It's not the first time the monastery here has gone through a cycle of destruction and regeneration – built in the early fifteenth century, it was pulled down by the Turks and then reconstructed in the sixteenth century. Largely destroyed (the Serbian Orthodox Church website says by Albanians) in the Second World War, reconstruction took place in the second half of the last century, until looting and vandalism destroyed more of it in the most recent conflict of 1999.

The police officer wanted ID so we handed over our passports – as if we were entering another country. And once inside the solid metal gate, it did feel like another country. With the help of Katarina, the Serbian friend and fellow volunteer from our charity, who was accompanying me, we spoke in Serbian, and when we went to the small monastery shop (*raki*, honey, incense, beeswax candles) the prices were quoted in Serbian dinars. We could even buy there a Republic of Serbia flag designed to be mounted on our car – but we didn't.

In fact, after the chat in the car and the weaving of traffic on the main road from Pristina, being in the calm of the monastery grounds felt not just like another country, but otherworldly. Even the gardens had the sanctified silence of a church, and we sat quietly waiting on a bench in the sunshine (I thought of Edith, who had noted here having 'sat on a stone by wall so as to get a break') while a soft-spoken nun with a glowing complexion went to tell the mother superior that we had arrived. Sitting on the sun-warmed stone, Katarina taught Sabri and me the Serbian reflexive verb, *gušterisati se*, 'to lizard yourself' – relaxing, soaking up UV rays as we were now.

The nun came back, apologising that the Igumanija would be busy for a while, but she suggested we look around the grounds and the church. We asked her a little about the community living in Dević now – just six nuns, she told us, and no guests staying in the extensive guest house where Edith had squeezed into a bedroom filled with mattresses on the floor, though the nun said that the guest house could sleep fifty people. I asked whether she had heard of Edith Durham and she shook her head. Was there a visitor's book? There had been, but it had been destroyed when the Albanians came. I asked whether pilgrims still came for the Feast of the Assumption, but she shook sadly once again.

Katarina confirmed that feast days in the Serbian church were not what they had been. She grew up in Belgrade and sang for twelve years in a church choir so she knows her church traditions, but she says that she really only learned about the church's feast days during the NATO bombing campaign. There's the briefest of silences while we both acknowledge what she is referring to – the 78 days when the British government which I helped to elect ordered its troops to bomb Katarina's home town. And then she explained how she came to learn the church's feast days, about how, when the bombings started, her parents sent her to stay with her grandmother in a remote village where she carried their cows' fresh milk to be sold in the shop, and learned to tell dates like her grandmother does, so that early August is 'between St Elia and St Mary'. 'But only the old people in the villages remember those any more,' she said.

We looked around the trim grounds. Off to one side was the graveyard with a few graves, all with new crosses. The dates ranged over the last fifty years but they had obviously been carved at the same time, very recently, before rain and lichen could work wrinkles and texture in the blank white stone, which was as clear of the ravages of time as the face of the young nun who had answered our questions just now. Here lay Poleksija Stankovic who had been 21 years old at the time of ED's visit, alongside Marta Jokanovic (29 in 1908) and Iguman Dimitrije Bodrov (24 years old when Edith was at Devič, so probably not the Iguman then, though I wondered whether he might have then been the deacon she mentions disturbing her sleep when he wandered into the shared bedroom looking for a comb).

Inside the church it was cool but not dark, as ED had described it – because the centuries-old frescoes, dimmed with age and candle smoke, had been destroyed by KLA soldiers in 1999 and most of them had been removed, with whitewash now painted over the destroyed sections. Some painting remained, patchy and scabby, and even in a few cases dabbed with lint as part of a restoration programme that seemed like an attempt to staunch

the church building bleeding its paint out. Above the tomb of the church's eponymous saint, Joannike, some remnants of the sixteenth century frescoes remained, and a picture of the saint stared down sternly from above a door; I imagined his steely gaze fixing Edith, and then fixing the looters and vandals of the KLA.

On the saint's icon had been left, in accordance with tradition, the modern day, everyday equivalent of the elaborate gifts (embroidered hand towels, slippers, *piastres* and Turkish pounds, a total of 150 napoleons) which ED describes being presented to the church during her visit; as Katarina bent to kiss him there was a rustle of 100 dinar notes.

We were joined in the church by the mother superior, along with her guests – a group of nuns and a monk from Deçan. I had been coached by Katarina in the appropriate greeting for men and women of the cloth and I prattled it competently now, while Katarina smiled proudly. It translates as something like 'may God help you', though hopefully without the desperate overtones the English phrase has. Sister Anastasija nodded politely at the greeting and moved on with her other guests, but the Deçan group made more eye contact with me and I ventured some conversation in my limited Serbian. They asked whether I had ever been to their monastery, and I thought of the multi-lingual welcome we had had there, and assured them that I had, and that it was beautiful.

That was the extent of our interaction, and I was sad. ED records some of the most significant moments of her two-way anthropological exchange (what now might be called 'participatory observation') with the visitors in this monastery –

Every peasant wanted to speak to me – where I came from – and why I wore a hat. Hat bothered them awfully. Thought it most silly. Did I wear if 'per chef' for pleasure; always? In the house? Was it because I was not married? I said it was against the sun. They asked why? I sympathised then with the many folk I have teased with questions. They said there was no sun – that they did not wear things because of the sun etc. I fell back on the stock reply and said I wore it because it was 'nas obicaj' ['our custom']. Everyone handled it and picked little bits off the brim. It gave me the chance of examining their clothing but was very fatiguing – on an empty stomach

She adds in her published account,

it occurred to me that if there were a Devich Anthropological Society it might report that it had found traces of sun-worship in the English, and mysterious rites connected with it that no questioning could elicit.

The disappearance of this two-way exchange, the mutual prodding of one another's headwear by women from opposite sides of Europe of course seems a loss to me. After all, as the old men in the white *plis* hats know, I'm the kind of girl curious about headwear. But on the way home, reflecting on it, I wondered whether it was really the monastic life that I was ruing, rather than anything more subtle or political. As Katarina said, 'nuns like peace and quiet' and that is why this doughty group of six had hunkered down in this verdant valley. I guess they didn't care much for English women coming down from Pristina to disturb them. I was welcome to come in and lizard myself here, or I was welcome not to bother them at all, but I shouldn't really expect them to ask intriguing questions about my hat.

Edith & I; on the trail of an Edwardian traveller in Kosovo

22 Prizren. A people scattered

If in Kosovo discussion turns to cobbled streets someone will say 'like in Prizren', although in fact the city doesn't have Kosovo's monopoly on quaint street paving. If you ask anyone in Kosovo about the country's history, they will tell you about Prizren. The League of Prizren, the beginnings of the nationalist 'rilindje' ('renaissance') movement was formed there in 1878, and put forward its demands for the independence of Albanian lands. The house where the League met, which ED must have been aware of, despite not having mentioned it in her notes, is now a small museum, though in fact it is not the original but a replica of the building destroyed by Serbian forces in 1999. In a country without a heritage industry, Prizren is the only place self-conscious of its past. Its streets are still called after the ancient crafts that were practised there – 'saddlemakers', 'blacksmiths', 'wheelmakers' – and they're labelled in three languages, as Turkish is still spoken here by many of the ethnically-Albanian population, as well as by a significant Turkish minority. When my friend's brother was getting married, and she as unmarried sister was in charge of buying the bride's jewellery and dress, and gifts for the family, it was to Prizren that she went shopping, even though I'm sure there is the same range of Turkish-imported bridal wear in the boutiques of Pristina's glitzy 'wedding quarter' and I know that there are women making better elaborate wedding waistcoats in the nearby city of Gjakova. Somehow belief in Prizren's traditions (Edith said 'the gold embroidery is not to be surpassed anywhere') persists, and Prizren has cornered the market of the imagination for Kosovan 'handmade' and 'authentic'.

I attribute part of this to what the city must have been like before the riots of 2004, and persistence of vision, a sustained memory despite the facts, from people who haven't visited in a while. Kosovo – and any country of course – is really multiple countries, the territory of the imagination of people now far away. The Italy of the imagination, for example, is lodged in holiday snaps and bottles of olive oil in kitchen cupboards around the world; the Kosovo of the imagination is, sadly, recorded in more detail in newspaper headlines of war crimes and ethnic cleansing, and the meager contents of refugees' suitcases.

The memories of pre-2004 Prizren are clear of the atrocities that marked that spring. It was well after the end of the inter-ethnic violence of 1998 and 1999 which resulted in NATO's intervention and bombing campaign, the withdrawal of Milošević's forces, and the arrival of the UN administration, but it was the occasion of a new – the last, let's hope – bubbling up of widespread inter-ethnic violence. Riots, mainly focusing Albanian fury on Serbian targets, left 550 homes and 27 Serbian Orthodox churches and monasteries destroyed, 19 people (8 Serbs and 11 Albanians) killed and over 1,000 wounded. Prizren suffered the most intense destruction, with seven churches or monasteries destroyed and the Serbian residential quarter burned. There is barely anything left of the Serbian population in the city now, all left to form another cluster of Kosovan diaspora across other Balkan countries and beyond, and the homes where they once lived remain a dark charred blot on the city's hillside. But before that, Prizren had probably changed little from what Edith saw on her visit – the first jottings in her notebook record it as 'highly picturesque with fortress and ruins of a castle on hill above it and river with several bridges flowing thro''.

The castle ruins are still there and give a view of the town where haze and distance smudge many of the twenty-first century edges. If you climb up and look down, you can no longer see the plastic shop fronts or the displays of bootleg Marlboro cigarettes piled in the windows, but you can see the pantiled roofs; the stacks of cigarette lighters with their misspelled slogans ('You Love Me' – who buys such messages, and for whom?) are not distinguishable on the tables set up by old men along the stone bridge, but you can see the men's white felt *plis* caps; you make out the flounced skirts of the village women squatting by their produce, and you can't spot that the milk is sold in reused Coca Cola bottles. Climbing to Prizren's citadel takes you back in time as well as up in elevation. I had stood there one autumn late afternoon a few months after our first arrival in Kosovo and

watched the years disappear; as the light faded, I had watched the centuries dim with them until the town was a blur of *hamam* domes and minarets, with little lights – who could tell whether they were tallow or electric – glowing from the windows of small houses, and the last glimmer of the day reflected in the silver river snaking through the city under the ancient bridges, and there was nothing to tell me where Edith's Prizren ended and mine began.

Prizren had been a constant refrain in Edith's experience of Kosovo, snaking like the silver river, or the filigree strands, through the encounters I'd had with her. Like my friend setting out to buy her brother's wedding accoutrements, Edith had done profitable shopping here – as well as the earrings I'd seen in Cambridge, it was in Prizren that she had bought the cigarette holders she'd sent to brother-in-law Godfrey and which I had then seen in the Pitt Rivers. It had been from here that my little micro-finance project with Syzana had sprung, and I smiled to read that the first thing Edith's notebook mentions her having bought here is 'good cards' which she went to post at the Austrian Consulate. I bet they weren't as good as our cards, decorated with a small fine piece of handmade silver jewellery.

But ED had arrived in Prizren on a Monday and for shopping in the city you really have to wait until a Wednesday. It was so then, and it is so today, even though the town has changed hands many times in between; it was celebrating the Sultan's accession day when Edith got there, but by 1912 the Sultan had no more call on Kosovo, and the country successively became part of Serbia, the Kingdom of Serbs, Croats and Slovenes, Yugoslavia, Serbia and Montenegro, Kosovo under United Nations Security Council Resolution 1244, and then an independent, self-declared republic. But market is still on Wednesdays.

My own first trip to Prizren's market had been in the hope of seeing the unique traditional costume still worn by villagers in the hills around the city. The women who wear this dress stand out for their long dark (often dyed – ED comments on the black nut that she'd seen on sale for hair dye) hair – worn loose even if they are well-past girlhood and even into widowhood – and the extraordinary hip ledges incorporated into their long, bright traditional skirts. The wooden yoke around their hips was originally designed for balancing buckets of water as the women made their way around the mountainsides where their villages nestle. Now they (quite literally) bustle and nudge their way through the milling crowds of shoppers in denim and designer rip-offs, and there is still demonstrable utility in wearing a wooden poking device at your widest point; the market equivalent of Boudica's spears on the wheels. No doubt Boudica had something of the look of these redoubtable old women with their black flying hair.

In the light of this I can't understand how ED could write 'costume nothing remarkable', but her attention was mainly taken up with the textiles in the shops, not about the shoppers' person. 'Embroideries finest have seen in the shops'. 'Silk and cotton tissues very cheap and good. Bought a whole lot of small embroidered cloths'. 'The embroideries of organe silk cord very fine. Gold work astonishingly fine'. She plays the part of orientalist colonial shopper, snapping up the good deals she ferrets out (she lists the price she paid for each), and adds in the published account of her bargain-hunting a regretful 'Had it not been for the difficulties of transport, I should have ruined myself' guaranteed to bring a rueful smile to the lips of cupiditous readers back home dreaming of such riches in their own hands.

I, myself, bought only a large paisley handkerchief, imported from Turkey like all the textiles I saw. I thought of all the cloth that had whipped around the former Ottoman Empire in the century between Edith's visit and mine – warp and weft shuttling out from looms, folding themselves into saddle bags and tea chests, unrolling in swathes in what ED described as the 'long wooden tunnels of the bazar streets, dark with hot, rich shadow, glowing with goods', then pinched and plucked for the quality to be tested before being parcelled up. Some went to Miss Durham's Hampstead dressing room, some to Miss Blackwood, and Judy at the British Museum, and all the curators in between them in England's museum stores and showcases; some went to the wedding chests of nervous local brides, who would grow old unfolding new layers from the painted boxes, working their way down the striata towards that shroud, and every Wednesday wrapping around themselves their best apron to travel into Prizren to market.

As well as the fabrics, ED also went shopping for silverware, and in this I was following her: I was expected at the filigree co-operative. I'd been working with them more since we'd moved back to Kosovo, and we were trying to set them up as a tourist destination for others who could be as fascinated as me by watching the swirls and squiggles (Edith's 'curlywurlies' and 'dingledangles') taking shape. We'd worked on the project in the

weeks leading up to Christmas, and now, on a cold winter's day I was going back to meet them again.

Faik had told me the co-operative had another present for me because they had heard about my research into Edith's visit. She mentioned in her account of Prizren the 'three-cornered amulets sewn up in velvet' and they had something similar waiting on the long workbench when Rob and I went into the workshop. It was a striking triangular charm, studded with a few stones and fashioned at the bottom with a slim sliding panel. Moving back the panel revealed the inside of the amulet as a space big enough to secrete a piece of paper. I asked them what I should put in there, but they didn't know. 'Words from the Koran?' I asked, but they shook their head again. After all, despite their skills, they were craftsmen, not magicians.

And they apologised for the amulet – they had wanted to give me something different: an animal's tooth amulet like the ones I'd seen in the Ethnological Museum and the Cambridge store, like the boar's tusk that Edith records having bought in Prizren from their great grandfathers. 'We've ordered a wolf's tooth,' they told me sadly, 'but it hasn't arrived'.

Ordered a wolf's tooth? From where? Some Satanic eBay? I held the silver triangle in my hand and assured them that there was no need for them to worry. This was an exquisite, unique and quite probably luck-bringing gift and would always be very special to me.

After Edith's day in the bazaar she went exploring around Prizren. She made her way out of the city tracking up the river on a visit on which I had tried, without success, to follow her. She records in her notebook after she had made her way up the valley out of Prizren, 'Went to see Tony Precha's daughter – is young widow with 5 children. Eldest boy fine lad. Very poor – mother and two children suffering from fever. Gave quinine.' There is no more explanation, but the name of Tony Precha rang a bell. I searched the electronic jottings I'd made since I started the quest for Edith, and 'control-F' found some matches. He had contributed to that Steinway Hall fundraising concert whose records I'd found in Aubrey Herbert's papers, and the accession notes from the Pitt Rivers gave an extract from the letter where ED had described the pistol I'd seen there,

My old friend Tony Precha who kept the Albanian restaurant near the Guildhall London and who began his career as a Bashibazouk in the Russo-Turkish war, told me that he used to ride with a pair of pistols in his sash, a pair in his holsters and a pistol stuck in each boot. Six in all 'just as good as a revolver'.

An Albanian restaurant in London in 1908! I had imagined 1908 London's cooking as all chop houses, pie and mash shops, or silver salvers at the Savoy – I couldn't imagine a 'fusion cuisine' thriving, right at the heart of Empire, near the Guildhall. Nor would there have been a large Albanian community who might have savoured the *mantia* sausage rolls, the layered pancake *flija*, the vast round trays of filo pastry *pite* pie or cornbread that I'd tried, and learned to make in Pristina. Even now there are few restaurants in London where you can sample Albanian cuisine – though in fact there are plenty run and staffed by Albanians, like that bistro off Charing Cross Road where I'd met Bejtullah at the Embassy function. Try saying 'faleminderit' next time you're thanking the chef or waiter for an 'Italian' meal you've enjoyed in London and you're likely to get a great response. Even less plausibly, given Athens' resistance to recognising Kosovo's independence, and ongoing political debate about contested territory between Greece and Albania, the restaurant where we were hosted for dinner once by the Kosovar Albanian Ambassador in London was 'Greek'. Its name was written in that script of angular capital letters, and it had the fake columns, the taramasalata on the menu but ... the owner and waiters were Kosovar Albanians, greeting me in the dialect familiar from Pristina cafes. After some glasses of wine there I plucked up the courage to ask them why they had made this politically surprising choice of national cuisine for their restaurant. They shrugged – 'no-one's heard of Albanian food, and everyone likes Greek food. Lots of the dishes are basically the same. It's business.' And the food was delicious.

So I had tried to find out more about Edith's Tony Precha, the beginnings of the Albanian diaspora and its cuisine in London, the great-great-grandfather of Agim and Bejtullah and the other Albanians I'd met in London. According to the 1901 census, 'Antonia' Precha had been born in 1852. His occupation was 'confectioner' and he lived on the Upper Richmond Road – a pancake's flip from where my own grandparents had moved half a century later. He was living there with his brother's family and a son. There was no mention of the daughter that Edith had visited.

By the 1911 census he is recorded as a 'restaurant keeper' born in 'Jacova' (Gjakova). His sixteen year old grandson, Nicol, is noted as 'assisting in the business' and as having been born in 'Prezran'. A large family of twelve, including grandchildren, and his brother's family, along with a servant, were living by then in Balham; it seemed that the preceding decade had been good to the Prechas. I tried to find out more about the family, using what my friend Lawrence calls the contemporary Domesday Book – Facebook. There were two (and only two) Prechas on there and I sent both of them a message, telling them I was writing a book and that I thought their ancestor might be in it. It turns out that they are UK-based sisters, and one of them gave me all that she knew about their family, saying that her grandfather had been from Albania and had made up his name to leave the country and 'escape the war'. She said that she didn't know the original name of her grandfather, Anthony, who never told his wife, still alive, anything about his life in Albania, and that all the ID he had turned out to have been forged.

I wondered at this 'other' Anthony Precha. It seemed too much of a coincidence that there were two Anthony Prechas, both Albanian, but perhaps the Facebook relative had heard of Edith's Antony and decided to borrow some of that early immigrant's biography for his forged identity. Perhaps 'Antony Precha' was becoming the generic name for an Albanian immigrant, like 'John Doe' for an NYPD suspect. It was very unhelpful.

I had reached the limit of what the internet could bring me, so my final avenue of exploration was back to the arch-archivist of the Albanians in Britain, the same Bejtullah who had whispered to me of Edith's relationship with Nevinson. I went to visit him for a coffee and yes, of course he had heard of Precha. He was even able to give me a copy of a letter written by Precha in the course of a dispute over his military pension owed. The letterhead announced his ownership of not one but three 'Albanian Cafe Restaurants' on Walbrook, Gresham Street, and Great Tower Street. It was extraordinary to think of all those Edwardian clerks and minor financiers getting their waistcoats grease-spotted on Albanian Cafe food in pre-war London. I wondered whether Edith would have gone there for lunch when her sick mother could spare her, savouring the evocative mouthfuls of proper coffee and Albanian nouns.

That far my imagination could follow her, but otherwise the Precha trail had run cold. I had no more information on this daughter whom ED had visited, or where exactly she had lived. So when Faik of the filigree co-operative offered to drive us back from the workshop, it wasn't to the Precha family or their former home – I had a different assignation with what I hoped would be a part of Edith's past. A Dutch friend in Pristina had told us about the Serbian monks who had befriended him and who lived in a monastery that lay out of Prizren in the same valley Edith had travelled to reach the Prechas. Archives and institutional memories were hard to find in Kosovo, but the Serbs excel at the past. I hoped that the monk there might be able to tell me something about Edith's Prizren of 1908.

I wondered what Faik would make of this destination, remembering the scar on the hillside like big black letters scrawling the attitude of (some of) Prizren's Albanians to (some of) Prizren's Serbs. But Faik was unbothered. After all, much of his earnings came from creating intricate silver crucifixes and incense burners for Serbian churches; there was more money in that than in amulets these days. He was happy to drive us to the monastery, and we puttered off over the cobbles in his Renault 4, with him changing gear with the stick by the steering wheel. It sounded more like carrying a bag full of car parts than driving a car.

I was glad of his relaxed attitude to the visit, but I hoped he wasn't so relaxed that he'd choose to come in with us. Our friend in Pristina had prepared us for Father Ksenofont – 'he's an educated man, hungry for educated conversation, but they have some radical views there. A senior international official was abruptly denied entry when he attempted to visit, a dictaphone thrust in his face and asked 'so what have you to say to us?" But Rick had said we should turn up there and when asked for our passports by the German soldiers who guard it, we should submit a note mentioning Rick's name.

Now that we were on the road I thought I'd double-check that this was going to work. Rick answered the phone,

'Yes, Father Ksenofont knows you're coming. By the way, he hates Edith Durham. Be prepared for some strong views.'

It was too late to turn back now – Faik was already driving us out of town. By now it was dark, and we drove along the Bistrica river, through a gorge where rock overhung the car. There were no settlements or houses, no light at all, and little traffic at this time of night, at this time of the year.

We saw the barbed wire before we saw the monastery and Faik pulled over. With some tact on all sides we established that he wasn't coming with us but he politely suggested waiting for us. Since we had no idea how short our shrift with the 'radical' monks would be, we assured him we would find another way home, and we waved him goodbye.

We made our way down a slope and over a bridge to a gate scribbled with razorwire, like a coarse parody of filigree. The river roared beneath us and as if the accompaniment of the white noise of the water, it started to snow. A young German soldier had spotted us and started to approach while Rob and I stood alone in the darkness, feeling very aware that we had no idea of the reception we would get on the other side of the hostile gate, and no idea how we would get back to the city when we were finished.

I pulled a notebook out of my bag and started to compose a message to Father Ksenofont. 'Our friend, Rick, suggested ...'. Rob spoke in German, occasionally cross-bred with Albanian, to the guard and we handed over our passports with the note. The soldier went away with our ID and once again Rob and I stood shivering in the black and white night.

The craggy rocks above us, the snowy setting, the sense of gaining entry to a stronghold where our identity (Rob's previous job as adviser to ethnically Albanian Prime Minister Çeku, the former KLA general, our fluent Albanian, our proud celebration of Kosovo's independence) could make things uncomfortable, all made me think of *Where Eagles Dare*.

We practised our elementary Serbian to each other as we stood there – we wanted to try to impress Father K and we definitely didn't want it to backfire by mixing ourselves up with inadvertent Albanian.

'Big river,' I said.

'Cold river,' Rob replied, making his adjectival ending agree with the gender of the noun. Bastard.

'Beautiful snow,'

'Old chur...' I was searching for the word. 'Krk?' I attempted? No, that was the name of a Croatian island. 'Hrk?' suggested Rob. 'Crk?' I elaborated. We giggled to be standing making noises like frogs in the middle of the silent night, attempting the noun that stood before us somewhere beyond the gate, in the dark. I fingered my amulet, hoping it would bring us luck.

The soldier returned. We were to be allowed in. He escorted us into the compound, right to the gate of the monastery, where a man with a thick black curly beard and robes with gold embroidery (I was developing Edith's eye for such things) stood waiting for us. We introduced ourselves. A smattering of Serbian – 'good evening, I am Elizabeth. It is my pleasure to meet you.' Father Ksenofont was unimpressed.

'Rick told me you would be coming during the day. Now it is vespers so for the next 45 minutes I will be busy.'

Would it be possible to wait? He shrugged. Or was that an inconvenience? We were so grateful for his time. He apologised, but there was divine service. I ventured, 'Would it be appropriate for us to attend the service?' He shrugged again. If we wanted.

We followed him round a corner and through a doorway. Suddenly it was the fourteenth century. Black-robed monks stood in a darkened room about the size of my kitchen. They were muttering and chanting, in the scent of incense and the light of just four candles.

If they were in the fourteenth century, I was still in the twenty-first. My mobile was on and in my bag. I must turn it off immediately – the idea of its shrill incongruous ringtone disturbing this sacred space with an Albanian friend calling gave me goosebumps. We would be thrown out to the night and the unquiet river with no more chances given. I rummaged in my bag. Where was the damn thing? In the darkened room I could only go by feel. I rustled the plastic bag also inside my handbag, fiddled with clumsy zips. At my side, Rob dug his elbow meaningfully into my ribs. I looked up and saw a beady-eyed monk staring at me with displeasure. Rob was pretty beady himself. I didn't dare start the rummaging again. My bag sat on the floor beside me like a timebomb, waiting to interrupt.

I stood (there were no seats except in an opposite corner of the room where I could make out space for perhaps two people) and looked round me. In the gloom I wasn't even sure how many people were in the little room, filled with prayer. First I counted six black robed figures, and then I spotted the knees of someone else sitting in the shadows. It felt like far more, because the walls were filled from floor to ceiling with gaunt faces staring at me, at my bag with its untamed mobile. The icons mostly had the same beards as the monks, the same fixed stare.

Meanwhile, the monks were sharing the readings that made up the service. One seemed in charge – he would select passages and offer them to a monk to mutter or chant. While one reading was going on he would line up the next, and move silently to another monk to alert them that their turn was coming. Often they started the reading or chanting before they even reached the lectern, suggesting these were all learned by heart. And as another came to take over, they would step back still finishing off the verses they had been reciting, leaving the texts behind them well out of eyesight. With this skill and memory the service was almost non-stop. The baton handed over in this religious relay was a tiny candle, the thickness of the sort you might put on a birthday cake, but immensely long and pliant, wrapped over and over in the shape of a skein of wool, from which the monks pulled out further inches as the candle was used up.

Occasionally, the monks responded to particular verses with fervent crossing of themselves – from head to foot as well as left to right. In the enclosed space, the sound of seven lean bodies describing a six-foot cross against their robes was reminiscent of the river outside. The candles guttered as the room stirred and swished to the bending and swooping of the men.

Eventually they stilled, and their voices calmed to silence. Each went round the room, kissing the icons – cold lips to cold glass. I realised this must be the only kissing they ever did.

A calm descended, and a great sense of peace on me. I wondered at the power of the amulet – we had survived the service without my mobile ringing.

Father Ksenofont invited us upstairs to a room again lit with candles, with one wall lined with books. We thanked him for the service, applauded the beautiful wall paintings. How old were they?

Only a few years – the chapel had been burned in 2004 by an Albanian mob. He got out a book to explain something of the monastery's history.

I had been wrong to hope that Edith might have been here. The chapel was first built in the 1340s but in the eighteenth century it was demolished and its stones used to build the Sinan Pasha mosque I'd admired from Prizren's citadel. It was only rebuilt in 1998. But Father Ksenofont did have some interest in Edith. I reminded him that from Prizren she had gone on to Pristina and been described by the Metropolitan there as the greatest friend of Serbia. He looked cross,

'Yes, but by then she had fallen in love.'

It wasn't the criticism I'd expected, and I asked him to explain. He said that he had learned that while ED had been in Gjakova (he called it Djakovica) she had fallen in love with an Albanian called Mark Krasniqi. Up until that point she had been pro-Serb, but after that her judgement had been clouded and the rest of her pro-Albanian life was the proof of it.

It's true that Edith's comments about the Albanians to the Turkish officer in Deçan ('they live like animals') are hard to reconcile with the ferocious championing of them later in her life in letters and articles I'd read, but this was an ingenious interpretation. I never subsequently found any support or evidence for the theory, nor any reference to Mark Krasniqi (her trusted guide from Shkodra was Mark Shantoya). It seemed possible that there was a modicum of sexism mixed in with the allegations of racism, as if the only reason an intelligent woman was likely to change her politics would be to fit with those of a man she had fallen in love with, but it was true that there was a shift in ED's commentaries and interests from the early years of Balkan exploration in Bosnia, Montenegro, Serbia, to an almost exclusively Albanian focus from 1908 onwards.

Father Ksenofont had been generous with his time and his learning, and we found after a while we had nothing else to say to each other. We thanked him and took our leave, wondering quite how we would travel on from here. Reunited with our passports, and out in the night, we looked at the road Faik had driven us on. It weaved round the course of the river and on one side was overhung with the rock, with no barrier between it and the river on the other side. There was no pavement, so any of the oncoming cars – which we would be unable to see because of the hairpin bends – would have no choice but to run us over. It was seven kilometres back to Prizren – too far to walk in the pitch black.

I stuck out a thumb.

The first car sailed past. Rob reminded me how he'd tried hitching in Kosovo before and had no luck whatsoever.

The second car stopped.

We couldn't even see who was inside it, but we called polite greetings through the dark window to the shadowy face we could make out beyond. Could we have a lift?

The man said he was happy to be able to help, and we had no way of knowing whether he was telling the truth.

He had teeth that were too big for his mouth, making his speech unclear, but we made the polite exchange of family histories which is the Albanian equivalent of talking about the weather in England. With a big Albanian family, our driver had scarcely finished his account of himself by the time we arrived back in Prizren, and he insisted on taking us for a coffee back in the city. Lamely, we offered to treat him but his hospitality wasn't having it. He parked up by a cafe and then we were able to see what he looked like.

He had said that his son in Istanbul (another scattered Kosovar) was a dentist, specialising in false teeth. I looked at the man's mouth and wondered whether he saw his son much. But he was more interested in talking to us about our own families and our homeland. He had followed in the footsteps of Tony Precha and so many other diaspora Albanians and had lived in London in the 1970s. Did we know Gloucester Road? Earl's Court? He had lived in Clapham for a year and was proud to tell us the exact route he would take to work – northern line, then change at Stockwell ... I wondered whether Tony Precha's daughter had ever been to visit her dad in London (why had she not moved over with him, bringing her 'fine lad' son, and the fever-ridden children to a country where Grandad with his live-in servant could have looked after them?). Might she and Edith have had just such a conversation about the route from Balham to the restaurant in Gresham Street? At least I was sure that Edith would have had the reverse conversation with Tony once she was back in London – the route between Prizren and her next stop – *strema* cart to Crnoleva; rest at *han* then to Shtime where the road divides to Gračanica...

23 Gračanica.
Heroes and villains,
and the uncomfortable
spaces in between

Edith left Prizren in a 'gold and yellow dawn' for her journey to Gračanica. She records some of the images glimpsed along the road, including the 'large, desolate' graveyard at Korisha which gives me goosebumps.

Korisha is a place that challenges our view of recent Kosovan history. In the fourteen years of newspaper articles, polemic and emerging 'facts' about the conflict in Kosovo from 1998 onwards the usual story runs as follows … Vicious ethnic cleansing by villains of Milošević's Serbia against poor, victimised Albanians prompts NATO intervention; bombing by NATO heroes of strategic Serbian sites results in villains withdrawing from Kosovo. Korisha reminds us of the grey areas in heroism – the 87 Albanian civilians killed there by NATO bombs during the campaign. They were not the only casualties of NATO – there were approximately 500 civilians killed by NATO bombs, including one incident when bombers mistakenly targeted a line of refugees.

The Albanians of Kosovo don't dwell on these statistics, and – understandably – nor do the countries of NATO. But I remember them whenever someone in Kosovo thanks me for what my country's done for their people. Korisha's graveyard is an uncomfortable place to travel past.

The rest of the road Edith took to Gračanica was 'being remade and parts finished good. Rest promising with solid foundations'. Her assessment has a shipping forecast ring to it, but is familiar for more reasons than that. More than a century later the road was, controversially, being remade again and playing out new forms of heroism along the way. The government of Hashim Thaçi (former KLA fighter turned politician) had put all its political eggs in a tarmac basket, investing a disproportionate amount of the country's budget in an ambitious road-building programme which left teachers without their promised pay-rise, and many other sectors of the national budget likewise underfunded, while the diggers and rollers and asphalters cut dark strips across the Kosovan countryside. As the opposition party, Vetëvendosje, scrawl in their graffiti across town, 'what do you call a man who promises a pay rise and then doesn't give it? a) a patriot b) honorable c) a liar' The stakes were high for war hero Thaçi trying out new forms of jingoism.

However, there was some fine patriotic rhetoric to the project – part of it was being dubbed the National Highway, linking Kosovo with its ethnic brothers in Albania (pictures of the premiers of the two countries shaking hands in hard hats as the ribbons of road met). At a party political level it is useful too – in exchange for the naming of the recently-privatised airport for the late Adem Jashari, hero of the village-based Kosovo Liberation Army successors' PDK party, the rival LDK party got the National Highway named after their late President Rugova – hero of the city-based non-violent resistance movement. But who cares about ethnic or party politics when there's money to be made, and the road offers that by the black tarmac bucketful. There are opportunities in the inflated contract (this is rumoured to be the most expensive road per kilometre in Europe) and in corner-cutting on quality (earnest international intelligencers have explained to me just how you – literally – skim off money from the top of the expensive road surfacing), and in the route (the National Highway required expropriated land which it was surprising to learn had in many cases only recently been bought by people with access in advance to the details of the route planned for the road. They were compensated according to law) and – for lesser roads – simply the fact of them being built in the regions and villages of certain people's political heartlands.

War hero Fatmir Limaj was the Minister for Transport in charge of the project and famously seen inspecting its progress in person on regular visits in the early hours of the morning. Heroic stuff. Then suspicions were raised and the EU Rule of Law mission, 'EULEX', launched an official investigation of allegations of corruption against the Minister. Dawn raids of a different kind were carried out and taxi drivers began to tut when I mentioned his name. War heroes can push their perks too far.

Then an interesting shift occurred when a new charge was laid against Mr Limaj, this time for war crimes. He was alleged to have committed crimes against Albanians and others during the 1999 war. The population rallied round Limaj again. It seems that loyalties could tolerate the imprisoning of a war hero for subsequent fraud, in the grey days of reconstruction and transition, but any investigation which threatened the heroic reputation of that black-and-white era was a step too far. A key witness, on whose testimony the case had relied, committed suicide and amid allegations of procedural error the case collapsed.

Mr Limaj is no longer a minister, although he is a member of parliament, but the road-building programme he oversaw continued relentlessly. Of course Kosovo needs roads as all economies do. The argument for the roads runs that by connecting Kosovo with Albania more quickly, the Kosovan economy would be stimulated. But roads run in two directions, and while one lane of the National Highway was certainly filling up with Kosovars heading to the Albanian coast to spend their money there every summer weekend, the opposite lane seemed much quieter. This road was certainly a mixed blessing.

Roads should open things up, but the community which was Edith's destination, Gračanica, was still often described as an 'enclave'. The word is politically-charged, with its etymology of 'locked-up'. Depending on who is using it, it can convey that the inhabitants of such a place are locking themselves *in*, unwilling to engage with the surrounding area. Or it can mean that they are locked *out*, prevented from accessing the benefits of the wider community.

Gračanica is only a short drive from Pristina, and is a community which was historically based around its stunning gothic Serbian orthodox monastery. After the war, when many of those Serbs who chose to continue to work in Pristina felt uncomfortable living in the capital, Gračanica offered the advantages of easy access to the city with the community solidarity of centuries-old Serbian traditions. The village became a small town and eventually its own majority-Serb municipality.

The monastery is one significant draw for visitors, and always has been, but there are other riches that belong to a Christian community. Bacon, for example …. In and around majority-Muslim Pristina, even where beer is drunk freely and few heads are covered, there are Muslim farming traditions which make it impossible to buy bacon. The Christian Serb butcher in Gračanica is used to hungry, slightly furtive ex-pats seeking rashers to take away for a sizzling Sunday morning taste of home. Likewise, a little restaurant with pretty garden on the outskirts of Gračanica is a favourite for an international clientele guzzling pork.

Edith might have understood – I remembered the description of her snaffling most of the tinned ham at dinner with the Metropolitan in Pristina – and she records her thanks to one of the creatures who supply this bacon and ham when she was in conversation with a Gračanica woman, her daughter-in-law and

Gračanica. Heroes and villains, and the uncomfortable spaces in between   219

unmarried daughter who began the ritual questions asking ED details about family relationships. It was here that her unmarried condition had led to the 'questions which – even in Servian – were most embarrassingly personal and physiological, when luckily one of the pigs got its head jammed in the petroleum can, rushed thus bonneted shrieking through the yard, and diverted the conversation'.

She turned her attention to the monastery, filling her notebook with architectural descriptions of the 'Queen stiff and gorgeous in Byzantine robes' in the medieval wall paintings, an interior 'dim and harmonious with faded colours and embrowned gold – old world, barbaric', 'frescoed with saints, gaunt, Byzantine and bizarre'. I walked around myself, echoing all her adjectives while the church made its visceral impact on me with careful stage-management of light and dark. Shafts of sun come in only from high cupolas which made me look up, squinting and humble, and dizzied to find, way above me, the hovering image of Christ Pantocrator.

It was a shared aesthetic experience, but the church means different things now. Although it has a joint UNESCO World Heritage Site designation with Peć Patriarchate and Deçan, the common vision implicit in that designation is undermined by the fact that the monasteries, and the history they represent, are some of the reasons why Serbia won't let Kosovo go. There could now be new explanations for the mournful expression of those icons, given the blood that has been shed around them in the last twenty years; but for Edith their poignancy came from the church's connection to one of the defining moments of Serbia's history, more than six centuries old, but picked at by poets and by politicians ever since. Her syntax comes over all Biblical or Shakespearean, her vocabulary alliterative and assonant, when she writes about the historical context of this monastery

And from its gates, it is said, went forth the monks who gave the communion to Tsar Lazar's army before the fatal fight.

The description is itself poetic, and it evokes the spirit of the epic poem which tells of the Battle of Kosovo in 1389, and which every Serbian school child knows: how Tsar Lazar had a dream the night before the battle in which he is offered the choice between an earthly kingdom or a heavenly one, how he chose the heavenly kingdom, and how he was killed the next day in battle in a defeat which ultimately allowed Ottoman (Muslim) rule across the Balkans. The heroic defeat is the Dunkirk of the Serbs, used by rhetoricians from the fourteenth century to today, in a line which takes in Milošević, who launched his bid for power in Yugoslavia on the six hundredth anniversary of the battle in 1989. In the shop attached to the church you can buy a saccharine Victorian painting of the battlefield and the heroic dying king, or – if your tastes tend to the ecclesiastical – an icon of Lazar.

I visited the monastery in the company of my nephew and niece. Young Cameron, then six, had an eclectic approach to heroism. He had spent much of his visit to Kosovo playing his Star Wars Nintendo DS game, and had a clear sense of hero, anti-hero and what was just 'perTHETic'. Scanderbeg, the Albanian hero of the fourteenth century, whom Cameron had seen in statue on horseback in the centre of Pristina, had newly been added to his pantheon, and during his stay in Kosovo he had acquired a plastercast bust of the bearded hero. In the monastery he had heard the story of Tsar Lazar too, and when we got to the shop he tugged at his mother's sleeve and asked for money to buy a gilded icon of Tsar Lazar as well. When we next went to visit their home in Warwickshire, we discovered that Cameron's bedroom, bristling with Transformers and Power Rangers and other articulated plastic models, held a bizarre Balkan shrine.

Indeed Cameron's bedroom is probably the only place on earth where a small windowsill is dedicated to the combined and contradictory heroism of the Albanian Scanderbeg, the Serb Tsar Lazar, and the fallen Jedi knight, Darth Vader.

24 Pristina

ED had negotiated a price from Prizren to include onward travel from Gračanica to Pristina, on the driver's condition that they left early in the morning. The next morning she got up betimes so as to be able to draw the monastery, and then they were off to what for Edith was a new town, and for me had been home for three years. They travelled by *strema* cart and the description of the journey is a new perspective on a journey familiar to me.

When I started cycling in London I learned to navigate the city in a new dimension. Previously, my sense of orientation located me in longitude and latitude, left and right. If you are a passenger on the underground, or even on a bus, it is only through N, S, E and W that your movement through the city is relevant. But get on a bike and, like a blind man reading a face with his fingers, you become aware of every wrinkle, pimple, promontory and rise in altitude. Hills can be blessing – exhilarating gift of freewheeling speed – or curse; on my Sturmey-Archer three-speed gear they could even put a stop to motion altogether. Travelling in a *strema* must have been something like this because Edith's account of her travels drew in contours I had never been aware of.

Of course reading the landscape has become harder with the cancer of building across Kosovo's countryside. This has accelerated following the recent war, with families who live abroad investing in bricks and mortar (but rarely in balcony rails or rendering) back in their homeland, and building vast houses either to show their wealth, at the sly suggestion of tricksy architects (who get paid here by the square metre) or in aspiration and perhaps nostalgia for the huge families of a generation ago. With one of these stuck in every field it's hard to get a sense of the breast of the land rising and falling in its natural pattern. But even so, it seems strange that I had never noticed the topography of the entry to Gračanica which Edith on her first and only journey there narrates ('On over more cultivated ground and up over low hills – dusty and hot and at last saw cupolas of the Monastery of Gračanica rising from valley below'). Nor had I, insulated by power steering and suspension, ever noticed the 'two low hills' which she notes between Gračanica and Pristina.

However, the sight of Pristina in the valley, viewed from the top of the hill on the road from Gračanica, is striking, whether you are a cyclist or passenger in a *strema*, bus, taxi or 4x4. The whole city is laid out in front of you, and still almost as picturesque as Edith's description 'From above most taking. Red roof, green trees, white minarets'.

She juxtaposes her sentence of praise for the view of Pristina from above with a brief, puncturing follow-up, 'Within, frowsy and dirty and ramshackle', and moves on immediately to some statistics. According to her,

houses vaguely stated to be about 2,500 of which about a quarter are Orthodox which includes Vlahs as well as Serbs. Also a considerable number of Spanish Jews – some said 60, others quite 200 houses. No Catholics. Rest all Moslem.

Pristina has changed almost beyond recognition from the figures she describes, and mostly in the years since the war here in 1999. No-one knows how many people there were in Pristina between 1981 and 2011 as there was no reliable census taken, but local residents talk about the city having doubled in size. The most recent (disputed) census reports a city of 200 000 people. Even if this is true (it is considered to be an underestimation),

Edith's description of 2,500 families can only be a fraction of that, even if an average family size of ten is allowed. My Pristina and Edith's are factors away from one another.

And things have moved on in other ways in that intervening century – more Catholics (their new Cathedral, inaugurated on the 100th anniversary of the birth of the most famous Albanian Catholic, Mother Theresa, towers above the Pristina skyline along with those minarets that Edith saw), far fewer Serbs, no Vlachs, and not a single Jew left, following the Second World War. There is only mute evidence of the Jewish community having once lived here, in their graveyard and a building believed to have been a synagogue, which now stands at the entrance to the complex of Pristina's Ethnological Museum and is used as a small exhibition space for modern art.

The museum is just along from the covered market which Edith describes. Nowadays the market will offer you dried apple slices from old men with faces as wizened as their wares, Chinese batteries that run out within minutes (the modern descendant of the 'foreign rubbish of the cheapest description – one of the benefits brought by the railway' that ED saw there), enormous knickers, and fecund piles of gleaming fruit and vegetables. Despite this range I've never seen an amulet for sale in Pristina, but it was here that ED bought the mole's foot that I'd seen in the stores in Cambridge. Nevertheless, her notes show none of the enthusiasm she reserved for Prizren's bazaar opportunities; she moves from description of the dirt to look up, as one is always encouraged to do in beautiful places or dramatic settings like Gračanica's church, only to note the market's 'bad roof all to pieces'. Following ED through Pristina on the basis of her rather dyspeptic notes was proving a dispiriting experience so I decided to take a different tour guide for my walk through the Pristina of 1908.

A future for Pristina's past, a powerful report published by the thinktank ESI the year I arrived in Pristina, gives unprecedented details of the twenty-one sites identified by a 1977 Yugoslav law as protected cultural heritage locations. As far as I could discover, all but two of these sites (the city library, built in 1930, and the house where the founding meeting for the Youth Communist Party of the district took place in 1941) would have been in existence during ED's visit, and one could assume that they were among the most significant buildings of her time.

Hamams and clocktowers would, of course, have been familiar to her in her travels elsewhere in Kosovo and the region, but I was surprised she hadn't mentioned any of the mosques that remain as a concrete connection between ED's visit and mine. Her artist's eye should have spotted the unique characteristic of the 'stone mosque', so-called because its minaret continues in stone all the way to the summit, without the usual conical metal cover pointing like a witchy fingernail at the sky, and finishing instead in a neat ogee which adds a stupa-like flourish to an otherwise conventional Muslim place of worship. It is apparently unique in Europe and one of only four such around the world.

Since ED's next stop after Pristina was to the site of the 1389 Battle of Kosovo, and given her interest in Gračanica's connection with the battle, I would also have expected her to have enjoyed the connection of one of the other mosques about which she also remained silent. In the grounds of the Pirinaz Mosque is, allegedly, the stone where Prince Lazar was beheaded in 1389, and the mosque was initially Lazar's burial place. The Turkish rule which was ushered in with Lazar's death may have formally ended in Kosovo in 1912 but the connections are still there. The fountain on the cultural heritage list is still called by its Turkish noun, 'shadervan', as is the clocktower – the 'sahatkulla'. And it is Turkish money which has recently restored another one of the protected mosques – the magnificent 'Great Mosque'. Empires take different forms, whether they are the benevolent colonisations of language (pots and plates and cushions and carpets, puddings and pistachios, 'come on' and 'slow down', 'again' and 'not at all', 'just so' and 'that's enough', aubergines and guns, the word for customer, the word for guest … all Turks still happily living in Albanian) or painful forced clearances (the magnificent protected town house now the Institute for the Protection of Cultural Monuments was the home of the Kocadishi family until their property was nationalised, whereupon they moved to Turkey. Likewise, the Gjinolli family – who had owned the glorious buildings that now house the protected Ethnological Museum – moved to Turkey in the 1950s at a time when Albanians were encouraged under Serbian Interior Minister Ranković to declare themselves as Turks and, through an agreement with the Turkish government, to move out of Kosovo to Turkey).

The Turkish restoration of the Great Mosque, revealing its cream stone like flawless skin glowing after a good bath, has been more successful than the attempts on another of the survivors from the Pristina ED walked through: the *hamam* opposite, where the workers on the Mosque in the fifteenth century were obliged to wash themselves each day. When I first moved to Pristina, my Albanian teacher told me that an old school friend of his lived in a house right next door to this *hamam*, and that the view from the friend's living room down onto the bathhouse cupolas was stunning. One day, passing the *hamam* by chance and with some time to spare, on an impulse I rang the doorbell. A young man came to answer it, politely curious at the sight of this foreigner on his doorstep. I explained my reason for coming round and found the householder one of those 'all kind good mans' of ED's *Pall Mall Gazette* article. The Albanian she presents there had described hospitality in his country – 'Perhaps you all lone, got no

The Ethnological Museum in Pristina

money, tired, hungry. You knock at door. 'Ullo, what you want?' 'I hungry.' 'Come in.' Then he give you bread, wine, tobacco, all what you want.'

Money I was fine for, and I wasn't even particularly hungry, but the hospitality was quite as overwhelming as advertised. I was invited up to meet the young man's parents, siblings and some aunts, who it turned out were in the middle of a family celebration. Pieces of cake, frothing with spray-cream and unlikely colours – the twenty-first century staples of hospitality that have replaced 'bread, wine, tobacco' were loaded onto my plate. I was asked carefully about myself, my family, my health. When I'd swallowed the final forkful of dessert (less certain now about my answers to the queries as to my health) and had convinced my hosts that I couldn't manage another mouthful more, I was taken upstairs to the bedroom with the best view down to the *hamam* below. It was a revelation; what, from the road, seemed a nondescript wall with blown twentieth century rendering, with the hint of cupolas bosoming above it, was here revealed as an extensive series of domes each pricked with a set of small glazed circles, or circles where glazing once was. The adventurous upper boughs of a sapling poked up at me through one of them and gave a hint of the spaces below.

Back home, talking to Rob about the little forgotten gem in the centre of town, we discussed how we'd like to let others know it was there. Rob decided that for his birthday he would look into renting the space one evening, clearing the rubble, lighting with candles, hiring a friend of ours who's a violinist, and hosting people there for drinks. Burim, the father of Adena, whose hair we had first cut, worked out how to go one better than candles and suggested he could also rig up theatre lighting above the cupolas, so that it would stream through the glazed circles (we discovered they are called 'elephants' eyes' and are not just circles but glazed tubes to create maximum light).

We organised some catering and take-home gifts of small soaps (which one guest bit into as they were handed round on a piled tray like sweetmeats). The *hamam* was cold, and the floor was earth at best, a small digger had been reversed into one small room that we made off-limits to guests, but there was an undeniable atmosphere to this ghostly place, with its arched chambers and beehive design details. Traditionally it was to this *hamam* that brides were brought the day before their wedding to be washed and prepared by their sisters. In the smoke from candles, like wraiths of steam, I imagined the women Edith had seen in the streets and on her visits around the city, stripping off the layers of clothing in unfamiliar design, the handmade wrappings and trappings that set them in a certain time or place, until they emerged as familiar cream-skinned creatures, just like me, in positions of repose with nothing except the occasional tattoo, the peculiarities of shaving, to show the century in which they were reclining.

The restoration of the *hamam* is still not complete. The sapling has been dug up (just as well, as it would be a tree of some girth by now) and work began on shoring up, replacing, filling in, the fabric of the building. However, one of the co-funders of the project (working together with the Municipality of Prishtina) discovered that the company who had won the tender for restoration were cutting costs and not sticking to the specification they had submitted. The discovery that the elephants' eyes were being replaced with plastic replicas was too much for them to keep faith in the project, and they pulled out so work stopped.

Continuing through my list of the physical remnants of Edith's Pristina, I discovered that if neglect and fraud, the sins of omission, had done for some of Pristina's twenty-one official cultural monuments, it was the graver sins of commission which had threatened others. The collection of manuscripts of the Islamic community was burned by Serb policemen in 1999.

Likewise, the St Nicholas Church and iconostasis together with the Metropolitan/ Archbishop's residence were badly burned (the iconostasis beyond repair) by Albanians in the 2004 riots. This was the building where Edith was hosted for the tinned dinner she described in her notebook as 'great feed'. Was it because her anthropological appetite was overwhelmed by the details of the ham that she makes no mention of the cultural riches of the now lost iconostasis?

Reading of all these failures to protect, my blood was up, and when I learned from the chance remark of a friend that the Hyniler house was to be knocked down in a few weeks I had the feeling of yet more of Edith's Kosovo, my Kosovo – Kosovo's Kosovo – slipping away. I imagined dust sifting between my fingers. The Hyniler house is a traditional 'konak' design and since even before Edith's visit it has been owned by the family who

The Hyniler House

currently live there. Projecting from the first floor is a traditional 'çardak' enclosed balcony to let in light and the warmth of the sun during the crisp, bright Balkan winters. Upholstered seating runs round the inside of these *çardaks* where extended families can gather for civilised living – drinking coffee together from tiny decorated cups, or tea in slender glasses that ring like bells when you stir them. Those are just some of the things that were to be destroyed.

More significantly, the Hyniler House is one of the twenty-one cultural heritage sites on the 'protected' list in Pristina. I went to visit it and asked the family how come it could be demolished. 'We had it taken off the list,' they assured me.

I went back to the law and confirmed what I had assumed – there is no mechanism for removing a building from the list.

I could understand the family's wanting to remove this tiresome safeguarding – their house was draughty, had no central heating, and despite the legal responsibilities of owners of properties on the protected building list, they had no corresponding rights or support through tax rebates or grants. Meanwhile their property occupied real estate in the centre of town where an apartment block (which is what was being proposed) would be worth millions. Traditionally, what developers do in such cases is to pay the owners of the land in one or more new luxury flats which they can then live in or rent out or sell. Needless to say, these flats would have central heating, but no *çardaks*. Indeed, Pristina would soon be completely devoid of *çardaks*. And with the house having been listed for legal protection there was a principle at stake.

I posted a photograph of the house on Facebook with a caption explaining that it was shortly to be demolished. Comments grew around it, along with calls to action. A friend convinced me to write an open letter in the form of a petition in the name of our now registered charity to the Minister for Culture. It called on him to take account of the house's listing on the protected register, and halt the demolition. Having been posted on Facebook, within three days there were 1000 signatories to the letter, and I printed it off and walked to the Ministry and delivered it to the Minister. I think Edith would have been proud, and I felt vindicated that this was a better use of my time than pimping the earrings from the Pitt Rivers collection.

I left the Ministry building some hours later with an uncompromising decree referencing the house's position on the list of protected buildings, and the penalty for demolition or other damage. The next day the decree was released to the media and the owners of the house. The house is still standing, though the family still have no support from the state and no incentive to care for their beautiful property (or to protect it from the 'accidental' fires which have claimed other high profile cultural heritage buildings in Pristina). It would be gratifying to think that our petition had 'saved' the house and the link between Pristina's history and today, but the reality is that this is just a temporary respite.

Three other of the 'protected' sites had not in the end been satisfactorily safeguarded: one is a Neolithic settlement on the outskirts of Pristina which was discovered during the construction of Pristina's first socially-owned enterprise, a yarn spinning factory. All excavation efforts were halted after the factory was built and the site has never been fully explored. Likewise, the ruins of another *hamam* were found during the construction of today's Government Building. They were apparently considered important examples of early Ottoman town architecture but were covered up, without due research. At least these sites are still there, under the feet of the ministers and civil servants charged with looking after the country. All that's needed to explore that other *hamam* is for the government – or at least its building – to fall.

The final building which had been admitted into the leaky ark of the protected buildings list is now gone – a private residence destroyed, without permission, for the building of the Post and Telecommunications of Kosovo headquarters. I tried not to think about those values and the apparent disregard for the past as I made my way to this same site on a very particular quest for Edith's legacy, mediated – through an unlikely series of circumstances – by the head of philately at the Post Office of Kosovo.

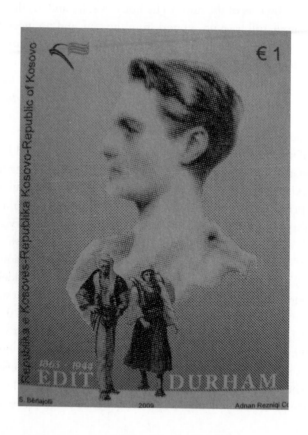

25 Legacy.
The Queen's head on
a Kosovan stamp

The issuing of new stamps is a matter of excitement for enthusiastic boys whose parents won't let them have a PlayStation, or for men in cardigans with pairs of tweezers. It's a cultural activity on the autistic spectrum, and something I had been snooty, if not snide about for most of my life. But perhaps we all have one stamp we could get excited about, and my philately moment came when I got an email from a friend telling me that Kosovo Post and Telecommunications (PTK) had just announced that they would be launching an Edith Durham stamp.

It was a huge honour – at that time only four individuals had been represented on a Republic of Kosovo stamp, and Edith was the first woman and the first Briton. The only Kosovan stamps I had seen previously had rather dingy pictures – a pigeon pecking in the dirt in the 'fauna of Kosovo' series, and some unphotogenic children with odd haircuts, in celebration of Children's Day. There had been some special issues showing individuals – first, President Ibrahim Rugova following his death in 2006, and then – inevitably, given the same tit-for-tat policy that governed the airport and highway naming, a stamp depicting the village war hero, Adem Jashari. The other individual who had been shown on a stamp had, uniquely, been commemorated while still alive – William Walker, the American ambassador whose stamp was issued on the tenth anniversary of his verification of the Raçak massacre in 1999. It was this massacre that fired international opinion about the atrocities being committed in Kosovo and led to NATO's intervention against the Milošević regime.

So this was quite a pantheon that Edith was being admitted to – a fantasy dinner party which I couldn't imagine ending well. Though former President Rugova – the intellectual, formerly head of the Kosovo Writers Union with an interest in mineralogy – would have had plenty to say to Edith, I could imagine her being more interested in Adem J whose swashbuckling hospitality and strong passions would have made him a direct descendant of some of the 'zoti i shpisë's' she describes indulgently in her accounts of her travels. Meanwhile, what William Walker would have made of her I don't know. I remembered seeing him on television as a judge of the Miss Kosova pageant in 2010 and wondered how much interest he would have had in Edith, of whom Aubrey Herbert had written – 'she cuts her hair short like a man, has a cockney accent and a roving eye, is clever, aggressive and competitive'.

I had wanted to learn more about the people who had brought this unlikely cast of Kosovo's heroes – and its one heroine – together, and this was what had brought me to the PTK headquarters in their glossy new building, constructed on the site of a house that Kosovo's law on protected buildings had failed to protect.

I'd had an electronic introduction to the Philately Manager through an ethnologist I knew whose sister worked at the post office headquarters. It seemed when I arrived that I was expected – the receptionist announced to the Manager 'our guest has arrived' and when I was shown up to Fakete's office she came to greet me with a kiss which is unusual even in a land where hospitality and physical contact are generously given to strangers as well as friends. The kiss wasn't really for me, I realised; it was for Edith. Fakete was enthusiastic about the new stamp and when she had sat me down and asked about my health, she started explaining how the decision to publish it had been made by the eleven-member Stamp Commission made up of Ministry representatives as well as noted artists, writers and scientists. 'It's a way of showing our gratitude, but also our countries' friendship; it's a way of saying thank you to Miss Durham, but also to the whole British people,' she said to me. And just as Miss Durham was a representative of the whole British people, I was treated as a representative of Miss Durham.

I tried to behave responsibly, wondering what ED would have done in such circumstances. She would, of course, have asked questions.

'How long have you been working here?' I prompted Fakete. But it was a stupid question – she reminded me politely that there were no Kosovar Albanians working in the Post Office in the 1990s when the regime expelled all Albanians from jobs in government-owned enterprises. She started work at PTK once the Philately division was founded by the United Nations Mission in Kosovo after the end of the war.

I returned to asking about the stamp and its accompanying first day cover. The cover shows a hand holding a pen scribing the words 'lobbying for the Albanian cause' in Albanian. Appropriately, the design is by Agata Çetta, the daughter of Kosovan folklorist, Anton Çetta, who is most famous for the reconciliations he pioneered for families in blood feud with one another. Çetta travelled around Kosovo in the nineteen seventies and 'eighties to collect folklore, published by him in a series of sixteen books, but – like ED – his impact among the Albanians was less through his writing and more because of the work he was inspired to do as a result of the needs he encountered in his travels. In the case of Çetta the need that became very clear to him from his extensive contact with village families across Kosovo, was for the reconciliation of bloodfeuds. The demands of the traditional *kanun* regulating feuds ruled that any male (including children) in a family was liable for any crime committed by someone else in the family, and the honour of the family against whom a crime had been committed was in question until that crime was avenged. The result was that Albanian men from the many families implicated in bloodfeuds were not safe to leave their homes, for fear of attack from strangers who saw them as legitimate targets because of their kinship; the same cultural attitude to proxies which had showed itself more attractively in Fakete's kisses for Edith planted on my cheek. The result was that the Albanian community in Kosovo was paralysed at exactly the time when they needed to show solidarity against the Serbian regime.

The *Kanun* does allow for reconciliation of families 'in blood', by means of a mediator, whose mediations are completed with 'the meal of the blood' (the translation gives a gruesome Titus Andronicus feel to the occasion) where the family of the murderer host a meal at their home for the mediator and the members of the family of the murdered. Çetta ate hundreds of such meals, having reconciled hundreds of families and liberated their menfolk from the self-imposed house-arrest that was the consequence of the requirements of the *Kanun*. Fakete pointed out to me how this idea of progress had been incorporated into the stamp, which is based on a pastel sketch of Edith completed in 1904, when she was 41 and had just made her first visit to Kosovo. The portrait is accompanied on the stamp by one of ED's own sketches of a man and a woman in traditional Albanian dress, the couple moving forward, as Fakete said oratorically that she hoped Kosovo will do. 'I know my country has some catching up to do; how many years ago did you have your Penny Black with a picture of your British Queen? Now at last we have a stamp with the picture of the British woman we call Queen.'

Fakete gave me a stamp and a first day cover, and I took a reverential photograph and pressed the wafer thin portrait between the pages of a book to keep it safe. There was something poignant about this fragile token of respect for Edith and her country from a nation scarcely acknowledged by Edith's compatriots on the other side of Europe; like a loveletter that had never been opened.

I thought immediately of someone I knew who would open such a letter, would value these professions of respect, and when I'd said goodbye to Fakete and was downstairs in the post office I scribbled a note to Antonia, who had set me on this quest three summers before. At the post office counter I bought some more Edith stamps and stuck them on, along with a Yorkshire address; sending on its way across Europe an envelope whose medium was its message.

I asked my friends in Kosovo about the stamp and they all agreed with the Stamp Commission that it was a well-deserved honour for Edith. 'Like the statue at the airport, and the roads and the schools', they said.

I had heard about the plans for the statue at the airport, though it still hasn't been produced. If it ever materialises this will be Edith's chance to spend a lot more time in the company of Adem Jashari. I was told that public subscriptions had been sought, and I even managed to meet with the sculptor who told me of his dream for it, but at the moment, when you arrive by air into Pristina there is no bronze of this doughty lady to greet you with her travelling trunk full of handcrafts. Perhaps one day that dream will take shape. But in the meantime, I wanted to see these Edith Durham Streets I was being told about. Where were they?

Well, there was the square named after her in the centre of Pristina – didn't I know? And what schools? The one in Tirana in Albania, for example, though my landlord told me about the television programme he had watched where interviewers at the school had asked pupils who this eponymous 'Miss Durham' was. 'It's our headteacher,' answered one boy – making me worried as much for the communication between the living members of the school's community as for the reputation of my long-dead friend.

'She was a woman from a society who founded the school and then went', another child said. None of them apparently knew about ED the tireless aid-worker or trenchant commentator or painstaking anthropologist of Albanian traditions.

'But you should ask someone from Suhareka about their school too,' I was told. I knew someone who worked in the education directorate in Suhareka, southern Kosovo, and when he heard about my interest he gave me a copy of a book about their Edith Durham School. It had a blotchy frontispiece with a portrait of Edith looking intelligent. The introduction pays only slightly more accurate homage to this school's namesake than the pupil in Tirana did. The biography printed at the beginning praises her 'spirit of field-based research of Albanian history and her presentation of the moral riches of the Albanian people' but gets her birthday wrong, says she came to the Balkans because she was suffering from tuberculosis, and makes no mention of her travels in Kosovo, or of *High Albania* where she wrote the account of some of those travels. The introduction concludes of ED, 'to the world she is a great woman, but for Albanians she was a great mother who cared for her children while she was alive and experienced the poverty and misery of the Albanian highland people'. It is a curious metaphor and rather sad commemoration that I sense would not have pleased the childless Edith at all.

I tried to visit this school, contacting the Municipal Education Directorate number my friend had given me. There was a thrill in asking 'do you have the number for Edith Durham' but although I was finally put in touch with the headteacher, on my trip to Suhareka, we couldn't find a suitable time for me to visit. Perhaps it was better for me not to be brought to an awkward face-to-face meeting with the mythical, tubercular Mis DourHAM, the 'great mother'. The teacher in me probably wouldn't have been able to keep from correcting the staff, and that doesn't go down well.

I had more success with the space named after her in my Kosovan hometown. The square in Pristina which bears her name turns out to be a place I walk past regularly. Like most locations in Kosovan cities, it bears no sign, which is why I'd never known its name. Most people would refer to it as 'the square behind the Grand Hotel' – the 'sixties hotel which is Pristina's most unlovely landmark (and where the rooms have so few bathplugs – as the woman whom I'd met in Edith's house in Hampstead had reminded me) though I learned later that it used to be called Trg Republike – Republic Square, in the days when the Republic was Yugoslavia and the word for 'square' was in Serbian.

In English, 'square' gives a misleading sense of the proportions and shape of this area, which has been hacked about with some fencing screening off the former army base, then the United Nations Mission in Kosovo headquarters, now a building of the EU Rule of Law mission – a history of power in Kosovo in miniature. Misshapen though it may be, the area houses some of my favourite businesses in Kosovo – the tables where secondhand books are sold, and where you can pick up an old copy of ED's *Burden of the Balkans* in linen binding for a few euros. Alongside an unremarkable series of bars which mainly cater to an international audience – the policemen come off duty from the Rule of Law mission, ready to down some drinks in locations where the television shows international sports or runs English-language quizzes – there's an excellent Mexican restaurant. I think Edith would have been happy to eat a *chimichanga* in a square bearing her name.

The next time we treated ourselves to a meal there I toasted her and we talked about the idea of legacy. I don't know what Edith would have hoped for as her legacy but I sensed she had

had enough vanity (hasn't everyone) to have been pleased by the road naming and the schools. And if she'd cared at all about the Englishwoman on her trail, I was feeling increasingly certain that our work with children on environmental projects, the campaign to save the old *konak* from destruction, the exhibition of historical photographs, stimulating sustainable tourism through Faik's filigree co-operative and the Roma women's income generating project were all much better ways to learn from her than my original filigree pipe-dream of a costly travelling exhibition. Looking again at the photograph of Edith's face staring out from the stamp, I felt I was now more ready to meet her gaze.

26 The Kosovo battlefields

1389 – a fateful year for all the Balkan peoples – that
the Serbs made their last stand as a united people.
Lazar summoned his chieftains, and they flocked to
his standard from Bosnia, from Albania, the Zeta, and
Syrmia, from every fastness and stronghold, with all
the heroes of the land – a list of doughty warriors well
known to every Serb child of to-day.

Sultan Murad and his Turks were encamped on the
broad plain of Kosovo, in the heart of Old Servia. He
swore to slaughter the giaours and to mark out the
frontiers with their heads. His tents spread all over the
plain; the lances of his warriors were like a black forest,
and their banners like clouds in the sky. So vast was his
army that, had God sent rain, it would have fallen, not
on green grass, but on horsemen and horses, spears and
banners. A desperate fight ensued; Murad was stabbed
in his tent on the morn of the fight by a Serb chieftain,
Milosh Obilich, who had sworn to kill him, but the
Turks were led by his son Bajazet. Lazar and his men
fought fiercely against heavy odds; the waters of the
Sitnitza ran red, and the horses splashed knee-deep in
blood. The Turks wavered before the wild onslaught,
and were falling back, when the divided state of the
Serb people was their own undoing. Lazar was betrayed.
His son-in-law, Vuk Brankovich, coveted for himself the
crown of the Nemanjas; he deserted to the enemy with
12,000 followers, and the ground on which they stood

has been barren evermore. Then fell Lazar and his heroes thick around him; and the Turks, though they suffered very heavily, remained victors in one of the decisive battles of the world – a battle from which the Balkan peoples still suffer, and whose consequences still threaten the peace of Europe.

ED's rich description of the Kosovo battlefield in *The Burden of the Balkans* which she published in 1905 contrasts strongly with the details she notes when she finally made a visit to the site three years later. The battlefield of her imagination seems to owe a lot to Byron's Sennacherib ('the sheen of their spears was like stars on the sea…/ Like the leaves of the forest when Summer is green,/ That host with their banners at sunset were seen') but in place of 'chieftains', 'fastnesses', 'barren evermore' and the elaborate similes, Biblical diction and inverted syntax of 'then fell Lazar and his heroes thick around him', Edith's contact with the reality of contemporary Kosovo Field feels bourgeois – though rather more interesting for it.

It reminds me of Gérard de Nerval's lament for the Egypt he had read about

I have already lost, Kingdom after Kingdom, province after province, the more beautiful half of the universe, and soon I will know of no place in which I can find a refuge for my dreams; but it is Egypt that I most regret having driven out of my imagination, now that I have sadly placed it in my memory.

Edith went to visit the *turbe* where the fallen Sultan's internal organs were buried (while the rest of his body was taken to the traditional burial place of the Ottomans, in Bursa, Turkey) but can talk only of its interior décor (to Nellie she wrote

appalling – decorated like a cheap lodging house – cheap Austrian curtain poles of shiny wood over the windows and cheap crimson curtains – walls stencilled

to look like 4 a piece wallpaper and over coffin a
large glass chandelier – rather a handsome one but so
absurdly out of place!)

There's none of the romance she summoned apparently so easily while writing her first book in Hampstead, and she moves swiftly (in the private account in her notebook she gives a reason for this – 'did not stop to draw as was afraid of catching cold') from the description of the wallpaper to the harem she visited.

This, too, she seems mercilessly determined to strip of romance. Readers in anticipation of Ingres' odalisques were to be brutally disappointed. Nine women there are, but they are not languid, nubile, reclining in exotic Latinate phrase – but described in solidly Anglo-Saxon terms as 'stout, pallid and collopy'. Déshabille there was, exactly as the reader might expect to be titillated by, but it is 'soiled, crumpled', 'messy', 'bulgy', and the only woman whose petticoats are mentioned is 'squatting' just as the only glands mentioned are burst ones (I don't even know what this means, and googling it made me feel sick). ED is happy to objectify these women, just as their male reviewers had done, but as cattle or zoo creatures, not as petted birds or indulged fancy accessories (she says 'I never discovered which belonged to whom' and lays on the animal metaphors, with the old woman's streakily dyed hair described as 'tigerish' in a 'monkey-house' atmosphere, which seems to convey something of stench as well as lasciviousness. Her scabrous conclusion about the women is 'their conversation is much what one would expect of a cow if it could talk').

It's powerful writing, with a clear message about Edith's positioning of herself on the battlefield of the sexes (indeed, for the published account she adds to the version from her notebook and what she wrote to her sister the significant phrase, just to reinforce this message, 'Marko was entertained by officers below, in which company I too should have felt more at home'). It reminded me of a line from an article she had written about experiences with other women in Macedonia – 'they have no doubt that I am their sister. For my part, I wonder if they belong to the same genus as I do – let alone species'. But I think there is another intention here too. This harem is not just any collection of women in any point in time and geography; ED is pedantic in the published account that this is the household of 'an Ottoman Turk (not Moslem Slav or Albanian)', and it is right on the field where the Ottoman Turks first established their sloppy, 'soiled', 'squatting' animal ways among the Albanians and Slavs in 1389. Even more importantly, ED makes reference over and over again in this passage to the new constitution which had just been agreed by the Turks, and by its association with these slatterns, the Constitution and the Turks alike are damned. Here it is Turkey itself which – worse even than being shown as the sick man of Europe – is presented as Europe's frowsy old whore.

The descriptions of unlovely undress are enough to get anyone pulling their stomach in as they read. My own experience of the Kosovo battlefield was dominated by consideration of my own physicality as it was the site of a personal battle of the bulge. The Pristina half marathon route goes across the windswept plain, where stands the tower erected by the Serbs to commemorate their battle, and where Milošević organised the nationalist commemorations on the 600th anniversary in 1989 which ushered in a decade of oppression and atrocity by the Serb regime against the Albanian population. Just as the battlefield's monuments stand as a permanent challenge to multiethnic Kosovo, a niggling reminder to anyone bowling along the main road from Pristina to Kosovo's divided city of Mitrovica (where Edith was headed next), references to the half marathon are bandied around as challenges to anyone sitting too comfortably on their well-padded, well-paid behinds in Pristina.

So the date in early May and the route marked out across the plain had featured on my mental calendar and mental map for some time before – a temptation and a possible proving ground. I had run a half-marathon before, in a friendly town in Kent, with the encouragement and accompaniment of my friend Lisa. Lisa runs half- and full marathons regularly, and had brought along her usual accessories – a pair of adult-size fairy wings (so that you can be easily spotted in the crowd of runners by any supporters who've come to cheer you on, she explained) and a sign she pinned to her T-shirt with her name on it ('that way, people watching the race know how to call out to you personally and it's really encouraging,' she said). Her running attire seemed unconventional, but it was nothing to the zoo of monkey suits, chickens and space men who jostled at the start line. There was nervous joking, self-deprecation, the occasional bit of self-conscious stretching.

I tried to transpose some of that atmosphere of the good-natured amateur, translate some of the comments into Albanian, to imagine some of the young guys you see drinking coffee in Pristina's cafes, but now limbering up and bouncing on air-filled soles. I imagined the crush of a similar huddle of people to those who had participated in my first half marathon, crowding together so that had God sent rain, it would have fallen, not on green grass, but on lycra. I thought I had an idea of what the Pristina half-marathon would be like.

But when I turned up at the starting line by the Scanderbeg statue outside the Government of Kosovo building, I realised I had got it badly wrong. There was near silence among the small gathering of runners. Perhaps 500 people were taking part – nothing like the crowds of thousands that had jostled and jogged happily alongside one another in Maidstone. I spotted a few women I knew and went to try to exchange the nervous jokes or self-deprecating comments I thought the occasion required, but they scarcely acknowledged me, too busy with infeasible warm-up lunges. One guy standing nearby had his mouth sellotaped in what could have been gimpish perversion, sign of a disability, or running science I had not yet been initiated into. Inconspicuously, I pointed to him and with a raised eyebrow asked a fellow runner what the sellotape might be for. She frowned at me, apparently not seeing anything bizarre in the sight, 'I think it's that thing to make you use oxygen more efficiently while you're racing'. I nodded sagely back as waves of panic rose in me; this was no Fun Run, and there would be no chicken suits here today.

I should have thought through the demographics more carefully before registering for this race. Kent has its fair share of slightly overweight women in their thirties; me, and Lisa in her fairy wings, had felt quite comfortable. Kosovo's population is famously young – the youngest population in Europe, with fifty percent of the country under 30 years old. In her first book, *Through the Lands of the Serb*, Edith described 'the Albanian' as having, 'many of the physical attributes of a beast of prey. A lean, wiry thing, all tough sinew and as supple as a panther, he moves with a long easy stride, quite silently.' The description, especially with its anthropological distance, its objectivisation and more animal-metaphors to go with those she used of the harem, isn't comfortable reading, but the physique she describes is familiar. And it was against these, not the mumsy runners of Maidstone, that I would be running today.

Of course it wasn't just Kosovars in the race; in fact with the disincentive of the entry fee, there were a disproportionate number of foreigners taking part. I think it was when I saw the gang doing star jumps together in their French Foreign Legion T-shirts that I realised just how bad I was going to look in this competition. Most of the foreigners in Kosovo are male (think squaddies and coppers) and young (pre-family, or with children of an age before incompatible education systems start to become problematic). The regime for the unadventurous single male foreigner in Kosovo is a bit like the regime for a prison inmate, but with drugs a little harder to come by. The consequence is the same – even if they're not fit when they come out here, young males posted to Kosovo soon become easily capable of running a half-marathon without breaking a sweat before their evening at the Irish Bar.

Thankfully, in the face of such competition, I had some other motivation to keep me going. Our charity was in desperate need of funds. We had managed to register more than 60 children from the Roma, Ashkali and Egyptian community for school, even though they were starting anything from a year to seven years later than they should have done. Now we realised that to keep them in school we needed ongoing academic support, Saturday classes, a local community advocate who could visit them at home each week and talk to their parents as well as to their teachers about any problems that were arising. We needed rent for the place where the Saturday activities would be held and fruit juice to serve there to children assessed by a visiting doctor as being malnourished. A number of volunteers and friends who were running the marathon had offered to ask for sponsorship for their efforts. If we could finish we stood to gain a total of about 4,000 euros. That would help me round thirteen miles.

The race was called and we took up our positions. With a starting gun we were off, and within the first kilometre I assumed a comfortable place among the last ten runners. After that there wasn't much further back I could fall. In fact, a kind of tranquility descended on me – the roads were closed to traffic and once the scrum of runners ahead had moved beyond my vision there was just me and a straggle of spectators on the sidelines shouting out my runner number (202 – *doo chind eh dooshi*, they chanted rhythmically, and I wished that – even though the Foreign Legion guys might have sneered – I had taken some of Lisa's advice so the spectators would have known my real name) and the regular thump of my feet on tarmac. My favourite part of the race was after I'd crossed the railway line that leads from Pristina to Mitrovica and was out past the power station (this, a pollution generating plant burning brown coal seems a surprising choice of route for healthy exercise or for Pristina PR) where there were not even any local residents to *doo-chind-eh-dooshi* me and just the frogs croaking in the choked river, and the thought of the children who'd be coming to class next weekend, and a light wind blowing possibly carcinogenic dust in my eyes.

Then there was a strangled wheezing with footsteps behind me and I realised I wasn't last yet – the guy with his mouth taped shut was just behind. From his race positioning it seemed that whatever the science behind his breathing technique it wasn't working for him. I tried smiling at him but the grimace he returned to me was a complicated creasing that I found unsettling.

Even if your escort has his mouth gagged with sticky tape, when you are running along an empty road with just one other person, it is hard not to fall in step with them. The psychologists of running say that it can help your speed and stamina, because you transfer some of the responsibility for effort to the other person; if you keep rhythm carefully enough you can begin to believe that it is not you who is moving your legs, but the other guy. The experience was not unfamiliar from my travels around Kosovo with this barely-acknowledged other guiding and anticipating my movements.

And thus it is was that I crossed the cursed, barren evermore plain of Kosovo, with someone else moving my legs, and him a respiratory freak with whom I wasn't able to exchange even one word.

I avoided the fate of Sultan Murad and Tsar Lazar on Kosovo field, running slowly and sometimes unsurely but always alive, and appreciating that every minute. When the Sultan's *turbe* came into view I thought of Edith and I thought of her struggle to position herself between the fleshy women of the overheated harem and the military men of action swapping war stories outside, and I newly appreciated, too, my twenty-first century opportunities for moving between these worlds, for jostling at the starting blocks with men and women all together and no-one deciding for me where I should stand. It was really all up to me; I wrenched a spurt of energy from my weary legs, and summoned the thought of the Fushë Kosovë kids to take me just a little faster along the road that led to Mitrovica, where Edith was to travel next.

27 Mitrovica.
Edith's – and Serbia's – last stand in Kosovo

'This is the first time in my life I have ever come out so far without a revolver. I have no weapon at all, and am not afraid,' commented Edith's travelling companion en route to Mitrovica. Her trip by rail was seen as a celebration of the new security regime. My own journey was more nerve-wracking; I went with a Serbian colleague from the project I was working on, which aimed to support schools in Mitrovica with inclusion of all children – whatever their disability, economic circumstances or ethnicity. The fact that this approach to education – indeed to life – was not currently shared by some of the residents of the town of Mitrovica had been made loudly – earsplittingly – clear a few weeks before, when a bomb was detonated outside the window of an ethnic Albanian family's apartment in the (majority Serb) northern part of Mitrovica, killing the father and wounding two children. Our visit to the city due that week had been cancelled.

We were now due to be visiting both the *ë* and the *a* – the contesting vowels grunting at one another across Mitrovica's dividing river Ibar, which are the endings of the town's name in the rival Albanian and Serbian versions. North is MitrovicA – mainly ethnic Serbs who don't recognise the Pristina government and consider Kosovo to be part of Serbia. Prices in the shops are set in Serbian dinars; the children go to schools run by Belgrade, taught by teachers paid by Belgrade, learning a curriculum (and worldview) set by Belgrade.

The half of the city south of the river is mainly ethnic Albanians who call their city MitrovicË and consider it – north and south – to be part of the independent Republic of Kosovo, whose institutions (schools, police, law courts, postmen) are run by Pristina. As a Brit, whose country had been vocally and actively supportive of the Republic of Kosovo, I might not be very welcome in the north. As a Serb, my colleague Mirjana might not be very welcome in the south. After the bomb had killed Selver Haradinaj we had waited a few weeks before rescheduling our visit. So today we, like the inhabitants of Mitrovica/ë, were jittery. If I'd owned a revolver, like ED's travelling companion had done, perhaps today would have been the day I would have brought it.

But sometimes more powerful protection comes from things that dial rather than revolve – the night before the trip I had phoned a friend of ours who headed the international diplomatic office's operation in Mitro (the jaunty nickname helps foreigners, particularly those working with communities both sides of the river, not to over-commit themselves linguistically). 'Will I be OK making this trip tomorrow?' I asked.

'What sort of transport will you be using in the north?' she wanted to know immediately.

'It will be a car marked with the logo of the international organisation,' I assured her. The organisation I was working for has been around for more than a century and has offices in 120 countries and a long respected presence in Kosovo.

'You'll be fine.'

I didn't tell Mirjana about my nervy phone call, and we travelled talking determinedly of other things. Mirjana is great company – an efficient colleague with an arpeggio of a laugh, played often through her conversation. She is one of the most happily multicultural of all my Kosovan friends, speaking near-fluent Albanian which she says she learned from the kids she grew up with in Pristina. We talked now in English. As I knew from my other work with Mirjana, in public in majority-Albanian Kosovo she always talks in English; even when her husband phones her, she talks to him in English, so as not to draw attention to those As where the people around us are using Ës.

While we were chatting she mentioned Facebook and, laughingly, I gave her a hard time,

'You're on Facebook? And you've never bothered to ask me to be your Facebook 'friend'?'

She looked serious and then she explained: the account she created is in her mother's name, and she uses it only for her old Serbian friends and family, 'It's hard when my Albanian friends are celebrating independence, and those Serbs I know in Serbia say this nationalist stuff ....' Even the international democracy of Facebook has its ghettos and its divided cities, its undercover citizens and its politics.

We arrived in the southern part of town which Edith had described as 'small, but cleaner and less hopeless-looking than Prishtina ... and fine vegetable gardens.' The vegetable gardens she had seen in 1908 were before the beginning of large-scale mining by a British company in the 1930s, and subsequently by a socially owned enterprise which was one of the largest companies in Yugoslavia. The Trepça company once extracted lead, zinc and silver messily but profitably from the land but the industrial complex straddling both banks of the Ibar is now as broken up as Yugoslavia – vast sheds with broken panes and rusting hulks, along with slag heaps and toxic dust. The result has been blood lead levels of more than six times the World Health Organisation's 'acceptable' 10 micrograms per decilitre in some children living in the worst-affected sites nearby. The vegetable gardens no longer seemed so appetising.

After our meeting in southern Mitrovicë, we were picked up by Mirjana's Serbian colleague who lives in the north, to drive through the northern part of town and on through the countryside to the village where we had a meeting scheduled with the kindergarten director. As I'd known he would, he arrived in the safe transportation pick-up truck of the organisation, but when I went to open the door I saw that all the organisation's logos had been taken off. What was this? My mind raced … A hijack situation? I quietly asked Mirjana about it.

'Ah, well organisations funded by European agencies had their vehicles burned here a while ago. That's probably the reason.'

Yeah, probably … On the back seat of our maverick car I strapped in carefully – as if a seatbelt would help against a grenade – and thought of Edith again, and her description of Mitrovica as 'tinder waiting for a spark.'

We drove from the south of Mitrovicë over a bridge and into a street in the north which is a tiny, still mainly Albanian, community. It was near here that the bomb had killed Selver Hajradinaj. My eyes flicked back and forth between the blood red Albanian flags with their mortal black eagles fluttering across them. The rows of flags came to an end in the middle of a street, and here our driver pulled in. Jumping out of the car he went round to the Republic of Kosovo numberplate we'd been displaying, and slipped it off, carrying it into the car. We had finished driving through the Albanian community, and now we were completely unmarked, stripped of our identifiers – and maybe of our protection.

We drove on slowly towards the end of the street where other flags were fluttering – this time the red, white and blue stripes of the Serbian flag with its superimposed crest. Looking down from the flags I saw why we were driving so slowly; ahead of us was a barricade.

The barricades had been erected by Serbs in Mitrovica a year before in retaliation for the action of Republic of Kosovo police who took (or secured, depending on your point of view) a border crossing which had previously been controlled by the European Rule of Law mission, and Serbian members of the Kosovo Police Service. A Republic of Kosovo police officer was killed in that action, and since then 65 international KFOR soldiers as well as a number of Serb civilians have been wounded. The barricades have been erected at various points and in various ways. In at least one case, a cross was put on top of a barricade and a Serbian priest blessed it, making it much harder for international forces to take it down.

Despite all the news I'd read about the barricades, this was the first time I had actually come face-to-face with one – unless you count what I saw on stage at *Les Miserables*. As we neared the ugly mound, I eyed it up. It was piled with gravel and topped with two broken kiosks; I imagined every spadeful of stones as a mean act of negative energy – a statement of what will not happen, rather than a statement of what will.

But there were an awful lot of those stones – I wondered what would happen now as our little car reached this obstruction. But our driver just drove the pickup round the low edge of the gravel pile, following the guy in front, who had swerved round it, in a track worn into the gravel which seemed to have got a fair bit of use. With this act of *realpolitik* we left the city behind, and drove on in Serbia – or as near as dammit.

We were now heading north, although when she had left Mitrovicë, Edith retraced her journey south again. She recounts

> To leave ..., I had to have my *teskereh* stamped. The
> official at the *konak*, in order to make a good job of it,
> licked the stamp three times and licked off all the gum.
> As it would not stick, he licked it four more times. As

it still would not, he put it in his mouth and sucked it patiently. It then showed signs of melting altogether, so he called a colleague to advise. He suggested the gum-pot. They searched for it high and low, and called in a third official – luckily that day there was no press of business in that department. The gum was found and the stamp stuck. It took half-an-hour, but was thoroughly done in the end.

No-one noticed my own departure from Mitro, slinking out along the road in our unmarked car. As we drove I noted plenty of other cars which didn't have numberplates; conducting a brief poll of 100 cars I counted 35 of them without any plates at all. This really felt like the badlands.

Our driver went too fast – undertaking or overtaking on blind corners. You wouldn't dare to do this in Kosovo 'proper', south of the river – the Republic of Kosovo police had become zealous in their monitoring and fining of speeding. Here, in a puff of exhaust smoke, we passed a policeman standing by the side of the road, and the officer watched us drive on with a look of bemusement on his face. I could see the driver's grin in the rearview mirror as he swerved onward; a rebel in a rebel state.

We passed the foot of the extraordinary solitary triangular hill atop which sits Zvecan castle. This castle was the grim site of the strangling of Stefan Dečanski who had built the exquisite monastery I'd visited with the Robinson family. I asked the Serbs I was with about it but they weren't that interested in the history.

'I go running up there, though' said the driver, flexing his muscular arms around the steering wheel, and his foot once more onto the accelerator. I gave him the appreciation that his driving suggested he was desperate for, but given the steep slopes I couldn't quite believe him. I thought Edith, who noted simply 'did not climb up', rather more sensible.

Our unlikely transport finally got us to the kindergarten where we were expected. The director there was brisk and although not unfriendly I wasn't sure she was very pleased about the project. On the way back with Mirjana we talked about the meeting and she explained a few more Serbian facts of life.

'You know that it's as hard for us to get meetings with these people as it is for you,' she said. 'They ask us what's the name of our boss in Pristina, and as soon as they hear the [Albanian] name – the surname – they refuse to cooperate with us.'

I thought of the man ED met on her trip here, 'who said that he woke up every day surprised to still find peace. 'We were living like snakes in holes, and now here we are all out in the sun!' A century later there were some spots in Kosovo where the sun still hadn't penetrated.

'Mitrovitza' (her phonetic spelling got her out of any accusations of favouring either Serbs or Albanians since neither would recognise the way she'd written it) was Edith's last stop of any note in her travel through Kosovo's sunspots. From there she went back to Prizren and spent a night before leaving for Albania. She never came back, but as she said at the end of the account of her travels in *High Albania*, 'I cannot write FINIS for the END is not yet.'

28 What went before

Even if it wasn't an end, it was a pause, and I stopped now to take stock of the woman who had accompanied me from Kosovo to the museums and archives of England and back again. Her life had started for me (and perhaps for her) when she was 37 and made that first transformational trip to the Balkans. However, as she herself wrote in *Twenty Years of Balkan Tangle*, 'the events seen by the casual traveller are meaningless if he knows not what went before. They are mere sentences from the middle of a book he has not read.'

So what should I know about Edith's life up to the age of 37, beyond the basic story of her middle adulthood going slowly mad with the frustrations of tending to an ailing mother? I'd seen the house she'd been born in and I'd known – from that Wikipedia article which Fatmir and I had pieced together at the beginning of my acquaintance with Edith – that she had been a watercolourist before she began her Balkan travels, but what of her schooling in between those two stages? Who had formed that unusual mind?

An article Edith wrote in the (*Manchester*) *Guardian* from 1934 gave a surprising potted biography. It was all the more surprising because the subject of the article was buses. It's a lively, quirky article including her thoughts on the sport of 'bus-jumping' and telling the story of the omnibus, which had just turned 100, and the more than half its life which ED herself had experienced. Along with some grumpy-old-woman-ising (buses nowadays 'run so often that many folk are forgetting how to walk', and you can't distinguish between the different bus lines, until a bus 'is in close on you and then you may miss it because it is only conspicuously labelled with Cheese, Chocolate, or Beer, its destination being hidden in small letters round the corner' unlike in the past when 'the red 'Ammersmith, the emerald green St John's Wood, the dark green City, the yellow, orange, brown, blue 'buses enlivened the street like a flock of macaws') she opens with an incident from her young teenage years at school,

> It never occurred to me to break a rule, and I was
> dismayed when told I was to appear before the heads
> on a charge of misconduct.
>
> Puzzled, I entered the room and was told sternly by
> three austere Fates that I had used bad language – low
> slang, in fact. I had been heard more than once to say
> 'bus' instead of 'omnibus'
>
> Anxious to please, I said that I did not know it was
> wrong and would not do it again. Then, wishing to be
> on the safe side in future, I asked timidly:
>
> 'Please, am I to say cabriolet instead of cab?'
>
> There was a pause. The ladies looked at each other. I
> was told to leave the room, and as I did so I heard one
> murmur to the other:
>
> 'I can't understand that girl. Does she mean to be
> impudent? Or is she only very, very stupid?'

In setting the scene for the incident she mentions that this was at Bedford College, when she was

> 14 and a half, the youngest student there, a law-abiding
> and hard-working child. I marvel now at the hours
> of work I put in every day and all day, and often on
> Sundays, too. Play was only for the holidays.

Another biographer's titbit was dropped by her in the correspondence I'd read between her and Marie Stopes. She narrates there her grandfather's 'practical' attitude to education which she says meant that 'I had a terrible struggle as a girl to learn Latin and was not allowed to go to the history class at school' – though the memoir of her grandfather, William Ellis, which I read later does mention that in 1876, when Edith was a young teenager, he took his granddaughter to 'some lectures on Political Economy then being delivered at the London Institution'. Her views on this element of her education were not recorded.

The grandfather in question seems to have been more of a liberal educationalist than Edith's reference to her battle for Latin would suggest – I later found information from ED about him, and his brief biography seemed like the beginning of another book. Indeed, it's a tale of Dickensian proportions: 13 year-old William was taken out of school because of his father's financial trouble (just a year older than Charles Dickens was when he was likewise sent to work when his father was imprisoned for debt). ED records of her grandfather 'he vowed at an early age to do all he could to promote the education of other poor boys'. Like Dickens (the men were near contemporaries – William having been born just twelve years before Charles), William Ellis worked his way up from this ignominious beginning of his career. Like Dickens, William Ellis was a great London walker; Edith's note on him records that 'When living at Brixton he used to walk to the City and arrive at 8am in time for a debating society held at the house of James Mill (father of John Stuart).' Edith may have been consciously drawing a comparison between herself and her grandfather when she included in her biographical note the detail of his transport preferences ('He provided a horse and carriage for his wife but went about on foot or in the few omnibuses and trains') as she seems to have achieved some renown for her own preference for public transport – not only in the 'bus jumping' article. I had read the speech on her eightieth birthday when the President of the Royal Anthropological Institute had presented ED with a cheque and asked her,

> We should like you, Miss Durham, to use it to mitigate
> the rigours of travelling in public conveyances, by
> hiring a taxi or private car whenever you wish to
> attend one of our meetings. We do not wish to exercise
> compulsion. We shall not audit the accounts. But, with
> all due respect, we must insist that you should for once
> restrain your charitable instincts and really use this only
> for your own benefit. If it enables you to attend more
> of our meetings than you could otherwise have done,
> we shall be amply rewarded.

More significantly than his preference for walking and public transport, William Ellis seems to have shared Dickens' zeal for social reform – which was inherited, in a different form, by his granddaughter Edith. She records

> Extraordinarily successful in business he amassed a large
> fortune and devoted the greater part (some £250,000)
> to the cause of Popular Education. Convinced that
> Democracy would rule in the future, he wanted to
> educate the people not merely in 'the 3 RRRs' but in
> the elements of finance and social economics and in
> the conduct of life. He built and financed schools in
> Bethnal Green, Kingsland, Gospel Oak and Peckham.

Reading accounts of her grandfather's life later I discovered that another of his schools had been built in Vincent Square, the address with a view of Big Ben where we'd had our flat when my journey to find his granddaughter had started. William Ellis School in Gospel Oak, which I had walked past on the way to many summer picnics on Hampstead Heath while I was living in London turns out to have been named after Edith's grandfather. (I am embarrassed that I had always thought it was named for the first rugby player).

Ellis also helped to finance the Birkbeck Institute and 'Trained his teachers and gave lessons himself in Social Science … He permitted no corporal punishment to be inflicted in his schools. … He used to say that a man who could not manage boys without hitting them was not fit to be a teacher.'

Mr Ellis' liberal views extended even to birth control, of which he was apparently a great proponent, but Edith wrote to Dr Stopes also of the family's other birth control activist –her mother's cousin, coyly referred to as Mrs X – like a chromosome – who

advocated, in company with a small society she belonged to, mechanical aids. They started sending some through the post and the post office stopped it as 'obscene' and there was a fuss and a scandal about it. Mrs X and her friends used to hold secret meetings to discuss ways and means. I remember she once asked me to one which was to take place in the basement of an empty house. But I was not allowed to go and quite reasonably so. For there was risk of a police raid and my father's practice might have been seriously injured if any relative of his was mixed up in such an affair.

Mrs X and her friends were not suppressed. They got a number of leaflets printed – I do not know where – and at night she used to walk miles and drop leaflets in to people's letterboxes. There was a row about that and complaints made to the police that an attempt was being made to tempt servant girls to an immoral life. I remember in the 1880s going to the house of a fellow student and finding her parents in a terrible state of mind about a leaflet that had been thrust upon them thus. I guessed it was one of Mrs X's or her friends and held my tongue.

Poor old Mrs X fought up til old age forced her to cease. She had no tact poor dear and dragged in the subject most unwisely at all places and times. I remember she got into trouble at the very first Club for Ladies started in London, the Somerville, long since extinct. She scattered her leaflets and pamphlets about ... She used to tell us of her exploits and burst into a great hoarse laugh ...'

It's tempting to have a 'great hoarse laugh' oneself – or at least a bit of a giggle – thinking of these women in bustles discussing 'ways and means' in a basement, and slipping condoms in the post. In another letter, ED reveals the contents of the pamphlets – 'some recommended use of syringe [douche]. Others withdrawal on the part of the man. And there was a leaflet by a woman who recommended violent coughing at the time of coition and declared she found it efficacious'. Along with 'poor old Mrs X' earnestly discussing douching at inapt moments, these references in ED's description prompted the patronising smile intended. But I realised this was also deadly serious and that these were brave women, to whom I – and millions others like me, with the number of children of our choice – owe our entire lifestyle. I thought of the woman who became my friend in Fushë Kosovë who was caring for 11 children aged 0-15, in a tiny house and with next to no money. I remembered her asking whether I'd come with her to the doctor to discuss some form of contraception, and the confidence of her smile when we came out after she'd had a coil fitted, saying 'enough. No more.' And I remember the tears of frustration – and the vision of continued grinding poverty for those parents and their 11, now maybe 12 or 13 children – when she told me less than a month later how someone had come from the mosque and told her husband that she must have the coil removed because it was against their religion. In the file of Marie Stopes' correspondence from eighty years ago, held at the British Library where I'd read Edith's letters to her, there had also been letters such as this, sent from a rectory address in 1931,

Dear Dr Stopes, Please have my name struck off the list of those to whom your poisonous literature is sent. I am ashamed as a Christian married woman and mother to receive it into our home. You are not married and cannot understand.

'Poor old Mrs X' was a heroine.

According to the note scribbled by Marie Stopes, or her secretary across Edith's letter in this file, Edith had, just like those ancestors of hers who had hoped that the postal service was the way to change reproductive habits, slipped something into the envelope with her letter – a cheque for a pound to support the Society for Constructive Birth Control, a generous gesture to a Society which, by 1931, had developed some unattractive eugenic views that I hope went further than Edith's.

Edith was a worthy granddaughter; her narrative of her grandfather's campaign elaborates, that he 'under the title of Parental Forethought would lead his pupils by question to realise how much greater was the well being and comfort in a home where there were but 2 or 3 children as compared with the family of a man who, with the same income, brought a dozen children, crowded and ill-fed into the world'. It was impressive stuff, and ahead of its time, but rather undermined by the sprawling family tree I'd sketched from what I'd learned about ED's mother – William Ellis' daughter's – family of nine children. ED wrote of her grandfather to Marie Stopes, 'that he sowed much good seed we cannot doubt for opposition to such teaching is fast dying'. It is an interesting turn of phrase, but the seed of all sorts which he sowed was certainly prolific.

It was apparently his teaching (though presumably not on the importance of birth control) that recommended William Ellis to Queen Victoria and Prince Albert (who had, like ED's parents, nine children). William Ellis gave lessons on Social Science to the four eldest royal children and apparently remained a friend of the Empress Frederic until his death, but ED was unimpressed by his credentials, writing in a letter 'as a girl I was often I confess bored stiff by the educationalists.'

Perhaps it was a lack of patience for academia that led to Edith going on to art school. Her *Guardian* article goes on to describe her bus (in fact, *'bus* – the 'low slang' of the 1870s has, of course, now descended even lower with the fall of the apostrophe) adventures when she joined 'the St John's Wood Schools'. Then

I was allowed some 'bus money, but was expected to walk the two miles one way. At this time it was a point of honour never to stop a 'bus. I was expert at running, catching the back rail, springing on to the step, and being shoved in by the conductor. All 'buses had doors, which were opened and shut for each passenger.

I could see how the years of 'bus-jumping' had prepared ED for *stremas* and for hours in the saddle across the Accursed Mountains. I could also see how the suspiciously impudent swot from the Bedford School could transform herself into the no-nonsense traveller whose sense of duty had kept her going despite lumbago, rheumatism and sciatica, not to mention blackbeetles, in delivering aid to the refugees of Shkodra.

I went to visit the St John's Wood Schools, having found an address for it at Westminster's art reference library in an artists' yearbook of 1890. Although the address still exists, it houses a building obviously constructed after ED's time there. However, the Art Reference Library had also given me something perhaps more concrete than an address, in the biography of artist Byam Shaw by a fellow artist, Rex Cole. Both men were at the St John's Wood Schools at much the same time as ED. Rex Cole's memories paint a fierce picture of art school in Victorian London – more Gradgrind than Pre-Raphaelite.

Our task was to draw from the Antique for five and
a half days a week, from 10am to 5pm ... We drew
the casts in a set order. First, a fortnight was spent
in imitating the light and shade of a cup and ball
followed by a cast of ornament in high relief. Next
came six outlines and one finished drawing, of each of
the features. After these, drawings of hands and feet, a
mask, the head and bust and, finally, a cast of the whole
figure.

Perhaps this was the piecemeal approach which had prepared
ED's eye as I'd watched it in Gračanica where her gaze had
seemed to swing, interpret, leap from interesting image to
thought-provoking detail, like a hand-held camera.

**Old woman most hospitable. Hair in great plait on
each side of face doubled back so as to make solid block
which with a flat drapery on top of head gave odd
square Egyptian effect. Shirt sleeves most beautifully
embroidered. Short black frill petticoat and red apron.**

The woman's face is left a blank – one of the drawings in
outline only.

Cole's description of the St John's School curriculum continues,

**The big 'Antique' room was packed with girl and boy
students, with the usual sprinkling of elderly folk,
the girls outnumbering the boys by about ten to one.
Silence was the order, and we were given printed
rules for observation. One, I think, ran thus: 'Talking
between male and female students is not allowed except
in the rests, and then only on matters relating to art.'**

**Casts of the Hermes and Illyssus, Theseus, Venus,
Laocoon, The Gladiator, Faun and Discobolus were
relieved ... against a ... wall, wainscoted with wood of
darker tint. On this hung a row of plaster casts – masks,**

and the separate features of the face of Michaelangelo's
David, spaced by numerous busts set on pedestals.
Everyone in the crowd got some sort of a view of their
cast. One standing at an easel saw over the head of
another sitting on a 'Donkey' – that long and narrow
four-legged stool, the head-end of which had a rest for
the drawing-board

I imagined a younger, lighter, softer-featured Edith balancing
her drawing on the St John's Wood donkey, little knowing
what preparation it might be for the other drawings she was
to balance, under the curious scrutiny of the Turkish officer at
Deçan, on the balcony at Gračanica monastery, poked at by the
schoolmistresses on pilgrimage to Devič.

The library offered other insights. *The Year's Art* yearbooks
listed Mary Edith Durham with studios in New-Court, Carey
Street (1892), Abbey Road (1893), Great Russell Street (1896),
Avenue Road (1897), Queen's Road Studios (1900) and having
exhibited at the Royal Institute of Painters in Watercolours, the
Royal Academy, and the Institute of Painting in Oil Colour.

But then, in 1902, the yearbooks fall silent on the subject
of ME Durham. By this stage she had made her first trips to
the Balkans. Her art now wasn't focused on Royal Institutes or
Academies but on capturing the details of tribal dress in dashed-
off ink drawings, hurried to be completed before she was found
out, or aquarelle to try to represent the colours of new worlds,
where she was now training her eye far from Great Russell Street.
She doesn't appear again in *The Year's Art* until her death in 1944,
when she is flatteringly listed as 'world traveler and accomplished
artist'.

As well as these biographical details, *The Year's Art* of 1889 has
a fascinating, sobering account (in frustrating black and white,
painted only with adjectives) of the 'action of light on water

colours' describing colour exposed in May 1886, August 1886, and March 1888

Carmine gone by Aug '86
Scarlet Lake – pink gone, vermilion left
Olive green had blue gone in Aug '86
and gone brownish pink by March '88

We like to think of art as enduring, but actually time works its ravages even here, leaving us only coarse vermilion from the Scarlet Lake, and a distorted brownish pink in our olive groves. Maybe what ED was looking for in the Balkan quest she embarked on at the turn of the twentieth century was something that would outlive her. I believed that that's what she found.

29 Communicating with the dead

I felt I had travelled Edith's trail as far as I could – through her books and her unpublished prose, her photographs and drawings, her homes and the objects she brought back. I'd heard her voice, I'd read her handwriting; I'd touched the things she'd touched and I'd visited the places she'd seen.

There was only one way to bring her an inch closer to life, which would be to meet someone who had met her. The chance came in a truly Balkan fashion. Rob and I were leaving a hotel in Kosovo one day, already in the car, when I heard my name being called by someone entering the hotel. It was Ela, a girl I'd met a few times when I'd run training for teachers in Pristina, though we'd not kept in touch since. She was with a woman in her seventies. As I waved and our car pulled out, Ela called to me,

'This is Mrs Carola. Her father knew Edith Durham!'

I grinned excitedly through the glass, but we were already pulling away, and late for a meeting. As we raced through the streets beyond the hotel, I wondered who Carola was. Once we were back at a computer I found the contact details of the woman through whom I'd been engaged to train Ela and her fellow teachers. Was there any chance she could put me in contact with Ela?

She replied conscientiously, and I contacted Ela who also replied conscientiously, and before I knew it I was on the telephone with Carola Scupham, nee Braunholtz. 'Oh yes,' she said in the careful tones of the former Classics teacher that I later discovered she had been, 'My father was head of Ethnography at the British

Museum for many years, till he retired around 1952, and also President of the Anthropological Society. Miss Durham used to visit us regularly and was very friendly to my younger brother and myself'. I remembered the name Braunholtz – this was the man who had read the speech at the Royal Anthropological Institute on ED's eightieth birthday.

We exchanged emails and Carola gave me more information. ED had apparently made her a scrapbook of Albania, which Carola no longer had, but she said she still treasured some silver dress ornaments she'd been given by Miss Durham. I thought about the other artefacts I'd seen that ED had brought back to England that were now in various museum stores, and guessed that unlike those experiences, I wouldn't be asked to wear gloves before handling Carola's treasures; it was tantalising, and I asked Carola whether there was any possibility I could come and visit her on my next trip back from Kosovo, and hear her memories of Edith.

Carola lives in Hitchin, which is where a British friend of mine in Kosovo went to school. I mentioned that I would be visiting and my friend shared a little-known fact – that the town was twinned with Bingen in Germany which is in turn twinned with Prizren. Prizren's spit-sister doesn't seem to have much in common with the cobbled Ottoman centre of filigree though. Despite slithering through the town in the worst snow Britain had experienced in living memory, just like the snowstorm in which I had visited Father Ksenofont in Prizren, I couldn't see any other similarities between the two towns. Where Prizren had seen inter-ethnic violence and its market hosts women from the nearby mountains with those wooden-yoked skirts, Hitchin is – as Bingen's twinning guide describes it – a cheerful town straight out of Agatha Christie.

And it soon became obvious to me that the woman who opened the door to me down the side street had the sharp mind

of a Miss Marple. Not that Miss Marple would probably have ever worn a red and black Albania T-shirt, with double-headed eagle splaying its wings across her chest, but the playfulness of Carola Scupham appealed to me. This is the kind of woman who might set off on a walk on a hot day in a tam o'shanter. Like Edith, she was straight talking (she told me off repeatedly – and not without justification – for being so late in replying to emails) and her sitting room was 'bunged up' as ED had reported having left her sister's house, with mementoes from Balkan lands.

The classical education Carola had both received and many times given was evident in displays of pottery from Greece, but there were also familiar knitted Albanian sock slippers, hanging above the gas fire like elaborate Christmas stockings. In front of the fire was a rug I was sure was from Kosovo, with the blood red designs I knew from the Ethnological Museum and from old collections like those Fatmir had described to me from his home in Preshevo before it burned.

I asked what she could remember of the scrapbook ED had given her and she grinned. 'I was a child ...' she said apologetically. 'The thing I loved most was a picture of a handsome 1930s man with big shoes, stuck in from an advert! But there were pictures of folk dances and landscapes too.'

Then she got out her own scrapbooks, like the granddaughters of that missing Albanian scrapbook she had been given by ED, and showed me the story of her travels in Kosovo and other Balkan lands. It was like hearing a cover version of a favourite song – the places I was familiar with, the towns that Edith had trod, now presented through another woman's lens, with her own stories of hospitality, perfidious taxis, unfamiliar food, playing variations on a melody I could sing along to. There was the mention of the village where she and I had so fleetingly met, the Ethnological Museum I so loved, and Carola had even stuck in a postcard with the sketch of the museum which Rob had drawn. This was not just someone else telling Edith's story, but someone else telling my own.

When we'd eaten a late mince pie, Carola laid out the jewellery ED had given her. It consisted of a series of crude silver tin alloy pendants which had been threaded together. I was illogically jealous of them. To have been given them from Albania sixty years ago was a treat — a story — in itself. But to have been given them by Edith Durham ...

I hid my cupidity as most of us do, with a series of zoomed in photographs, showing every detail.

There was more, though. Carola had remembered that for Christmas 1942, when she was nine, ED had also given her a book, *The Insect Man*, about the life of the entomologist Fabre. She laid the book on the table in front of me. Inside the front cover, 79 year-old Edith (just a little older than Carola, sitting in front of me now) had cut out and shaded a butterfly, across whose wings she had written 'Carola Braunholtz from MED. Xmas 1942'. It was a sweet, thoughtful gift from an old lady, and despite what I knew of Edith's love of scrapbooking (from the albums I'd seen at the Bankfield, at the very beginning of our acquaintance, and those at the RAI) I was surprised at the care that had been taken.

'Oh yes,' said Carola. 'She was very good with children'.

This was new information for me. I had imagined that ED's impatience with stupidity would extend to frustration with minds not yet entirely logical, and I knew that her lack of sentimentality wouldn't inspire her to the mawkish romanticisation of children from that era of hair ribbons and Mabel Lucie Atwell. Then I remembered that of all the scathing description of her visit to the Turkish women's quarters by Sultan Murad's tomb her only approval had been saved for the children ('Awful pallid stout collopy females and a lot of children too. The children quite nice. The women terrible.'). And one of my favourite passages from *The Burden of the Balkans* had her describing a feisty four-year old boy who asked the gendarmes

for a 'fisik' (cartridge). This he solemnly wedged into the handle of the tongs, and, at the word of command, went down on one knee and brought his weapon smartly to his shoulder.

'Oganj bit!' ('Fire !') cried his grandfather, and the
child dropped flat behind a cushion and aimed at us
over the top.

Arsov, the local leader, had taught him this trick, and
he repeated it over and over again to the admiration of
the company. Even after we had ceased talking to him
he wandered round the room uncannily, and continued
to cover us with his weapon from different points of
vantage till the gendarme restored the 'fisik ' to his belt.

Poor little 'oganj bit'! His father had been shot, his
mother was quite destitute. I almost volunteered to take
him home with me.

She goes on,

But in the next village was a little girl who called me
'auntie' straight off and went to sleep in my lap, and I
nearly took her too ...

The Turks, she said, were very naughty people, and
had stolen her new red stockings and the little shirt
her mother had made her. Now she had to wear odd
stockings, and was very cross about it. If the Turks
came again she should hit them very hard.

The style of ED's description of the children doesn't differ
from the way she writes about others she met. I couldn't decide
whether this reflected a respectful treatment of children, refusing
to patronise them, or an infantilisation of all those other Balkan
adults she described with their funny ways. I wondered whether
Edith would have liked to have had children if it had been possible
on her terms. In a letter written on the subject of birth control
when she was in her sixties, she mused on the implications of
religious celibacy,

The best types both men and women with a high ideal
of duty and power of self control were the very ones
debarred from reproducing their kind.

I wondered whether there was a hint of regret for her own situation, and – entirely selfishly – I wished again that her genes had been perpetuated.

Having reached the limits of Carola's memories from 60 years before, we turned to her father's. Carola still had her father's diaries and we looked through them together. The writing was scholarly and difficult to read and the process was time-consuming, though fascinating, tumbling us into the Second World War home front. Carola offered to go through the diaries with more time when I'd gone, and send me what she found.

Shortly after my visit, she wrote to me with careful notes of the references to Miss Durham. Along with details of unexploded ordnance in Russell Square (I thought of the threat to those purple slippers from the British Museum's collection) and the RAI windows being broken by a bomb, and the one and a half pounds of runner beans he had harvested, HJ Braunholtz had noted Miss Durham coming to tea at the family's home in Harpenden, and in one case staying a couple of nights.

By 1941, amid 'air raids and gunfire all afternoon' Braunholtz had called on Miss Durham at the Hampstead Nursing Home in Belsize Grove. I hadn't known she had been ill there so long before she'd died.

The diary even included her phone number, 'Primrose 1457', like a paint colour chart reference. Evidently things had moved on in ED's communication since the 1928 letter I'd read from her to writer Joseph Swire – a letter which had given me a glimpse of what daily life was like for Edith in the final decades of her life, back in North London. It launched straight into something that was clearly bothering her deeply.

I hope you will never again commit such an
indiscretion as to ask the exchange to put you on
to a complete stranger in order to reach someone

else. Surely the fact that I am not in the telephone book should have been sufficient to prove I had not a telephone. I live in four small rooms at the top of this house. Some people called Barton have rooms below and have a telephone. As you must know when several people have apartments in the same house one must be most careful in no way to inconvenience ones neighbours. Some months ago an aged relative of mine broke down and is in a nursing home. He is in a state of senile dementia and is a great source of anxiety. Mrs Barton hearing of this very kindly said that I might give her telephone number to my sister and the nursing home in case of an emergency. Otherwise I have never given her number to anyone.

I keep no servant myself and just as I was cooking some lunch the Bartons servant came hammering at my door saying 'Be quick; I am afraid your bad news has come. They are calling you on our telephone.' The Bartons fortunately were out and the maid let me into their dining room … I was stunned by the impertinence of anyone using the Bartons telephone without their permission and felt what a fool I should look if they came in and found me using their instrument in their dining room. And how difficult it would be to make them understand that I was not guilty of giving the number … And meanwhile my lunch was getting cold at the top of the house.

I remembered Carola's comments on my own breach of the etiquette of long-distance communication. After a full typescript page of such recriminations, Edith gave Swire some paragraphs of the analysis of recent Balkan history he had asked for and then switched her tone abruptly in the final paragraph.

> **If I can assist you with your work I shall be glad to
> do so. Perhaps you would come here to tea one day?
> I cannot offer you much choice as I am about to have
> my sitting room papered and painted. ... Please let me
> know if [the date] will suit – and for goodness sake do
> not ring up the Bartons. Sincerely yours ...**

It's the letter of an aging woman, living on her own, with all the proud independence (the repapered sitting room and self-prepared lunch) of that situation. It's also a letter through which the basic urge to share knowledge and opinions can't quite be repressed despite suspecting bad manners in her correspondent.

Most significantly, it's a letter from an accomplished networker (perhaps not, yet, through the telephone lines, but making connections in every other way, whether with neighbours or cold callers wanting advice on Albanian history). I could understand how this woman could have continued as a welcome guest at the home of H J Braunholtz and his family right up to the end of her life.

The last entry in Carola's father's diary which references Edith is for her eightieth birthday, when Braunholtz was due to meet with Sir Edward Boyle (former acting British Commissioner to Serbia) at the Grosvenor Hotel 'to go to Miss Durham'.

Less than a year later, Miss Durham had died.

Carola and I continued an email correspondence. Our messages were enlivened by having met in person, but they still remained just words, or less than words – the pixels on my screen. I started to ask existential questions about how this differed from what I was reading of the words that Edith had written once, also at a time and place from which I was distanced. Of course, there was the knowledge that Carola could respond to me, even with delays, but there was also something significant about the fact that we had met in person. The lack of such face-to-face contact was the gap in my knowledge of Edith which I could never close, the space enabling all kinds of misunderstanding and omission. Emails with Carola were only a fragile substitute for bridging that gap with Edith.

'But what about her family?' she asked.

She was right; there was one other way in to Edith, a way that her genes might, in fact, have been perpetuated, that I had not yet explored.

30 Meeting the family

What *stremas* were to Edith, trains were to me in my tagging along behind her, a century later: it felt like every new Edith experience was bought with a small orange ticket from British Rail, and there was jolting 'something hideous' as the train pulled out from London on the line to Cambridge once again. I was back for a visit to England, and as we passed signs for Hitchin, where I had visited Carola, and for Ely – my own birthplace – I had the sense that I was going back through time, travelling along the sleepered coils of double helix DNA to find out where Edith had really come from: I was going to meet the family.

I had learned of surprisingly few descendants from the nine Durham children. I knew that Herbert hadn't had surviving children, from the obituary sent me by King's College Cambridge, and ED's letter to Nellie which I'd read at the RAI referred to 'the Hereford catastrophe' and 'I was so looking forward to a Durham baby' suggesting not only that there had been a miscarriage but that none of the other sons had had children. I had gathered that Arthur had died early, so that left only Frank to perpetuate the family name.

Even leaving aside the name-bearing Durham sons, the genes hadn't travelled as far as you might imagine, considering the six Durham daughters. From the mentions in ED's will where her sisters Florence and Frances Hermia were referred to with their maiden name it seemed that, like Edith, they had never married. But Nellie, of course, had married – because I knew that her husband, Godfrey Hickson, had been the recipient of the filigree pipes from Prizren. And ED's will mentioned a niece and nephew surnamed Hickson. They would now be dead, of course, but perhaps they had had children?

The Royal Anthropological Institute had helped me here with the details of James Hickson, a don at Pembroke College, Cambridge, now in his seventies, and ED's great-nephew, known to the RAI because he is also ED's literary executor. I hoped he might have the memories, papers, or photographs which could plug some of the gaps I still had in this incomplete picture of Edith.

He was welcoming by email, and so it was that I was sat on the train on my way to see him and some of his great aunt's 'papers' he had vaguely mentioned. As the train hared across the flat fenland, like a ruler laid across an exercise book, I made notes of the questions I had for James.

There was factual information I hoped he could help with – the lacunae in the family tree I had drafted, where because the census results from beyond 1911 were not yet public, I had lost some trails or tendrils. I wanted to know what other survivors there were from Arthur and Mary Durham's line; who was Joan Durham Trethowan, referred to in the will, and how was she related to Edith? Who was Mr Sharon Turner, one of the beneficiaries of ED's father's will?

And then I was curious about some more subjective information about Edith herself. I couldn't decide where she lay on the scale of quixotic to ruthless. Her no-nonsense attitude of not suffering fools gladly could be played as a Lady Bracknell, breaking up the trophy-hunters among the Montenegrins with a brolly, and we love to hear stories of doughty daughters of Empire uncompromising and fearless in foreign lands. But how to reconcile her sharp tongue with the obvious compassion which led to her going to unnecessary lengths to offer humanitarian aid in Albania and Macedonia, and then during the First World War in the Pyrenees and in Egypt. She was someone with a fairly sturdy sense of herself and her own importance yet the quality of her books depends on being a good listener, a silent observer, the stenographer of proceedings, not the presiding judge. If you met her, which of these characteristics would be most evident?

Arriving at James' house, he made me a pot of unpronounceable tea he had brought back from a recent trip to China.

'I'll help as much as I can with what I know of Aunt Dick,' he said, and then paused as if he'd said something rude. I smiled – I knew this family nickname from her letters to Nellie. But it put me in a difficult position, as I had been with Carola on my visit there. When she had talked of 'Miss Durham' and I had responded with 'Edith' it sounded like I was being disrespectful, or that I was trying to claim greater acquaintance. For goodness' sake, she was the one who had met the woman. But now I couldn't bring myself to say 'Aunt Dick'. It sounded stupid, and even James seemed to get self-conscious about it after a while. Occasionally I referred to 'Edith' but most of the time we both lapsed into 'she' in our discussion. It was already confusing enough that Edith had two names. She was fierce about them – I'd seen the letter to the Society for Constructive Birth Control where she'd barked

please ask the secretary to fill in my membership card correctly. As I write and publish a good deal I much dislike my name being wrongly quoted. I am NOT Edith M Durham but yours sincerely M Edith Durham.

Edith had many more names than I'd realised.

Then he began his story. It was a narrative of which I knew only the middle section – I was ignorant of ED's (and James') ancestors, and I was ignorant of the generations who'd come after her. James explained the long-term friendship of the Durham and Hickson families, going back at least to ED's grandfather's generation when some of the Hicksons were boarders at 'Grandpa Durham's school', and that it had been at the Hicksons' home that ED's parents had met. I tried taking notes and keeping track of the generations in the story but my carefully inked-out family tree was getting tangled. I wondered how I would ever understand the linkages between the families, the family names which recurred in each generation … and I still didn't understand where Trethowan had come from.

'Well, maybe this will help'. James showed me a pile of books. One of them was the Cambridge Natural History reptile volume which ED had illustrated competently. Underneath were signed copies of her books, complete with marginalia (ED's distinctive hand grumbling in pencil alongside the printed text of her own narration of the history of the Great Powers' interference in the Balkans – 'what gulls we were': an old lady looking for a fight with anyone who would listen and in the absence of other correspondents, with her younger self). I handled them respectfully, but I couldn't see that this pile was really going to help with the questions I had.

Under these, at the bottom of the pile of books, was a hardback notebook with a moiréed cover. The cover had a wafer of paper cut in the shape of a shield on the front – the same scrapbooking technique which had given Carola's book its 1942 Christmas inscription on a cut-out butterfly. The paper was the same austerity quality and was lettered in ED's own hand dating the front cover one year later than Carola's book. What had the old lady produced now? Might it help me with my outstanding questions?

The book was titled 'A family history; Fatio, de Vesian, Durham and Hickson Compiled by MEDurham 1943'. Opening it greedily I leafed through the pages, finding a family tree, narrated family anecdotes, the reasons for the names given to each of the Durham children ('I was named after Mother and Grandmother

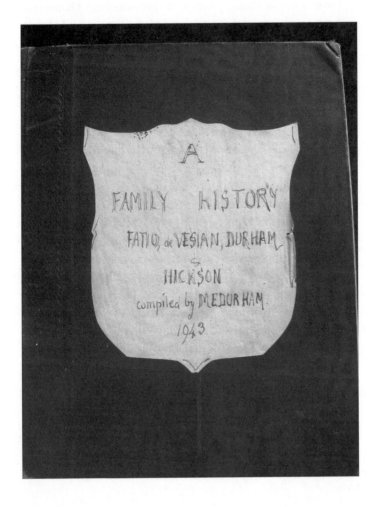

A

FAMILY HISTORY

FATIO, de VESIAN, DURHAM
&
HICKSON
compiled by M.E.DURHAM.
1943

Mary, Edith a name then popularised by Lytton's novel *Harold*'),
descriptions of homes and grandparents, political views and
academic achievements. Edith might as well have written me a
letter, saying 'Dear Elizabeth, I heard you needed some additional
help for your book and I hope that the attached is useful'. I
couldn't believe my luck.

I read avidly, bemusing James with my excitement. He hovered
– in the familiar role of curator-turned-medium – while I took
notes on my laptop. I lost track of time, looking up occasionally
in disorientation. The clock on my computer was still on Kosovan
time, so I was used to the sudden squeeze around the heart when
I was in England and checking the time, thinking I had lost an
hour. The computer clock was one of the many small signs of
returning home, when I got back to Kosovo and found myself
truly in the right time zone once again. But this dislocation was
more significant than that – not just one hour out of joint, but
surfacing from the twentieth century, and even further, thanks
to the histories ED was relating, to the present century, when I
would look about me in confusion before I returned to her story.

A full family tree had been drawn by ED and updated in biro
by someone since, and I copied it down in its entirety. There
was my story, reduced to a neat diagram; family trees are blunt,
wooden things, with no space for subtlety. There, next to the neat
number (1) as the first issue of the marriage of Arthur and Mary,
hung Mary Edith Durham. I was interested to see that she had
characterised herself as 'author and traveller'. The second part of
the description was a bold claim, since she hadn't been back to
Albania since 1921, and as far as I had discovered, her travelling
(apart from more typical Hampstead lady holidays in Italy etc)
had only begun in 1900. Roughly forty years of (albeit enforced)
stay-at-home, followed by twenty years of regular and wonderful
travel, followed by another twenty years in north London – I
wondered how much ED's descriptions were wishful thinking.

But as I well knew: if you are writing the history, you get to decide on the adjectives.

Beyond the diagram was the prose, and it seemed that in this unpublished book all ED's anthropological skills had been turned on her own family. I had winced at the implied distance, power dynamic, the treating of foreign peoples as specimens, implied in writing such as this in *High Albania*:

> The characteristics of the small, dark type are: …
> eyebrows level, often nearly or quite meeting over
> the nose, which is usually short and straight, maybe
> slightly aquiline, but never has the long, drooping point
> characteristic of the fair type of Maltsia e madhe, and
> the fair people of Montenegro, Bosnia, and Central
> and South Albania. … there is often a distinct trace
> of hair along the temporal bone to the outer end of
> the eyebrow. This small, dark Albanian type differs
> markedly from the large, dark type of Montenegro, in
> which the skull is extremely wide at the temples and cut
> straight off at the back

But in this manuscript ED turned on her own family exactly the same cold scientific eye for unflinching physiognomical detail, the reduction of people to their skull-shape, which is so uncomfortable for a post-Hitlerian audience. Each genetic strand (Fatio, de Vesian, Durham and Hickson) was concluded with a section headed 'Physical peculiarities'. For example,

> All the men of the Durham family so far as I knew
> them, were tall – over 6 ft. Frank Sheppard was 6 ft 3
> inches. Lean and bony, loosely built. Hair brown; in
> most cases dark brown and did not turn white. Old
> Grandpa Edward Durham was extremely active up to
> a great age. His hair remained thick and had hardly
> turned more than 'pepper and salt' when he died in his
> 91st year.

I (Mary Edith), Herbert Edward and Alice Lilian
took after our mother and inherited one of her
peculiarities, a projecting upper incisor. In respect of
hair we all resemble my father's family in as much as
none have gone white. Whereas in my mother's family
was a tendency to whiten young and become quite
white.

She drew some conclusions – perhaps the final commentary
on the embarrassingly naïve enterprise she had embarked on forty
years previously, and from which so much important work had
come, an enterprise contextualised by her thus: 'It occurred to
me that the vexed question of Balkan politics might be solved by
studying the manners and customs of each district and so learning
to whom each place should really belong'. In the summary to
her family history notebook she wrote

Few families can trace their mixed origins in such
detail. It is a good example of how futile it is to talk of
'pure races'. That a 'pure race' exists anywhere is in the
highest degree improbable. In England which has been
for centuries the home of refugees the population is
very mixed.

She concludes with a fair summary of the family, which also
hints at some of the values she prized,

The history is a fine one. A record of honest struggle
and much intelligence. A refusal to submit to
oppression and a power to suffer for conscience sake.
… On the Durham side there are no distinguished
ancestors but it is a record of small lives honestly lived.

As he watched me reading, James filled out some detail. Did
I know about the surgical implement invented by ED's father?
He suggested I read the Guy's biography of Arthur Durham,
which subsequently offered a rather odd, wriggly picture of
A Durham FRCS – 'he particularly excelled in operations for

rectovaginal fistula, harelip, lithotomy, and abdominal surgery. His remarkably long fingers, that seemed to have eyes in their tips, his flexible wrist and sinuous movements of the hand made him powerful, searching, and graceful in all his manipulations, while his invention of the lobster-tail tracheotomy tube has proved of great value.'

James also mentioned bits of family lore that couldn't be found in anyone's biography. We discussed the Montenegrin exhibition which ED had helped to curate in 1907 and James told me the family story of how the delegation from the exhibition came to Ellerdale Road (I remembered my own visit there; the boys trampolining in the garden and Marianne Faithfull played to me). I wondered what they'd made of it. James said his father would have been about five years old at the time but that what he remembered was the visitors' great admiration for the bathroom mirror and taps.

I remembered ED's comments in *Through the Lands of the Serb* on her offer of marriage which an intermediary was attempting to negotiate with her. He'd said

ces Messieurs **don't mind where they live; they will leave the Servian army and live in England – or America. Perhaps Mademoiselle lives with her father and mother? They wouldn't mind that at all.**

She remarks in the book, 'The idea of 'them' – for it seemed 'they' had to be taken wholesale – arriving at my suburban residence was too much for me'. I wondered how she had handled it when one day some of 'them' really did turn up, bursting into the family bathroom to wonder at the plumbing arrangements.

James told me that for a long time Edith had not got on with her sister Caroline and I did some more research about Caroline and her husband, with whom I knew I should have been more familiar, having heard him referred to as 'the great geneticist Bateson'. From my reading I realised I really should have known more. Given ED's fascination with skull shapes and inherited hair colour, I would have thought that she and Bateson would have had much in common as I learned that it was he who coined the word 'genetics' and was a key populariser of the work of Mendel – even naming his son Gregory, in what was presumably homage. Gregory himself went on to a noted career in cross-disciplinary work, including anthropology, and married anthropologist Margaret Mead. I imagined ED would have enjoyed having her nephew and his clever wife to dinner to discuss tribal adventures – though the way Mead's accounts of Papua New Guinean sexual relations were used to inform the 1960s sexual revolution, and her ethnological field research into breastfeeding which was taken up by her paediatrician, Benjamin Spock, seem a long way from ED's careful watercolours and notes of bloodfeuds.

The Bateson family history that I read was brilliant but very sad – Gregory's brother (Caroline's eldest son and ED's nephew) having earned a Military Cross was killed in the First World War only a month before the Armistice. The second brother, Martin, apparently argued with his father over his ambition to become a poet and playwright, and the resulting stress, when combined with a disappointment in love, led to him shooting himself in Piccadilly Circus on the birthday of his older brother. The event is noted in ED's family tree without euphemism or elaboration: 'killed himself'.

The sister who was more important than Caroline to both James and me, was sister Nellie, and it was as I sat at James' fine dining table – strewn with a feast of documents – that I was introduced to her. She was important to James because she was his grandmother; for me her significance was in the fact that it was she who had been the correspondent who accompanied ED (in one case literally, on the Montenegro journey of 1902) around the Balkans. The letters to Nellie seemed to have been rehearsals, often differing in no more than the occasional word choice, for what became the published accounts of ED's journeys. It suggested closeness, and of all of ED's siblings, it would have been Nellie that I would have wanted to have met.

As we talked about her, James nodded casually: 'That's her,' and the woman smiling down at me suddenly became more than a portrait. The larger-than-lifesize painting was hanging right opposite me, a sweet-faced girlish study. She was softer, more fragile than Edith, though the distinctive long, straight, determined nose which both girls shared with their father was still in evidence.

The other sister I'd had a particular interest in was Hermia. I knew from the Dictionary of National Biography that she'd been awarded the CBE for her work in the First World War in organising women's services in the army, munitions and agriculture, and that she was the first president of the council of women civil servants – though none of this featured in ED's potted biography. Instead, I got potted crabs – in 1873, when ED was 10

Hermia was named because I was an eager student of marine creatures – kept sea water aquariums and specially cherished hermit crabs. My entreaties that the baby 'the little crab' should be called Hermia were granted. She was born at the sea-side – Aldwick near Bognor – and I had a large collection of hermit and other crabs!

Along with the brothers and sisters, there was more about Edith's grandfather, William Ellis. I knew as well as anyone, that the information chosen to reveal someone in a biography tell you at least as much about the biographer as about their subject. It seemed relevant that Edith chose to include details of her grandfather such as that he taught by 'the Socratic method, leading his pupils by questions to arrive at conclusions' (I thought of her endless questions in the course of anthropological study), and that he had 'a keen sense of humour; was witty and could be sarcastic.'

Another element in the William Ellis story answered my final question – learning that his wife's father was Sharon Turner – the name I had seen in ED's father's will. Presumably the legatee was a descendant of this Sharon Turner (who was two generations older than ED's father), but having been drawn by the name I learned that while researching for a book in the British Museum, Turner made the acquaintance of Isaac Disraeli 'with whom he became fast friends and it was owing to the influence of Sharon Turner [ED's great-grandfather] that Benjamin Disraeli was baptised'. Indeed, you never know whom you'll meet when you start researching a book. I put away ED's manuscript and smiled up at James. He had been extremely generous in sharing his family with me and I wished that I had some way to thank him. When he brought out of an envelope the final image he had to share with me from his archives, I realised that maybe there was one thing I could give him that he'd appreciate. The image was an original print which I recognised because it had been used as the basis for the ED stamp in Kosovo. Opening my bag I brought out for him a miniature version of the drawing, on sticky paper overprinted with a '1€'. I handed James the light wafer reverently, as if it should be accompanied by communion wine.

He hadn't heard about the Kosovan stamp and fingered it with genuine interest. At least I'd been able to bring a little bit of Edith back to her family from Pristina.

He said regretfully. 'You had some other questions about what she was like as a woman. I can't help with those as I have no memories of her, but one member of the family had strong personal memories …'

I held my breath, pencil hovering over the questions I'd jotted 'how quixotic vs ruthless was she?', 'how far did she romanticise/

patronise the Albanians when she was back in London?', 'what was her relationship with her mother?'

James continued, '... but Anne died 18 months ago'.

It was a fitting foil to my extraordinary luck in being offered the family history notebook to read. And it was a lesson; ruthless Edith's voice admonished me – 'if you had only got on with your research a little quicker'. I remembered the letter Edith had written to a woman she had met at a public meeting and who had then asked her for some information on her grandfather. Edith had followed up the discussion by letter though regretting that she had none of her grandfather's papers which he had burned shortly before his death, and reminded her correspondent that at the meeting where they had spoken to one another she had lent her a light with the comment, 'I was able to lend you an electric torch I am sorry I cannot throw more light on the past!'.

Some things can be salvaged – some things can be written and diagrammatised neatly in moiréed notebooks, passed on by bequest to nephews and their sons for safe keeping. But other memories live only in the wormholes of our intricate minds, chance recollections, images triggered by a particular perfume or a strain of music, mental geography which is lived in three dimensions and five senses and can't be captured or retrieved except by direct contact. Anne had been 17 when ED died; older than Carola had been when she'd met ED, old enough to make judgements, to wonder, to compare. And she, unlike Carola, would presumably have visited ED at home and could have told me whether the rooms were stuffed with her imported treasures. Did the house have the smells and the goathair scratchiness of her Albanian travels? Did she take her shoes off at the door?

But I was too late. Anne was dead, and with her died the last memory of Miss Durham's sitting room, of what it was like to kiss Edith hello, of what kind of food she would have served, of how she held herself in a chair, whether she listened, or whether she talked too much; whether the head tilted back in an open-mouthed laugh which I had seen captured in one photograph was a characteristic pose of joie de vivre or a one-off glimpse of something that usually sat below the surface. All that were left now were the two dimensions – fragile documents, and pencil markings in the margins of history books; the tappings at my own computer keyboard.

$\mathscr{31}$ Meeting the family II

Getting off the train at the tiny Devon station I did a double take. I recognised the man standing ready to meet me … At least I half recognised him, or recognised half of him – this was Paul Hickson, James' brother. Now that I'd met a living member of Edith's family, the Durham/ Hickson genes were imprinted in my memory, where I'd worked away at them, trying to retro-engineer what a woman who shared some of them two generations previously might have looked like.

In fact, I had remarkably few images of Edith to help me – from 80 years of growth and illness, travel and experimental haircuts, I had seen only five images. One of them was the Seymour Lucas drawing reproduced on the Kosovan stamp, and I never trusted drawings. It shows what could be a handsome young man in profile, with short hair and Byronic collar. It was dated 1904, when Edith was 41 but she looks much younger – and I trusted the drawing all the less for that.

Another image – as I'd seen on the Wikipedia page – is a photograph from 1886, when Edith was 23. Here her collar is just as full and lacy, but the photograph was taken before she had cut her hair, and she sits with flowing pre-Raphaelite locks and a conventional print dress pinned with brooches, against a background of what could be rhododendron leaves. This is the model of a slim, demure and rather beautiful Victorian daughter with what you could fancy to be an evaluative distance in her steady gaze and perhaps a secret smile; maybe she was thinking of somewhere else at the time.

The next picture I knew was undated but the hair was short, and the jowls filled out from that young lovely in the suburban Victorian garden. There is no romanticism in this picture and this is the image I had most carried in my head of Edith in the Balkans. She is determined, no-nonsense, but still staring out beyond the picture and still with something of the Mona Lisa about her mouth.

I knew only two other pictures of her, one showing her in conversation in the field, where she seems to be roaring with laughter; the other more serious, doing war relief work in northern Albania in 1913. She is positively stout now, and bundled on a fine white horse like a sack of potatoes topped with a tam o'shanter. She isn't looking at the camera, and her face is in shadow so it's difficult to get a sense of her, other than her physical discomfort (probably nothing to the feelings of the beautiful mare carrying her).

That's it – five images. Imagine only five pictures – and two men, now in their seventies – being all that was left of the shape of your face, the glint of your laugh, the sculpting of muscle and fat at your form over eighty years. And you don't even get to choose which five pictures they are that will be left – the Seymour Lucas drawing was no doubt one that she commissioned and chose to sit for and keep. Likewise, my favourite, though less flattering studio portrait was obviously one that she sat for. But the chance photos of her in conversation or on horseback (probably while she was calculating how much quinine was left in their stores, and dividing by the number of villages she would be visiting that day, and the likely rates of malaria she would encounter) are possibly not even ones she liked.

These are the really cruel ravages of time – not just what it does to your jowls and your waistline, but its vicious acts of random violence in editing the memories and traces you leave behind.

The man whose nose may have shared the line of Edith's, who may also have inherited her projecting upper incisor, and who knows what habits of mind … this man, Paul Hickson, came forward to greet me. He was with his wife, Alison, and together they walked me through the village to their home.

None of us was quite sure why I was making this journey. After my day with James Hickson in Cambridge, with its discoveries and its frustrations, James had suggested I could get in touch with his brother who was the executor of ED's niece, Anne. 'He may have her papers and may be able to tell you any stories Anne remembered of Aunt Dick before she died,' he said. It turned out that Paul lived in Devon, and lay roughly on the route I'd travel from our house in Cornwall up to Gatwick to fly back to Kosovo, so by email I had politely asked whether it might be possible to drop in, and Paul and Alison had politely agreed that I might.

These were fine threads I was catching at – old memories, dead people – with the Hicksons, as with Carola, but they seemed to be the only people who might be able to share some first-hand memories of ED. I told Paul and Alison about Carola, and it turned out that the Hicksons had lived in Hitchin themselves. I wondered again about what Balkan leylines ran through this small town.

As Alison settled me with a glass of water she said, 'I don't think that we'll have anything of interest.'

It was obvious she was being modest, as she gestured at an ornate flintlock,

'This is a gun which Edith wrestled off a man on a train from Zagreb'. She then got out a heavy turquoise and amethyst cross which was one more of the chance survivors of ED's travels. She explained that the cross had been brought back from Albania and had been among Anne's possessions.

'When she died we looked all through her belongings for this, but we couldn't find it. In the end we gave up, and we brought in a firm of house-clearers to take away all the furniture we weren't keeping. I was downstairs as they were carrying out the furniture and one of them came to me and asked me whether I knew that the desk had a secret drawer stuffed with jewellery. That's where we found this.' The cross, like a symbol of honesty and selflessness, lay on the side. So this is what I had travelled to Devon for.

I smiled brightly. 'And did Anne leave any information about Edith in her papers?'

Alison and Paul rolled their eyes ever so slightly at one another.

'Anne was very passionate about her family history research towards the end of her life. She'd been a librarian and she spent a lot of time cataloguing everything to do with her father's family and following up leads. Whenever we went to visit her she'd want to tell us about her latest find. But I'm afraid we didn't really pay much attention – after a while you just stop listening.'

I felt a new pang of sadness for Anne's death. If only ... If only I'd got in touch with the family at the beginning of my research; if only I'd been able to visit Anne while she was still alive and could have let her ramble on as long as she wanted about her memories and discoveries of Frank and her aunts and uncles.

I heard a little about the life of this woman who had cared about some of the same things as I did: after the death of her father, Anne had apparently lived with her sick mother to look after her. Her painstaking interest in Edith made sense; I knew how inspiring it could be to follow the footsteps of someone who seemed to have dealt with the same challenges you faced yourself, and triumphed over them. If Anne hadn't negotiated two months away each year from her mother's sickbed like Edith had eventually managed to do, perhaps the scrapbook Alison passed me now was her substitute, travelling back in time rather than out across wild Europe.

While Edith had been the collector, Anne was her curator. Librarians know a lot about what you leave behind at death, and

Anne had set out the information she had gathered clearly and conscientiously in a file bulging with photocopies and print outs.

'I'm really not sure it's all relevant,' Alison said apologetically, as I started leafing through. It was wonderfully thorough – much information about Edith that I knew, but also detailed biographies of her brothers and sisters, letters of enquiry to the schools they'd been to and the places they'd worked, along with newspaper clippings of tangential relevance. I learned that sisters Hermia and Florence had lived together in Devon until Hermia's death, that Florence (whom I also learned was nicknamed 'Coo', like a dove) had died five years after Edith, of a heart attack on the steps of the National Gallery (I imagined the scene, the panic, the littleness of life amid the gallery's timeless beauty and the screech of Trafalgar Square's motor cars; a spirit taking flight like a pigeon lifting up, up, up the steps, beyond the Caravaggios and Velasquez, leaving the Botticellis and Rubens flesh behind, lighter even than Seurat's dots now, suspended in a shimmering stratosphere, the heaven of the Wilton Diptych, all gilt stars and azure, with Renaissance cherubim in the clouds, and maybe – who knows – her family gathered to greet her). She was cremated among the columbaria of Golders Green.

I found the same census information I had pored through – its stark summaries and occasional inaccuracies (when sister Alice's details were recorded, her mother Mary's name was given as 'Emry' – the Albanian word for 'name'). I flipped the pages, watched with curiosity by both Paul and Alison. A particularly heavy page flopped back, and with a skipped heartbeat I saw that it held a glued-on sepia family photograph. Looking more closely I had once again the half-sense of recognition I had had on seeing Paul at the station. I knew this picture – or I knew something just like it. But bigger. And in reverse.

Sure enough, the image revealed itself to be the photograph from which the familiar picture of 'pre-Raphaelite' Edith had been taken. There she was by the rhododendron bush, in the same dress, the same pose – but now revealed around her were the rest of her family. And she was not sitting on the left of the picture, staring ahead of her to the right, but sitting on the right of the picture, staring ahead to the left. It was a small metaphor for the dangers of research – I had had just one part of a much bigger picture, and up till now I'd seen only a mirror image of the truth.

All the stories that had spilled out of the pages of the moiréed notebook in James' dining room and before, now had an illustration to go with them. Here was Herbert, whose will had established the fund which had later enabled the trip to Kosovo of Cambridge student, Neil Robinson, whose trail I had followed along with his widow and daughters. Herbert was shown wearing a rakish cap. Here was Nellie, ED's confidante, looking rather worried and clutching a book. The young woman to her left is marked as 'Bee' (my own family nickname), presumably Caroline Beatrice, who went on to marry Bateson and lose two of her three sons to war and suicide. Looking at her here, all puppy fat, with a tam o'shanter gripped in her hand, I didn't like to whisper to her of the tragedy that lay ahead. Hermia, the future CBE, looked suitably solemn, next to the other siblings, and in the midst of them all, round-faced, smiling and plain, sat the woman who had given birth to this varied brood, comfortably hunched over herself. I wondered about her – the woman whose illness had so blighted her eldest daughter's life that she had had to take off to the other end of Europe to recover; the woman to whom Edith had dedicated her first book, the woman who, with nine such high-achieving, fearsomely bright children, must have been quick of mind and bold of spirit herself – the woman who was the daughter of educator and philanthropist William Ellis. But she gave no clue of any of this.

The picture fleshed Edith out – no longer alone in reverie, she could be seen now as part of a group. I could even see what the Wikipedia image had cropped – that she, like Caroline 'Bee' was holding in her hands a tam o'shanter.

'This is really exciting,' I told Paul and Alison, explaining just how few images I'd seen of ED.

'Oh, if you're interested in photographs then maybe it's worth getting the others down from upstairs,' said Alison. I tried to sound casual, and failed.

'That would be wonderful!'

The extent of the Durham girls' fascination with tam o'shanters was soon made clear in the envelope of photographs Alison brought down. Here was another photograph with the Durham sisters in elegant dark dresses and snowy collars. Florence and Caroline both wear black tam o'shanters – ridiculous berets with a prominent bobble on the top, which quite undercuts their classy evening wear. In a subsequent photo, it is Edith and Lilla wearing the hats, which were clearly considered suitable for all occasions, and perhaps proof against everything, as ED had said of wearing it in Kosovo,

I was the only one of the party who did not require sun protection and gave my umbrella to Radovan who was on foot and hot. I found my tam o'shanter quite sufficient and was surprised at my companions.

This tam o'shanter photograph brought to life another character from Edith's letters. This picture, too, was neatly labeled, and 'Dora' was shown to be an attractive, smiling, sensible-looking woman sitting on a wall. Exactly the sort of person you'd want minding your flat while you were in Albania – which is what I had gathered Dora was doing in 1908, from the letter from ED to Nellie at the RAI where she mentions Mrs Childs' teeth

Mrs Childs must certainly go if she has been making scenes. Neither Jenny nor Dora gave me any hint in their letters – or at any rate none that I understood. … I really was an ass to take the flat but – as you

know – I was cornered with the Exhibition and did not know what to do. I couldn't plant myself on you and had nearly decided to go to a hotel and then I saw Dora looked so ill and everyone seemed to think being alone down at Shere [?] was wretched for her and I had promised Mama to try and look after both her and Turkey.

And your house was all bunged up with my things. But as soon as I had signed the agreement I felt I had tied a stone round my neck.

… Ever since I got out here I have been cursing the flat. My only consolation was that it might be a happy home for D and T.'

I mentioned this letter to Paul and Alison. 'So this is Dora at last,' I said. 'But who was Turkey?'

Alison went out of the room again and came back with a small painting of an orchard.

'Paul's mother said that the family had always assumed that this was painted by Edith's girlfriend', she said. The painting was clearly signed, 'Isabel McTurk'.

At last, perhaps, I'd turned up something concrete about Edith's love life? But subsequent googling, and examining of the census for 1901 and 1911 gave me no hint of any more information about Isabel McTurk, or whether she knew Edith, and if so, in what capacity, and whether she had house-sat for her in King Henry's Road.

As well as the group photographs there were single portraits of each of the girls at various times, all softened by youth and old camera lenses and printing, each a theme and variation on the same determined nose, each neck hung round with a demure pearl necklace, of various lengths and subtle differences in the way it hung as if it was the essential DNA varying in each girl by choice or chance, nature or nurture.

There were other holiday photographs of the family together, marked as from stays in Wales, Lyme Regis and the Isle of Wight – while the girls assumed more or less whimsical stances. Edith always seems composed, smiling carefully, perhaps a little removed. This was the sight that had so eluded me at the British Museum, among the photographs taken *by* her where not a single image was taken to represent her. Around her, like props in the story I'd been following, the other members of the family assembled themselves in varying poses. Dora carried an ancient tennis racket, Punna and Carlo, the dogs, wandered on and off Lilla's lap; in most, 'Mater' sat smiling pleasantly if rather distractedly, and looking straight at the camera.

There was just one image where Mater is caught as if in mid-conversation. Her husband is turned towards her with a smile, and she looks like she's answering him. Well, I guess they managed to produce nine children – they must have had at least a few quiet moments smiling at each other through his big Victorian beard. That look and smile between this Victorian husband and wife may have been the precise starting point for the long and extraordinary life I had been following. I grinned back at them.

32 Full of purpose

Journeys have destinations, and there's an obvious end point for a biography. In this case, it was the missed teatime appointment with Beatrice Blackwood of the Pitt Rivers Museum on 15 November 1944. The Queen of the Mountain People escaping once again from the restrictions of Hampstead, liberated to roam the mountains; now free in time as well as space.

I ordered her death certificate online and held the surprisingly intimate official chit. Cause of death was coronary artery disease. It was a surprise to me, as much as it perhaps was to her. The year before her death she had compiled a list of 'cause of death in members of the Durham line, as far as known'. It was a scientific approach to what may be a growing preoccupation for an 80 year old. The family is laid out as in doctor's notes – the prose a sad corollary to the family photograph I had seen at Paul Hickson's house; her father's chest, under that double-breasted jacket covering the lungs that would eventually fill with liquid and drown him, like his father before him, in pneumonia; the strokes, tuberculosis, diphtheria, and the sad end of uncle Frederic, who had lurked in the shadows of one of the pictures I'd seen, and whose 'senile decay ended in dementia and suicide' (he had thrown himself out of a window. I presume this is the elderly relative whom ED mentioned being 'a great source of anxiety', in her letter to Joseph Swire).

Nellie, the sister who seemed to have been the closest, whose correspondence from Edith had turned itself into more than one book (and to whom *High Albania* had been dedicated) had died of a 'ruptured blood vessel' in the heart, but otherwise, there seemed to be no family history that would prepare Edith, the family historian, for that squeezing pain that would presage oblivion.

Of course, as ED had written at the close of *High Albania*, 'I cannot write FINIS'; that wasn't the end. There was a household of 'effects' (the word suggests that the nicknacks with which we surround ourselves are somehow brought into being by us – that if they are our effects, we are their causes), and beyond that her family, and thousands of other families, whose names she probably didn't even know, who were, together with their descendants, now living because they'd been saved from famine and disease by her work. These were truly her effects.

There was also the treasure trail she had left in museum storehouses from London to Halifax, wolves' teeth and hens' claws wrapped in tissue paper, and guns laid to rest in the safehouses of university towns. As rivers flow and silt up, lay down sediment and throw up spray, the current of her collections moved items slowly around Europe – from mountain villages and refugee columns, the workshops and bazaars of Ottoman towns, into saddlebags and packing crates, travelling trunks and the holds of vast ships, up the Adriatic and in the guard's van of international trains to rest in a parlour in north London, before travelling on to professors and curators, to great-nephews and friends' children now grown up, grown old, and retired in sidestreets.

But what of the other river she had navigated and sailed upon; the river that had eventually been dammed and burst its banks. What of her body? The complete absence of any UK memorial to ED's life was paralleled by the silence I'd been met with in trying to find out about what happened to her body after her death. Her will had specified that her body was to be cremated and the ashes scattered, but I wanted to know where. And I remembered someone who ought to be able to help me.

Robert Elsie is from Vancouver and now an expert on Albanian, living in the Hague where he works as an interpreter for the International Criminal Tribunal for the former Yugoslavia (ICTY). Paid to be the accurate mouthpiece of war criminals by day, by night Robert collects and publishes Albanian folklore. Somewhere in between it was inevitable that he would develop a detailed knowledge of Edith Durham; I emailed him, the Englishwoman sending a small pulse of electricity from Pristina to the Canadian in the Netherlands about the extraordinary eighty-year-old's long-dead body. These, too, were her effects.

Robert replied quickly and with information: ED had been cremated at Golders Green crematorium (as I remembered learning her sister, Florence, had been).

If this had been the last step of her journeys I felt I should go and visit, but I wasn't enthusiastic about the trip. I had only been to this crematorium once before, a few months before I set off for Kosovo for the first time. It had been for a memorial service on the untimely death of Maureen, a neighbour and friend. I had read one of my poems at the service, and barely got through the lines, such were my gouts and gobbets of grief. I had only the haziest of memories of the 1930s buildings and the municipally-moderated environment of commemoration.

The size of the complex is striking – the scale of the lives, and deaths, of North London in the century since it was opened takes one aback. When ED's stout, raddled body had been taken there the setting would have been only 5 years old. The names marked in the book of remembrance for that time were all Anglo-Saxon; now the plaques shaded by recent flowers were accompanied by the Star of David, by Buddhist symbols, or the names themselves showed South East Asian heritage. I saw no Albanian names, but in the multicultural mix there must have been some.

Among the hundreds of thousands of ordinary Londoners cremated here; along with Maureen, were a dazzling cast of other thought-provoking names. I tried to imagine them on Judgement Day in conversation – Sigmund Freud and Sid James (probably talking about breasts), Joyce Grenfell giving Ivor Novello a piece of her mind, Edwin Lutyens and Erno Goldfinger assessing the memorials, Anna Pavlova pirouetting while Ronnie Scott riffed and Joe Orton scowled at them both. And Edith? And Edith?

I was looking for some trace, some connection with Edith. There was no reference to her in the memorial book, and the seventy years that had passed since her old body was carried through these gateways suddenly seemed a yawning gap. What trace could I expect there to be of an event so long ago? I went to the crematorium office to ask for help and the young woman there said she could go and check for me what records they held. She asked me to wait on the tasteful, wipe-clean chairs – the same that you get in nursing homes, proof against any incontinence of the bereaved or the physically frail.

As I sat waiting, the other staff chatted amid their work. A query had come in about a well-known racing driver and whether his cremation had been held at their crematorium. They'd had difficulty finding him on the computer 'but he must have been done here,' the girl said to her colleague. I thought about the fats and bone particles, the pieces of bridge work which have to be sifted through manually, the reduction of a human being to a light grit; perhaps it was just easier to talk about people being 'done'.

A strain of organ music floated through the open window from the chapel of rest and the staff's talk moved on to the closing-down sale at a nearby dress shop. It must be hard to keep your conversation appropriately tactful and euphemistic, respectful and sombre all day. The cloying perfume of lilies is too much for every day, but I found the combination with the shopping bargains unsettling, so I was glad when the woman who'd offered to help came back from the archives with information for me. ED had been cremated two days after her death. Arrangements had been made by Mary Hickson (presumably Wilhelmina Mary Hickson?). And the ashes? 'Dispersed' she said. I asked what this meant and the clerk explained that they wouldn't have been taken elsewhere, but would have been scattered in the crematorium gardens. I thought of the caption on ED's drawing of Shkodra, 'my beloved land'; for a woman who had had and had shared with others such a strong sense of place, having her mortal remains scattered here seemed an anticlimax.

'Would they have been scattered in any particular place?' I asked.

'They could be anywhere' she said.

Seventy years later they certainly could. The particles of what had once been Mary Edith Durham wouldn't have taken long to blow away, become soggy parts of the well-tended lawns, of the worms – and the blackbirds who were tugging at the worms – in the crocus memorial lawn beyond the window. There she and Anna Pavlova and Sid James and Enid Blyton mingled and commingled, were broken down further into molecules which could then be part of gases, melted 'into air, into thin air'. And that air would be inhaled by the visitors here, the solemn children (scared into unnatural slow movement by signs saying 'It is inappropriate to let children run or play in these revered grounds'), the mourners, the people who came for the cremation here of TS Eliot, of Vivien Leigh, HG Wells and Amy Winehouse. And then those molecules would be breathed out, excreted, rubbed off, in homes and streets around north London, northern Europe, the northern hemisphere and the rest of the world. That's where Edith was really scattered.

Philosophically, the idea held up, but psychologically it was unsatisfactory to be here with nothing more than the note in my hand from the clerk to say that it was in this place on a dreary, wartime November day that Edith Durham's body was reduced beyond recognition. I had thought I would leave something on a stone, a flower tucked into a columbarium, say some Albanian optatives over a plaque, but there was nowhere to focus me. In an attempt to mark my visit somehow, I picked a small daisy from the lawn and closed it between the pages of my notebook. Yet again, I had taken more than I could give in my odd asynchronous relationship with ED.

I wandered the grounds a little, out beyond the columbaria holding urns, beyond the 'Section 1 dispersal area (visitors are asked to keep to the grass paths)' signs, thinking about these things and feeling empty. Edith's life, and her death – all of our deaths – seemed too marvellous and enormous to be framed adequately in the neat lawns and trimmed rhododendron bushes. It was reminiscent of the 'cheap boarding house' decor ED had described in the fallen Sultan's tomb on Kosovo Field; I didn't want this to be the end.

My phone in vibrate mode mewed against the hard cover of a book in my bag. It wasn't communication from Hecate's cat, the guardian of the underworld, but an SMS from a colleague in Kosovo; the children attending classes at our Fushë Kosovë centre were well, but the municipality had still not replied to our request for state-run classes to begin; could I draft an email to continue the pressure? I'd hoped for a free afternoon to spend at the crematorium, but I realised I was being indulgent. I glanced up at the statue near which I stood, the figure of GD Birla, the Indian businessman and philanthropist, at whose home Gandhi was staying when he was assassinated. The inscription might have appealed to ED: 'What we call life is a wonderful journey, full of purpose.'

The phone was reminding me of the purpose, and the journeys I could be making, and this crematorium didn't feel like even a part of a journey; certainly not a destination. It was a siding, or an ox-bow lake, a becalming for your ship; the frustrating halt while your passport is taken by the Sud and you can't get on to

Gjakova. Staying here would do no good to either Edith or me – it is no use having a purpose if you won't make the journey towards it. I got out my notebook and jotted down some lines, and, as someone from near here had done before me long ago, I walked purposefully off to the station.

Glossary of foreign words in the text

Çardak   A glazed balcony

Çifteli   A plucked instrument with two strings

Flija   A traditional dish of Kosovo and Northern
                    Albania, baked in a large round tray and made
                    of layered strips of batter so that it resembles a
                    thick stack of pancakes

Gusle   A bowed single-stringed instrument found
                    across the Balkans

Hamam   The Turkish word for bathroom, in Kosovo
                    used to denote the public baths and steam
                    rooms which used to be common

Kanun   The Kanun of Lekë Dukagjini is an originally
                    oral code of laws dating at least from the
                    fifteenth century and regulating social and
                    civil affairs in traditional Albanian society

KFOR   The Kosovo Force of NATO – international
                    peace-keeping force based in Kosovo since
                    1999

Konak   A traditional house; the Turkish word for an
                    official residence

Kulla	Literally meaning 'tower', this is the word used for a style of fortified stone houses in Kosovo and Northern Albania
Kumbar	A role like that of godfather, and the name given to the man who first cuts a child's hair
Motokultivator	A basic tractor made up of a seat above an engine, used to cart goods and sometimes people
Ndrikulla	A role like that of godmother, and the name given to the woman who first cuts a child's hair
Nizam	Turkish soldier
Opinga	Raw-hide slippers made from strips of leather
Plis	Traditional white felt hat, now worn usually by old men, in Kosovo and Northern Albania. It has become a symbol of the Gheg Albanians
Raki	Grappa-style firewater made usually from plums or grapes
Strema	Covered horse-drawn cart used by ED on her travels
Turbe	Turkish word for tomb or mausoleum

If you enjoyed *Edith and I; on the trail of an Edwardian traveller in Kosovo,* read Elizabeth Gowing's first book, *Travels in Blood and Honey; becoming a beekeeper in Kosovo* (Signal Books, 2011) available in Kindle and hard copy.

The book was described by *The Times* as

'A sheer delight; a beguiling, bittersweet story of a lively love affair with a traditional world, as ancient as apiculture, in transition to new nationhood'

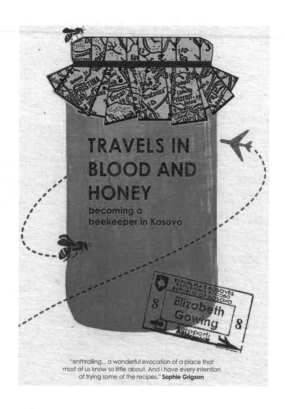

TRAVELS IN
BLOOD AND
HONEY
becoming a
beekeeper in Kosovo

Elizabeth
Gowing

"enthralling... a wonderful evocation of a place that most of us know so little about. And I have every intention of trying some of the recipes." **Sophie Grigson**